AF732638

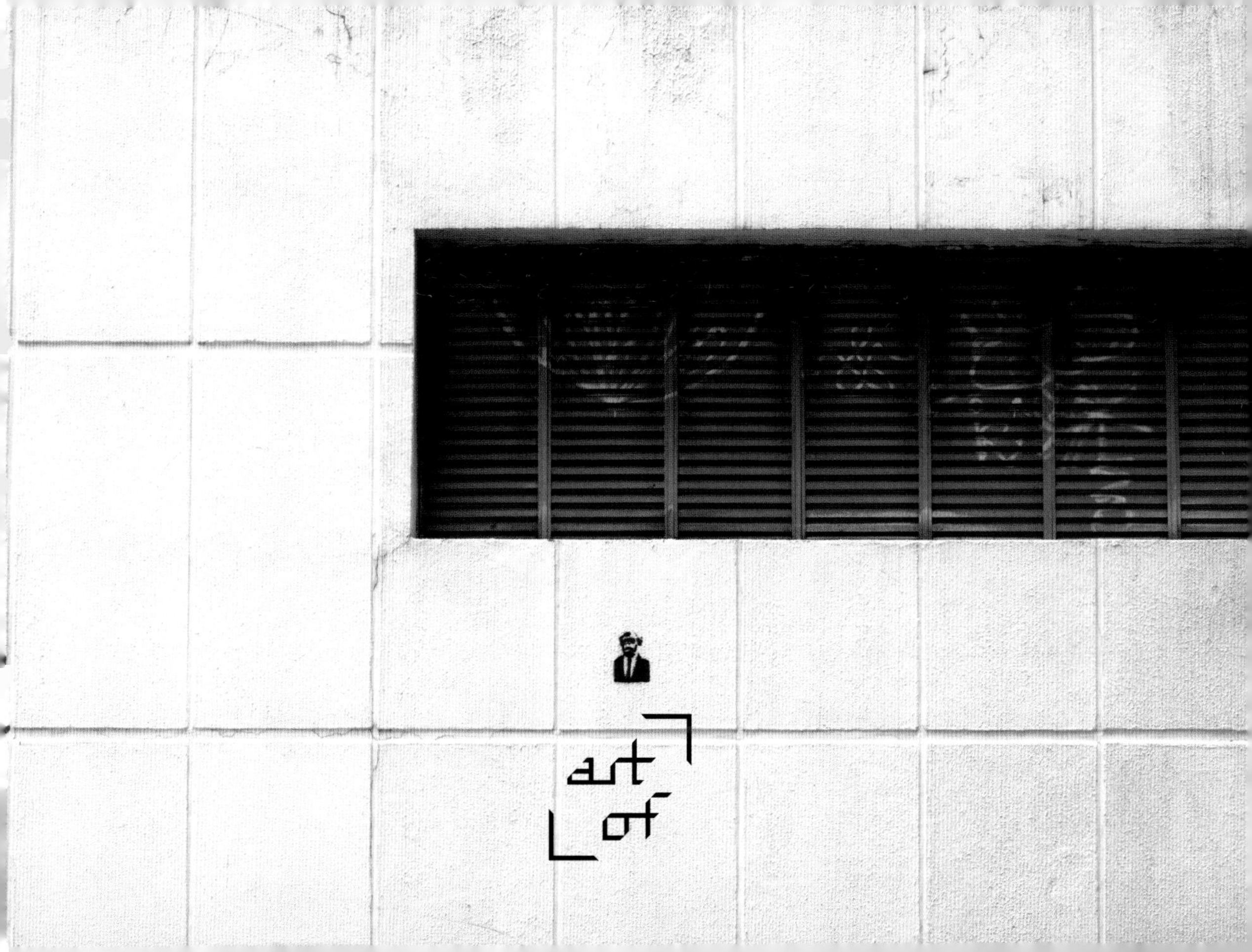
art
of

First published in the UK in 2016 by
Art of Publishing Limited
London

WWW.ARTOFPUBLISHING.NET

Copyright: 2016 Art of Publishing Ltd.
All rights reserved. No part of this publication may be reproduced, stored in a retrieval system, or transmitted in any form or by any means, electronic, mechanical, photocopying, recording, or otherwise, without the permission in writing of the publisher.

ISBN - 978-0-9932407-4-4

Photography: Andy Cantillon
Editor: Andy Cantillon
Assistant Editor: Nina Chini Gani
Design: James Bunce
Publishers: William Fulford/Bill Fulford/Andy Cantillon

ART OF THE STREET

RIO DE JANEIRO

Art of the Street, Rio de Janeiro is book 3 in our mission to capture the best of street art across the world's greatest cities. From tackling 'local' strength Caipirinhas, to being chased out of 'no-go' favelas, we've gone the extra mile to document and preserve these works in an ever transient and evolving scene.

Special thanks to Nina Chini Gani and the Fabrica de Arte e Cidadania for taking us to those secret places.

Featured artists include Santa Crew, Kovok Crew, Toz, Wark Rocinha, Vhils, Nata Familia and Smael.

We hope you enjoy the book.

Andy Cantillon is Co-founder of Art of Publishing Ltd. and photographer for the entire Art of the Street series.

Also available from Art of Publishing:
Art of the Street, London and Art of the Street, Berlin.

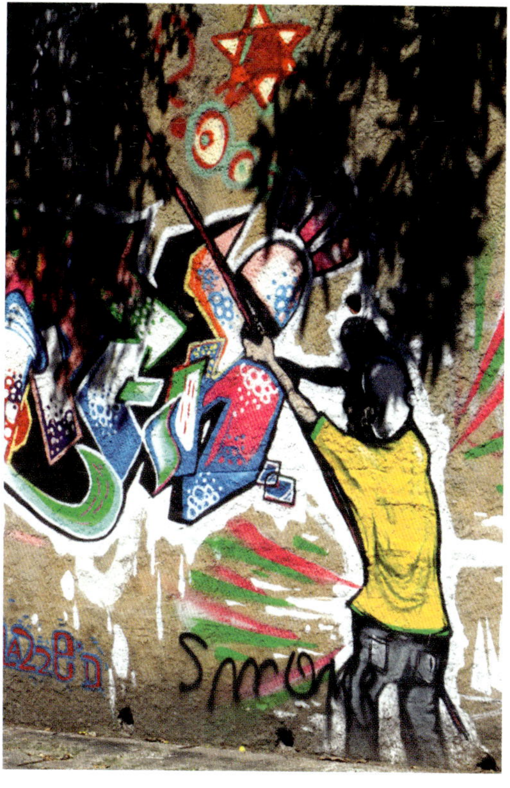

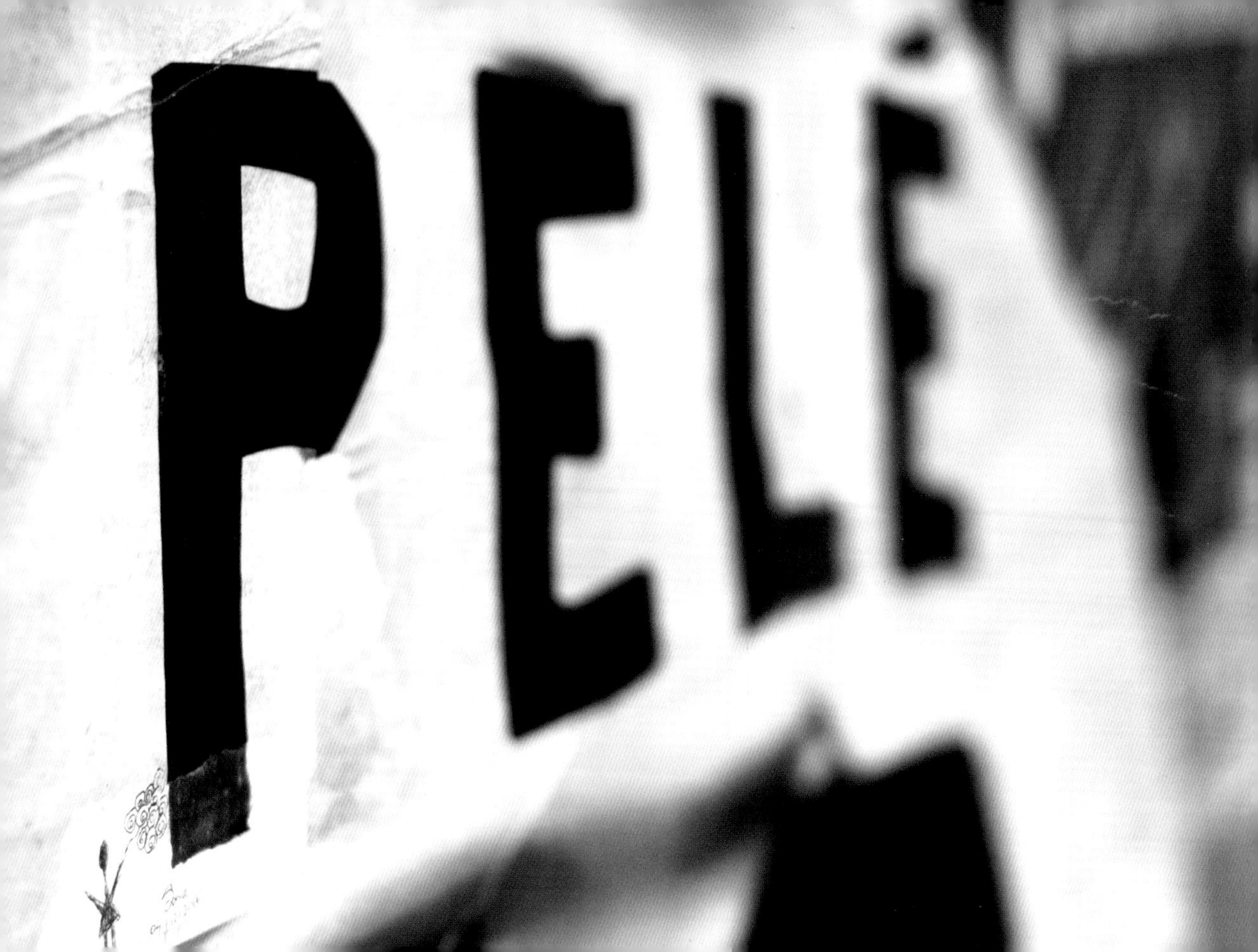
PELÉ

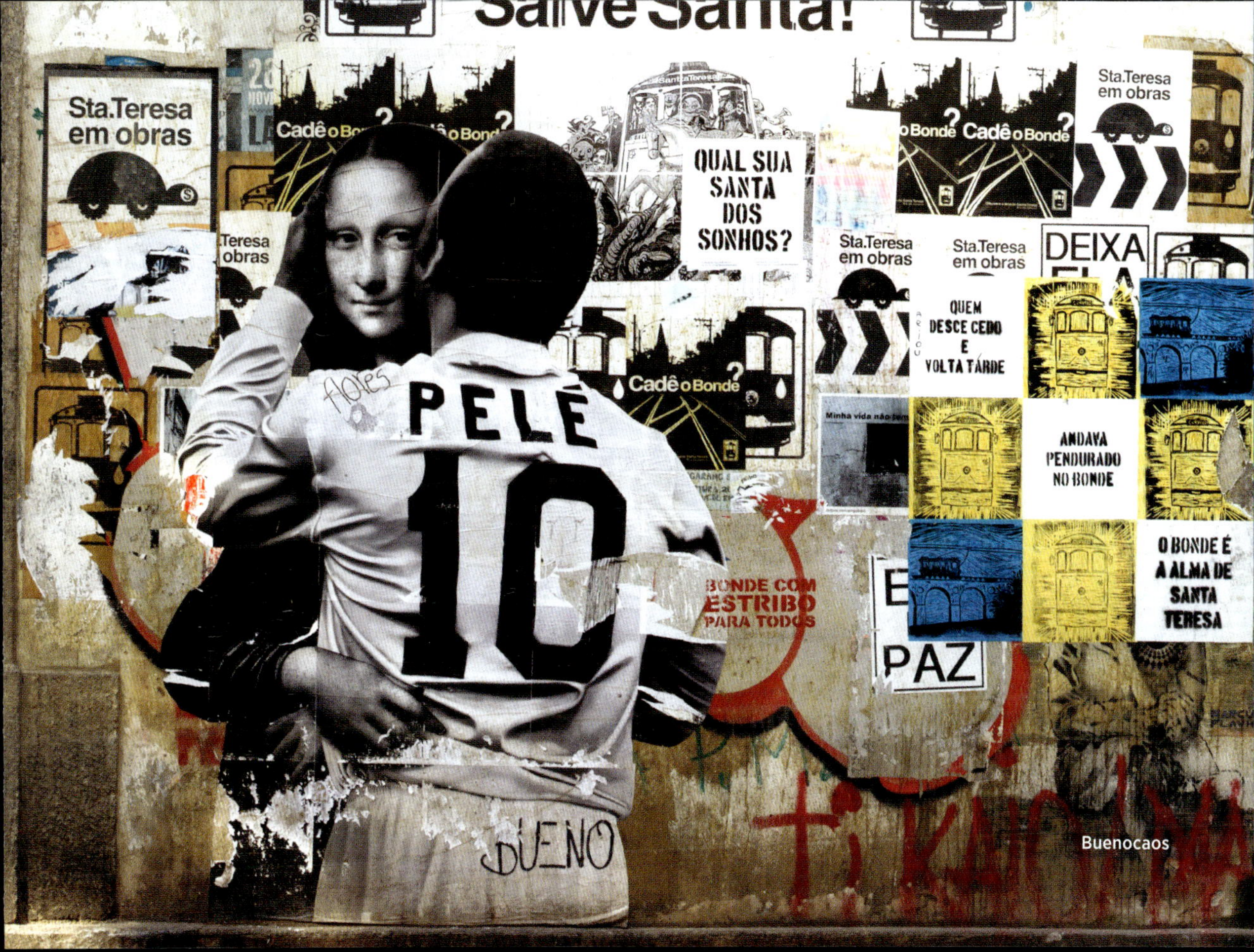
Salve Santa!
Sta.Teresa em obras
Cadê o Bonde?
QUAL SUA SANTA DOS SONHOS?
Sta.Teresa em obras
Sta.Teresa em obras
DEIXA
QUEM DESCE CEDO E VOLTA TARDE
Cadê o Bonde?
PELÉ
10
Minha vida não tem
ANDAVA PENDURADO NO BONDE
BONDE COM ESTRIBO PARA TODOS
PAZ
O BONDE É A ALMA DE SANTA TERESA
BUENO

Buenocaos

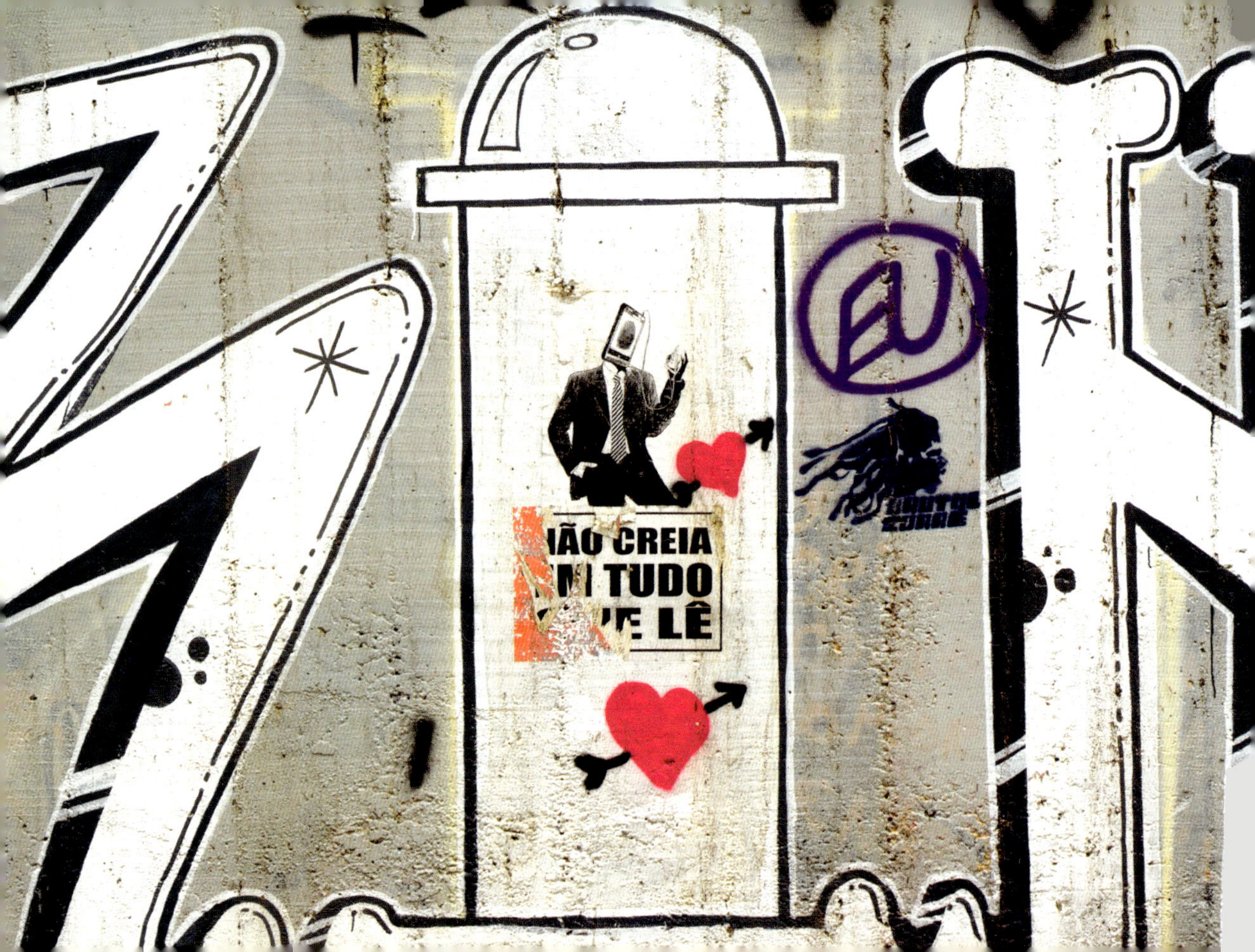
ÃO CREIA
TUDO
E LÊ
EU

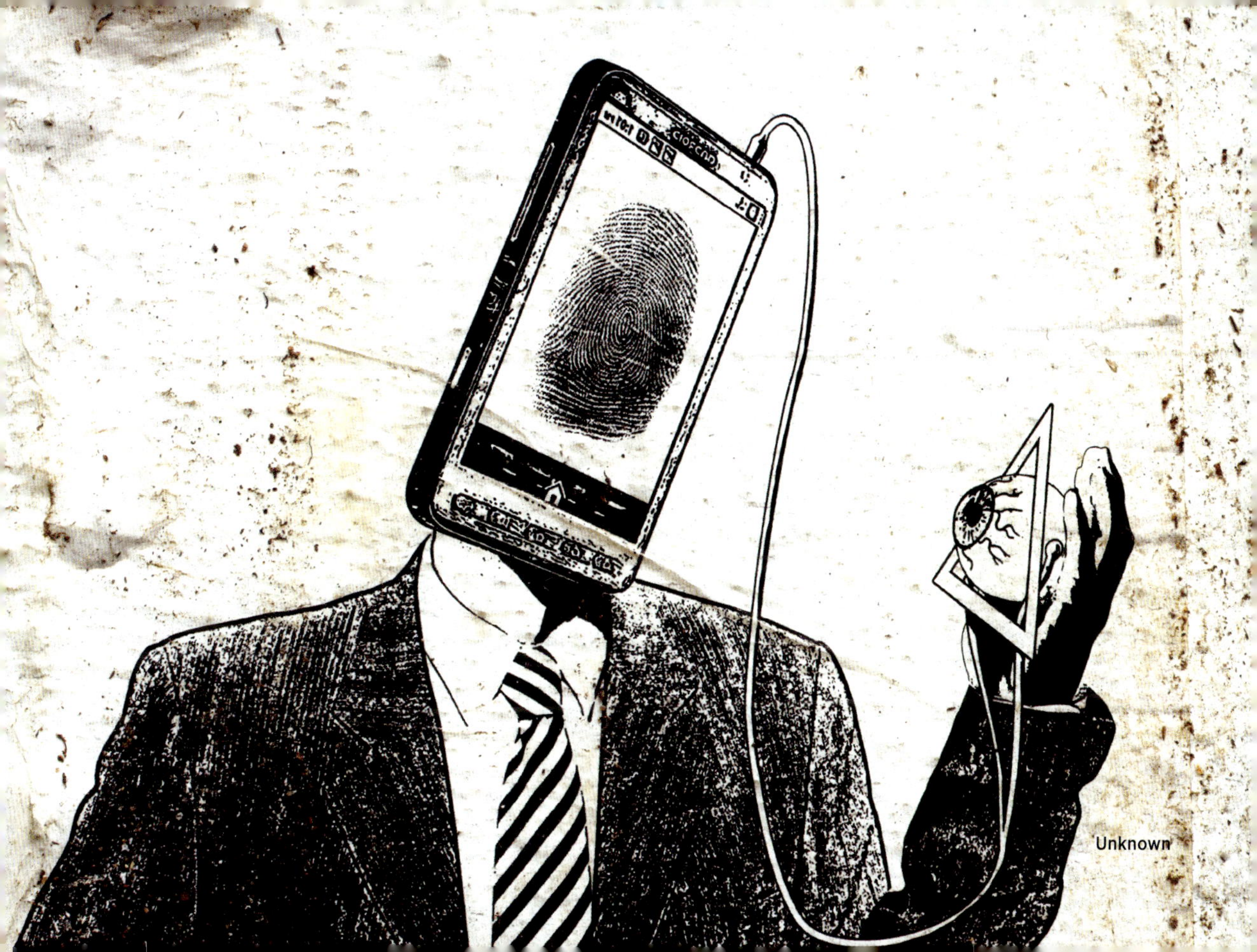

Unknown

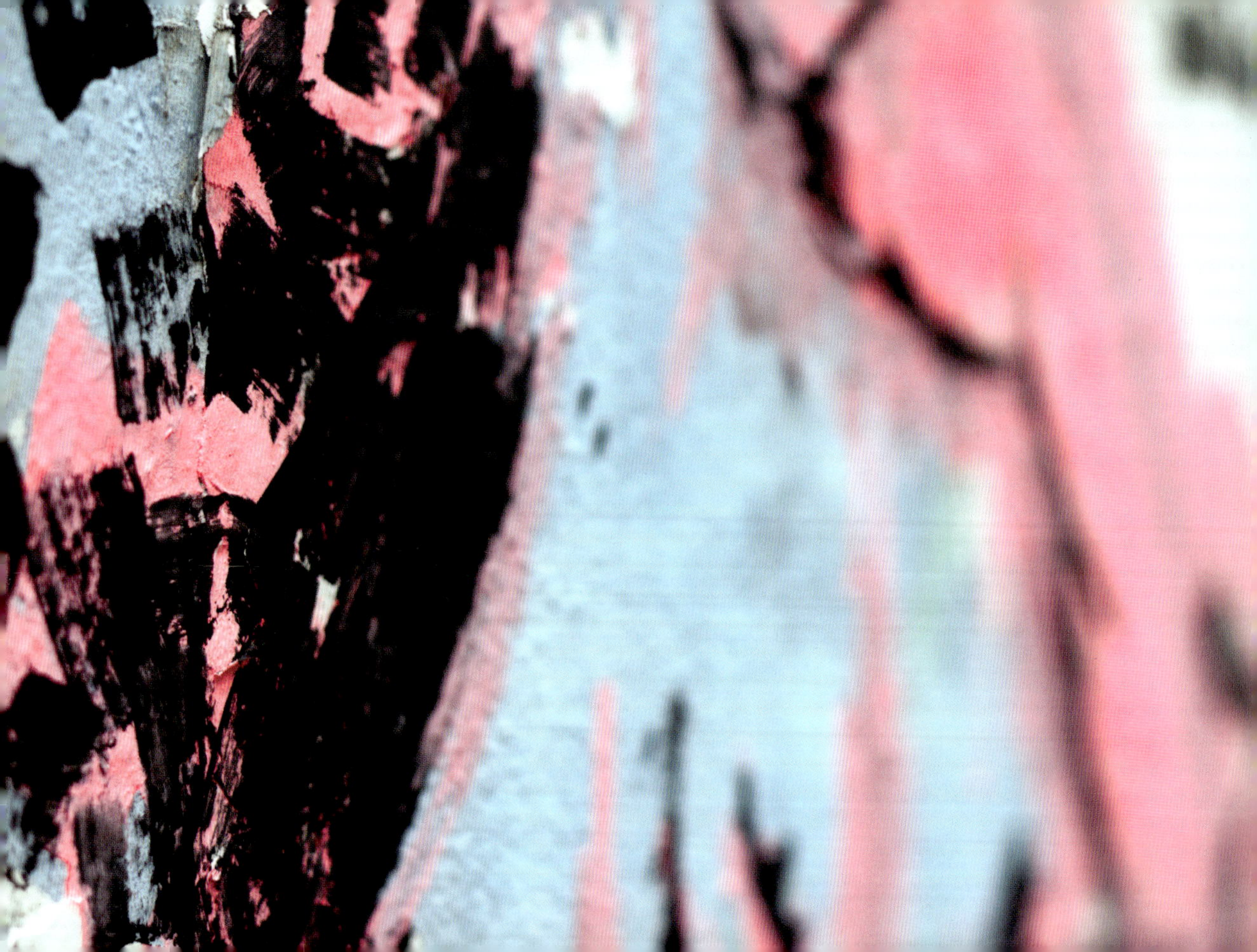

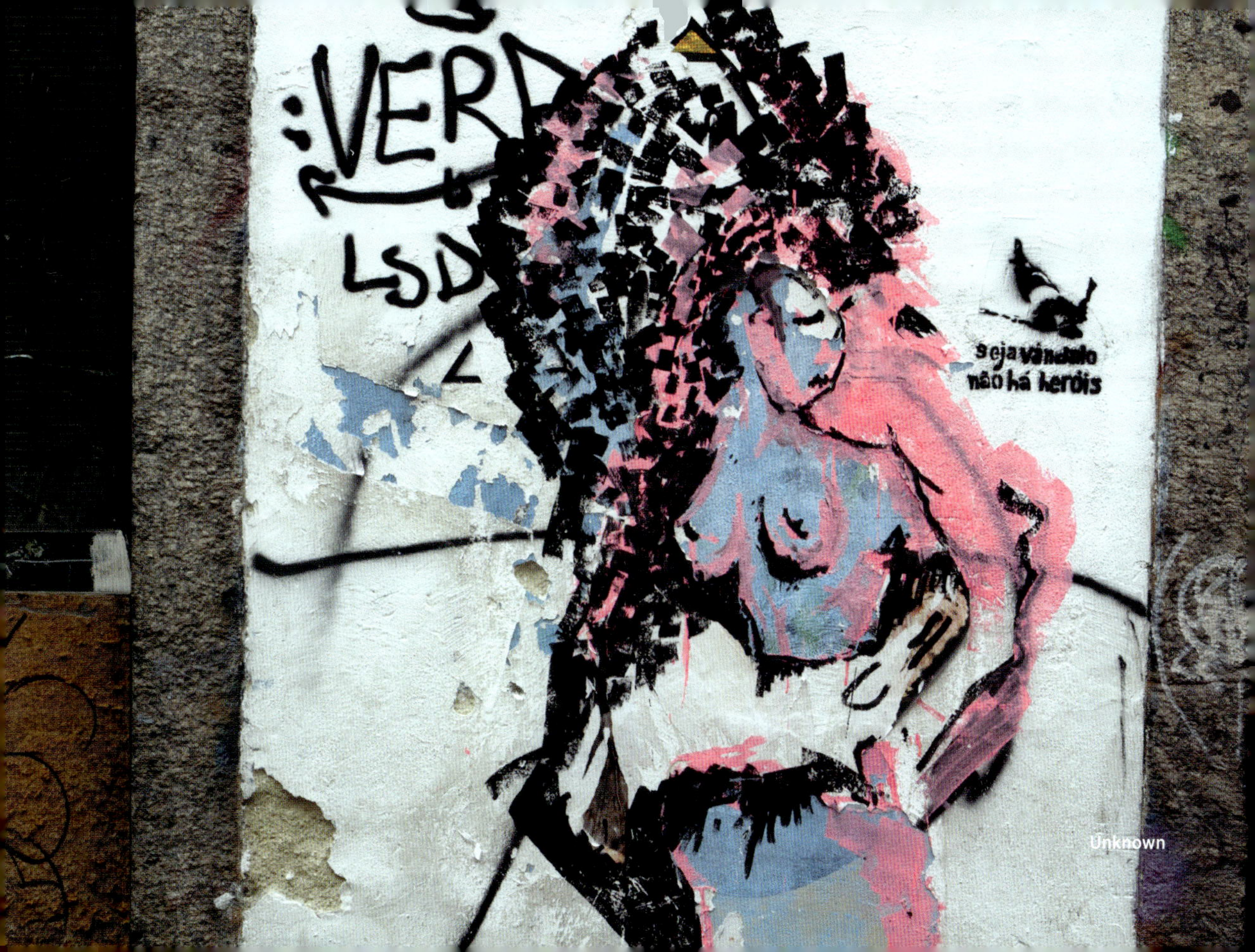

Unknown

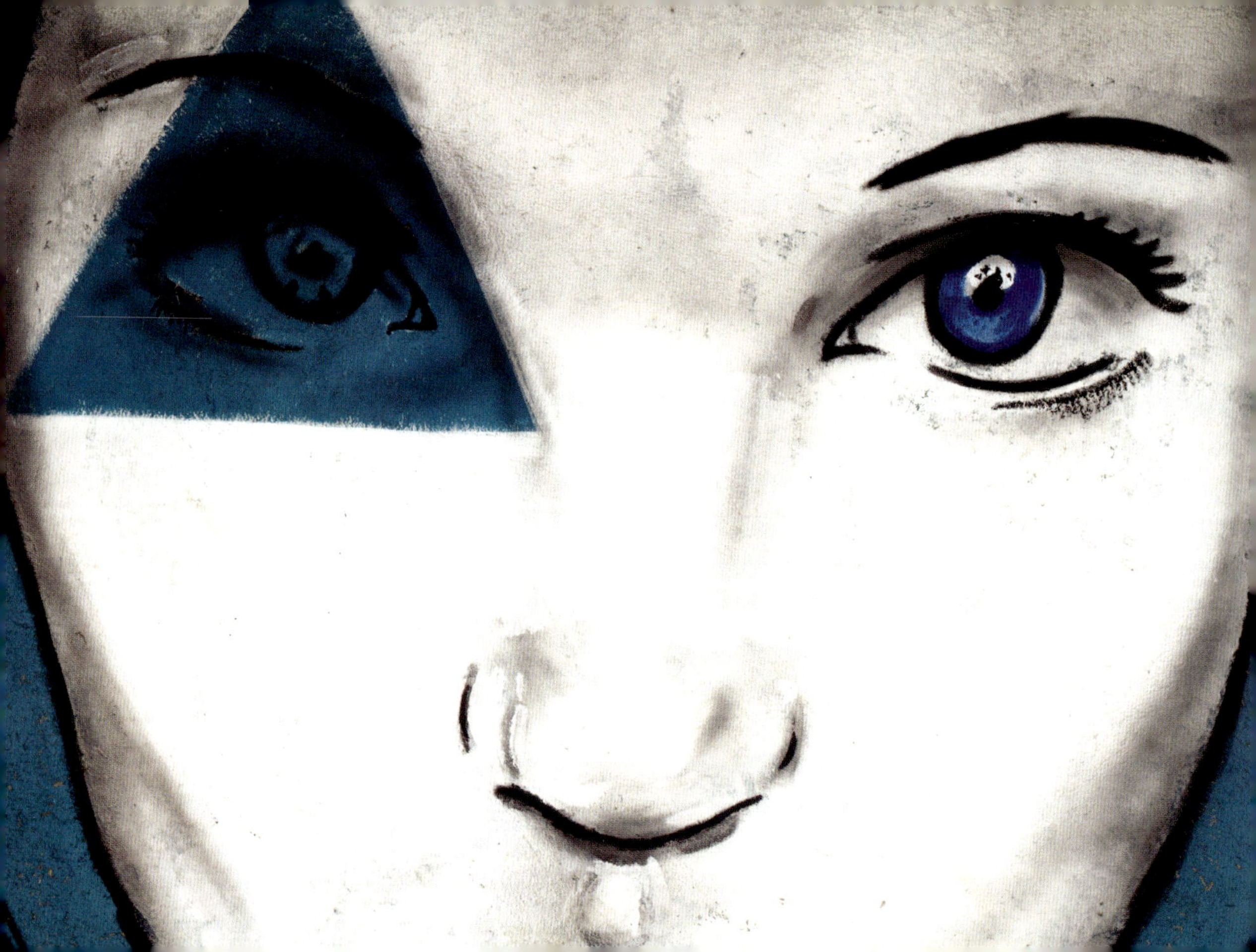

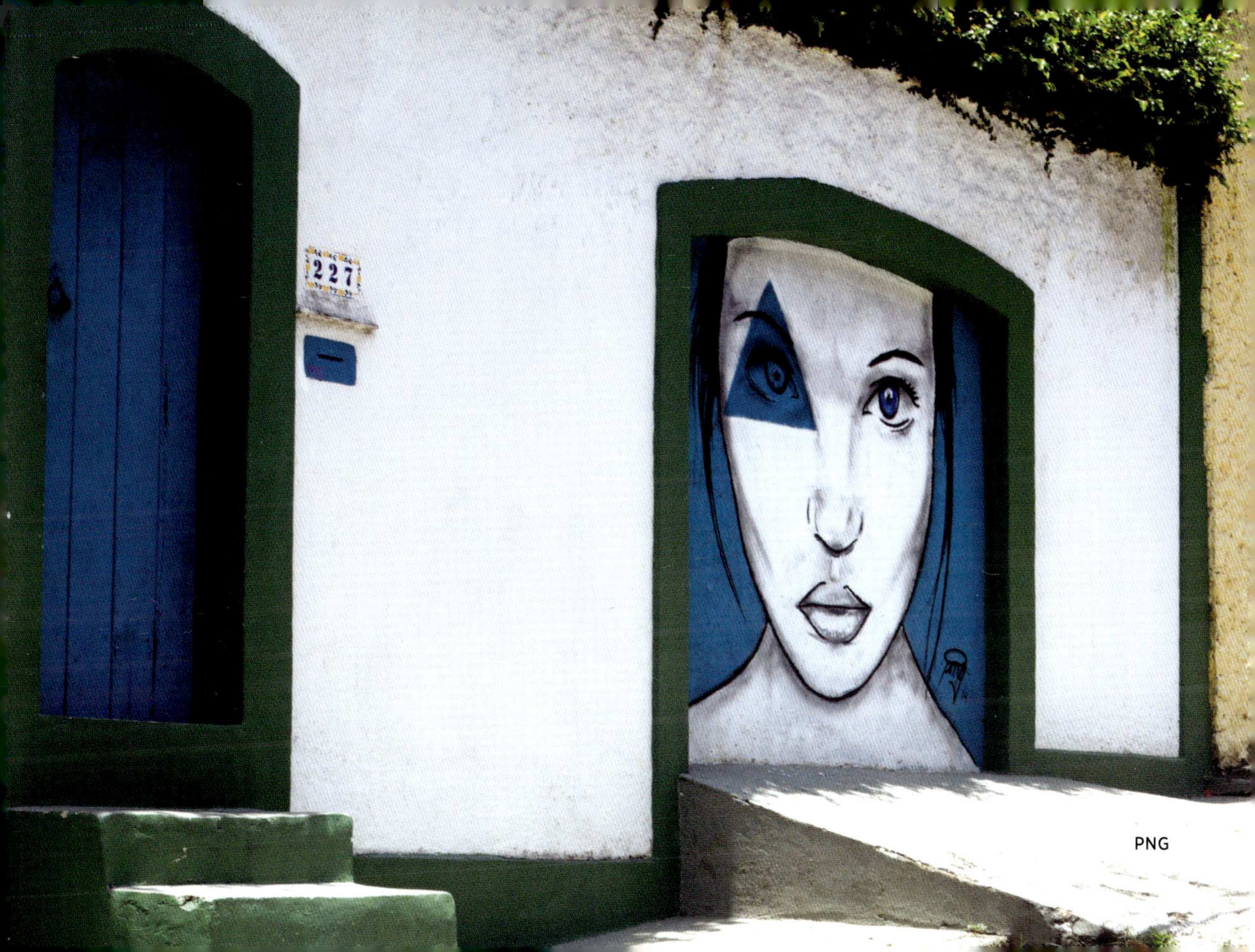
227
PNG

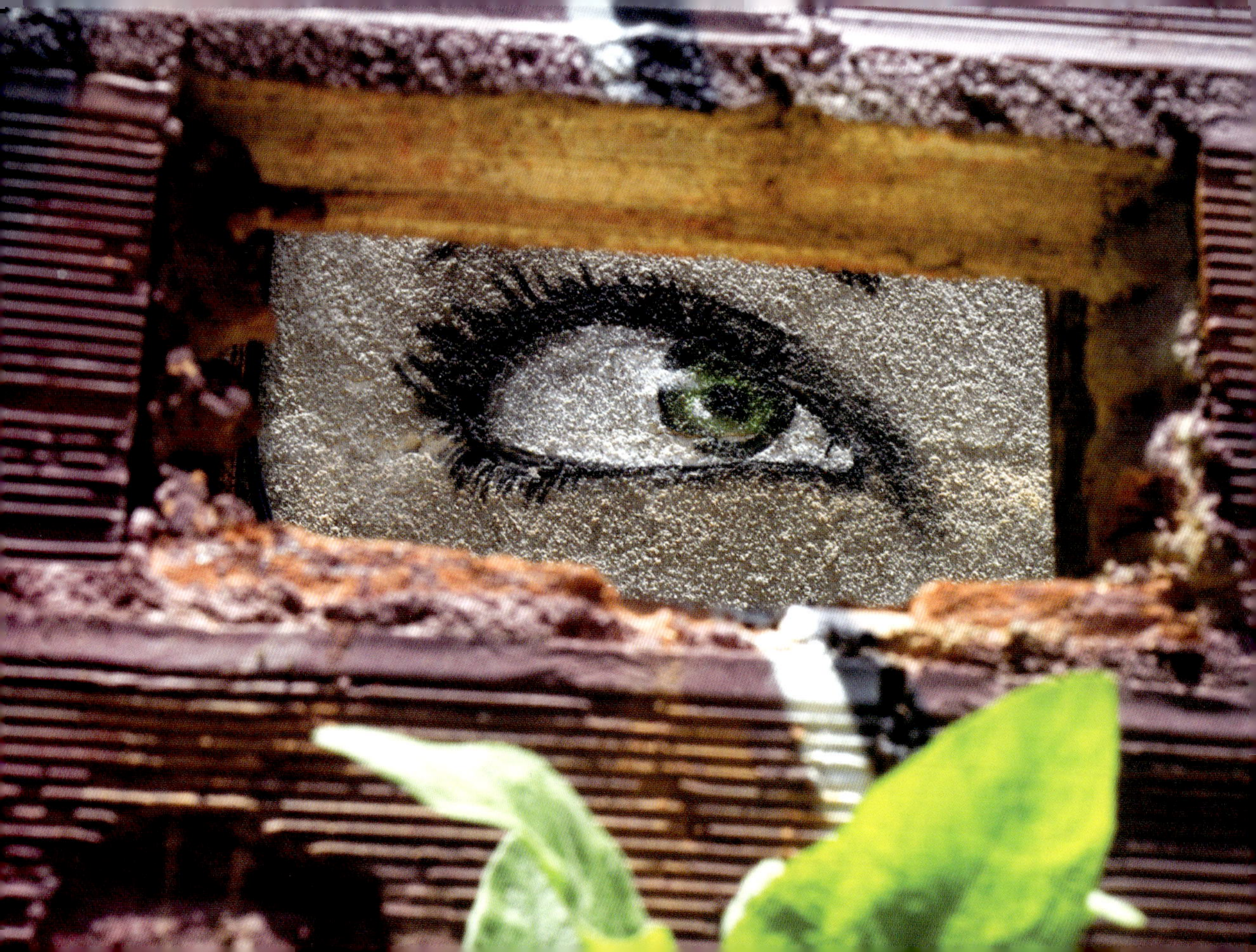

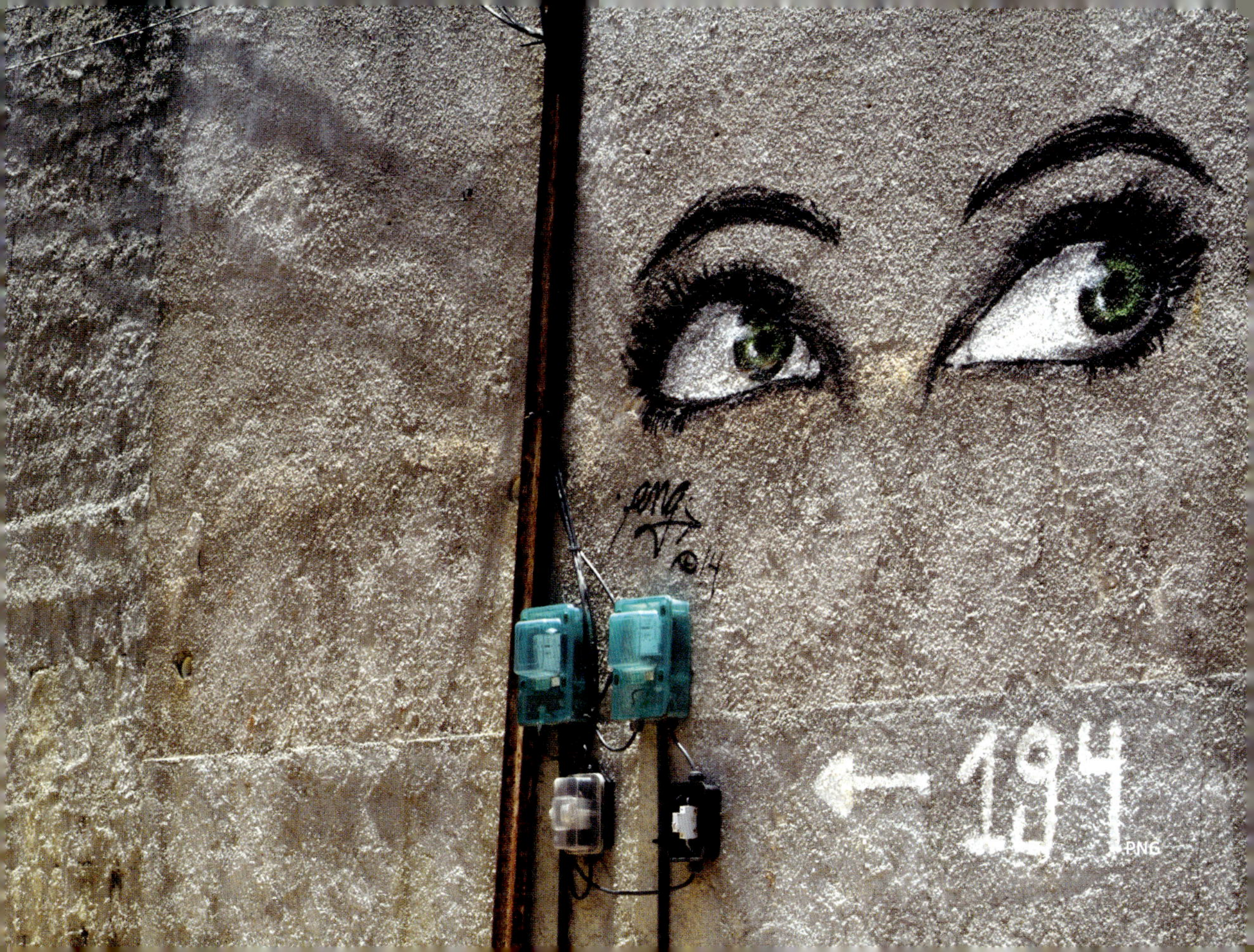
194
PNG

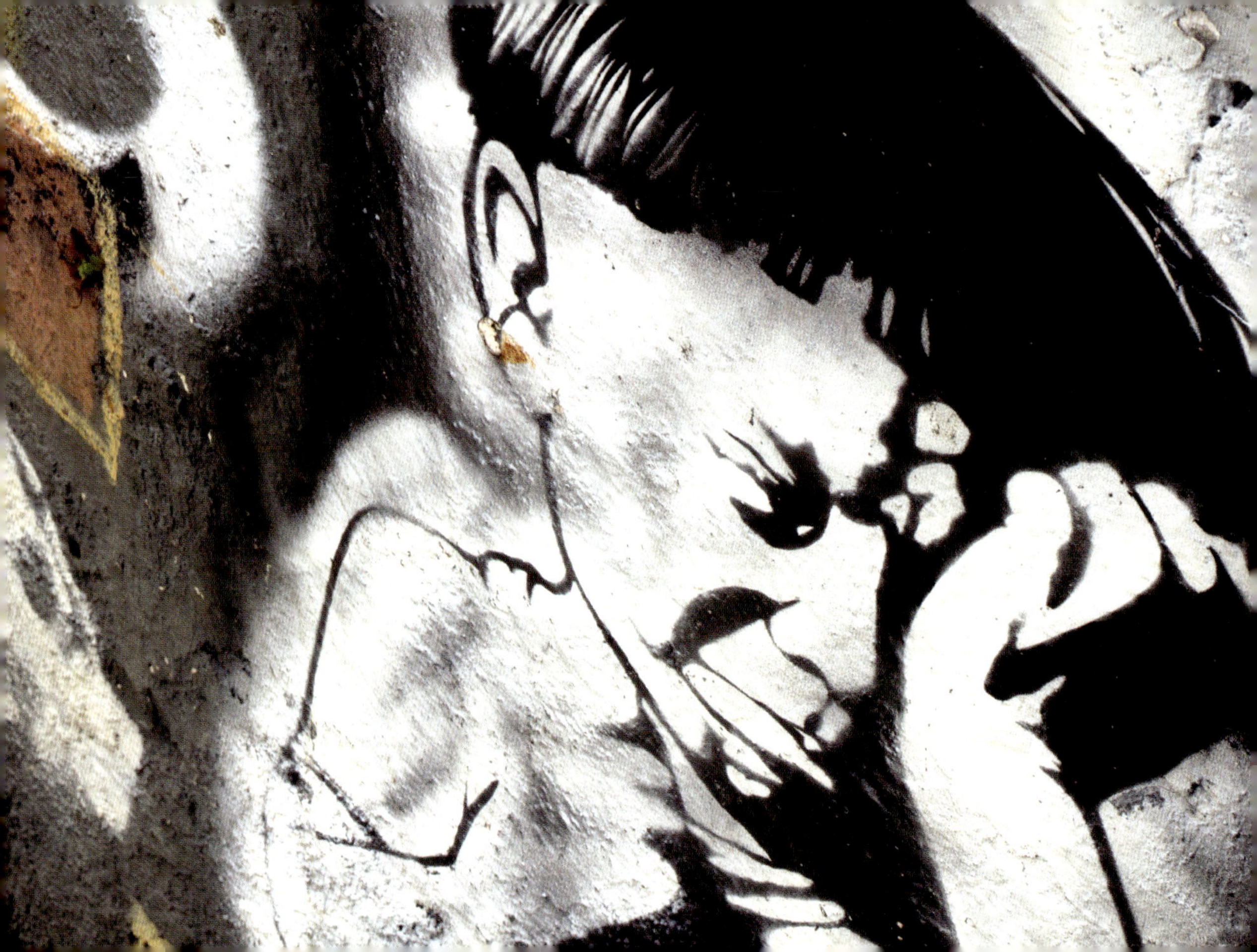

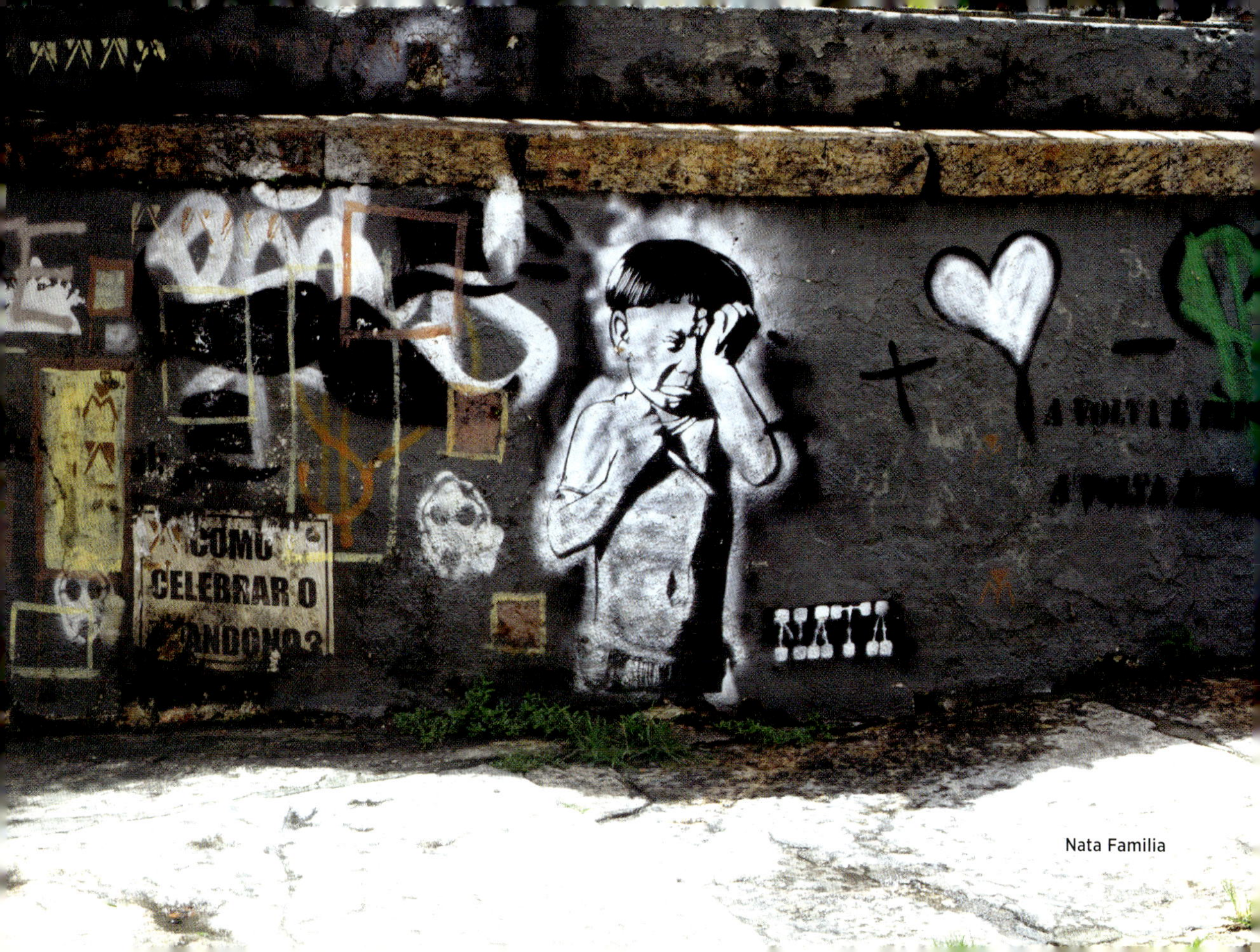

Nata Familia

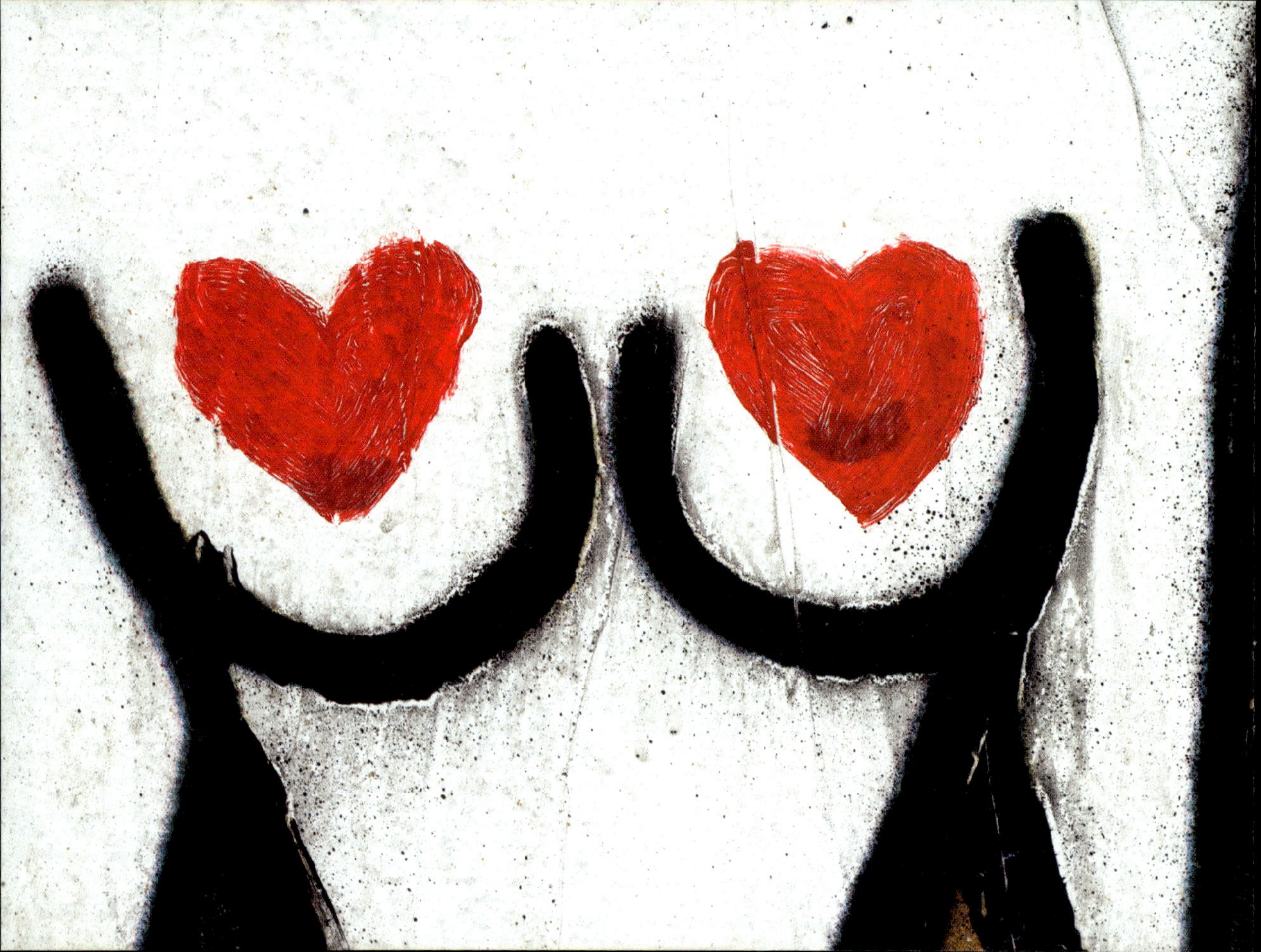

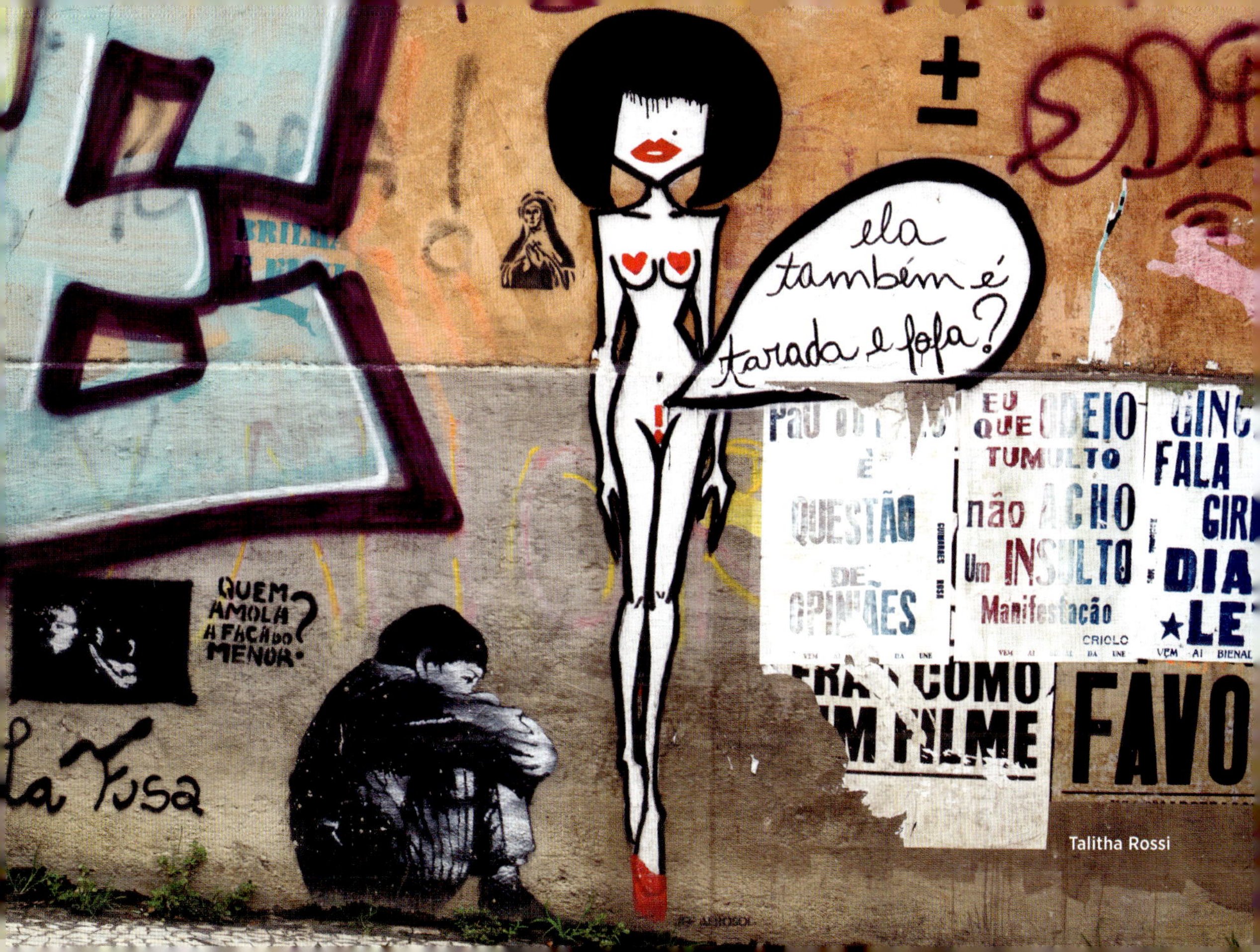

Talitha Rossi

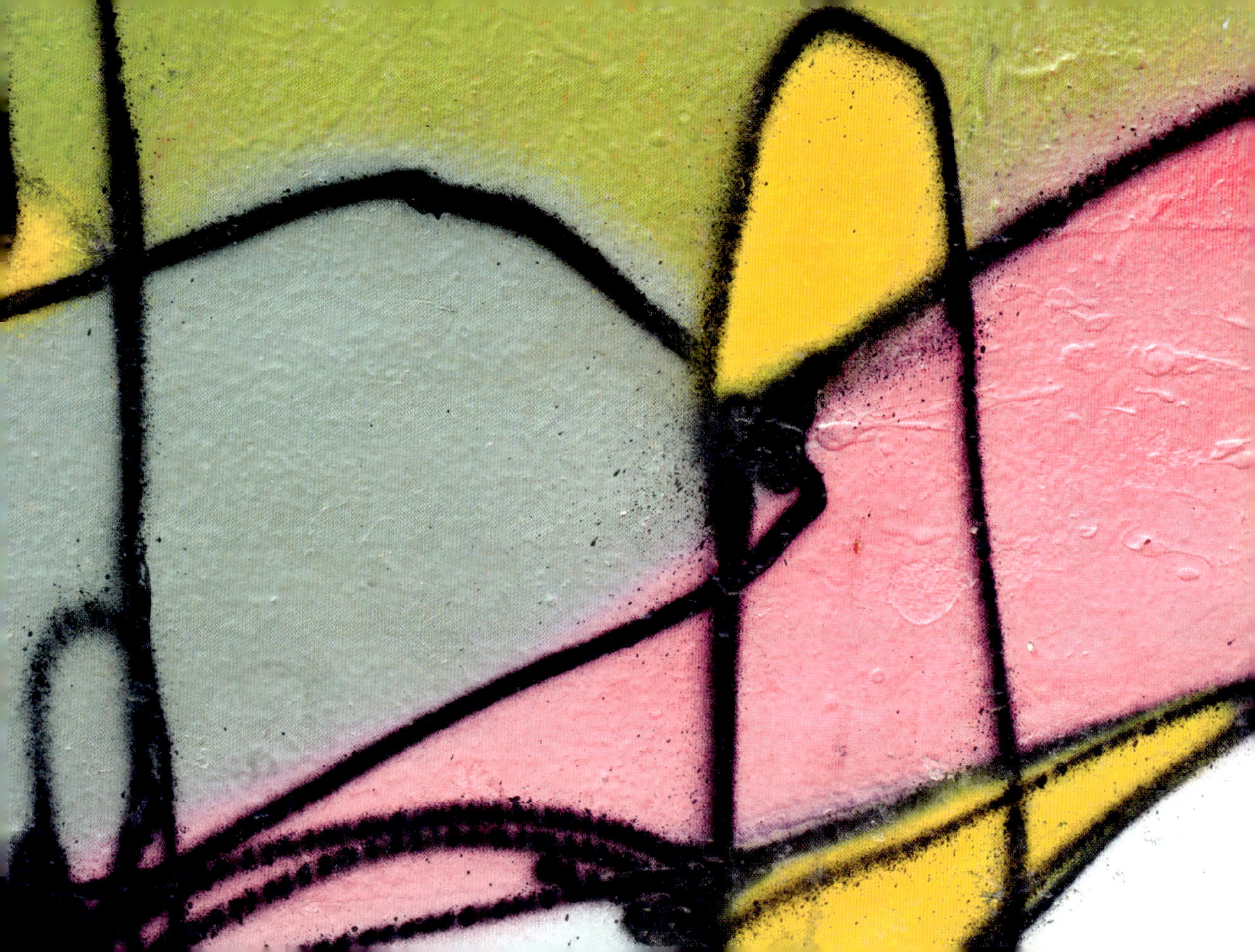

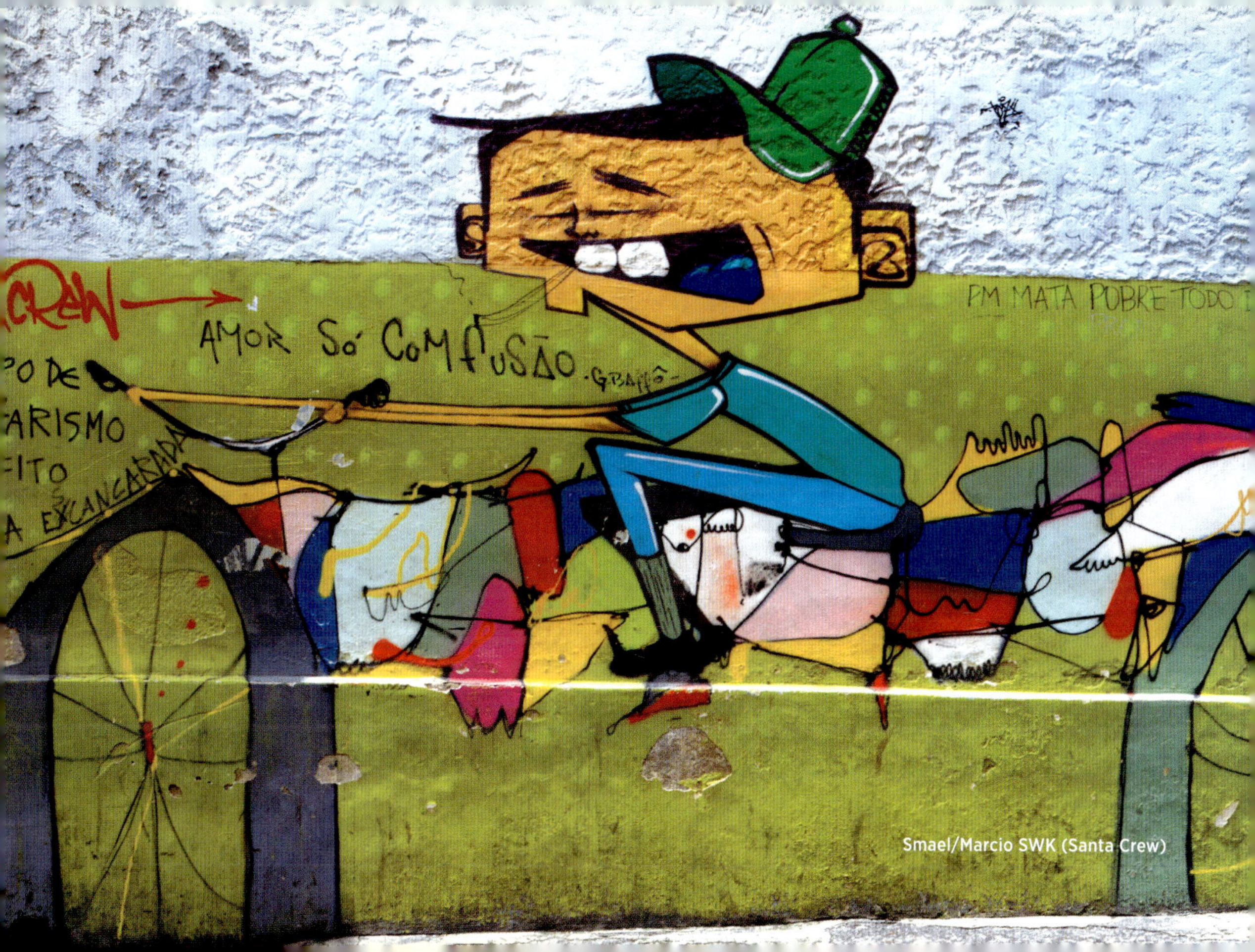

Smael/Marcio SWK (Santa Crew)

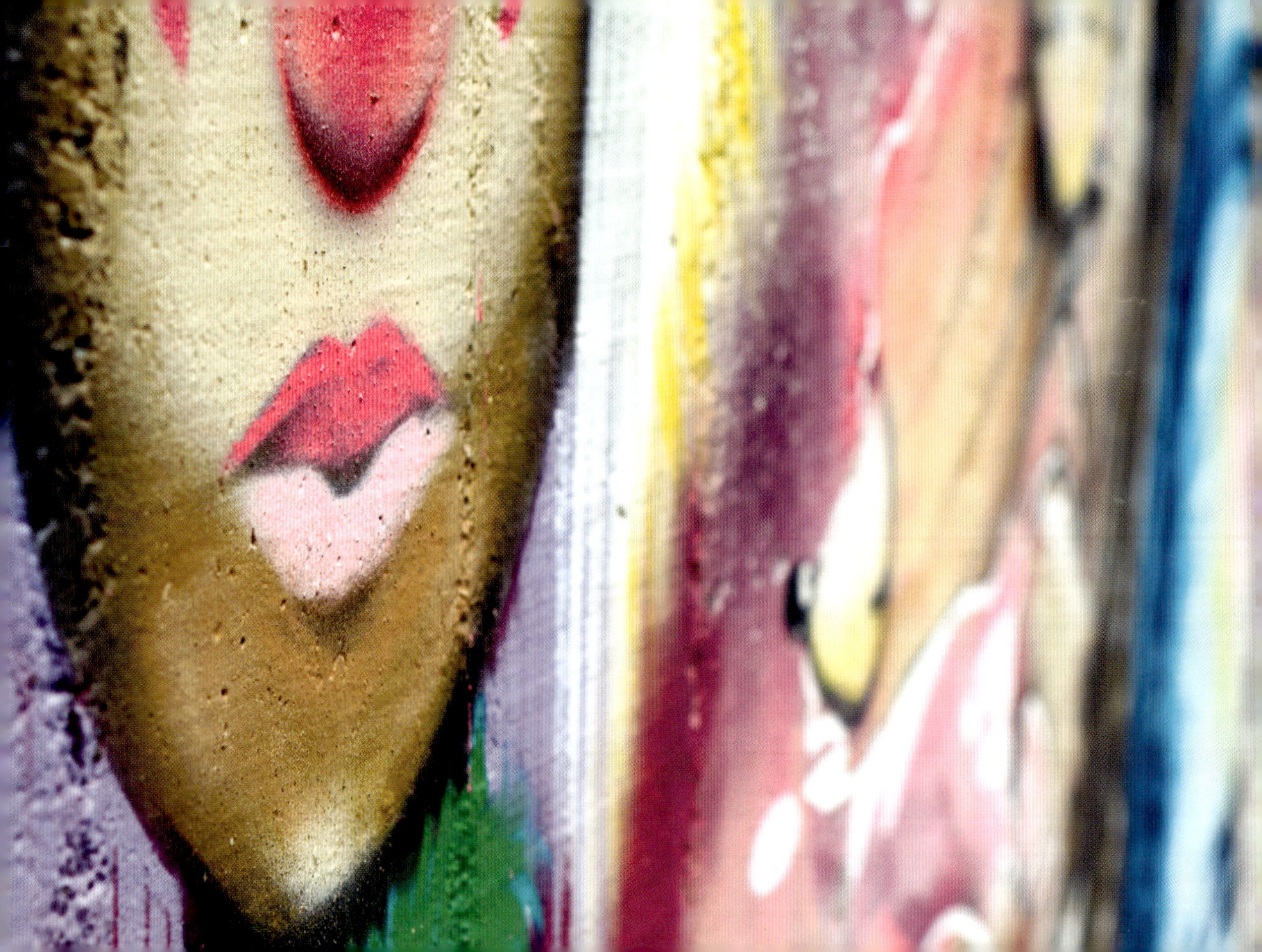

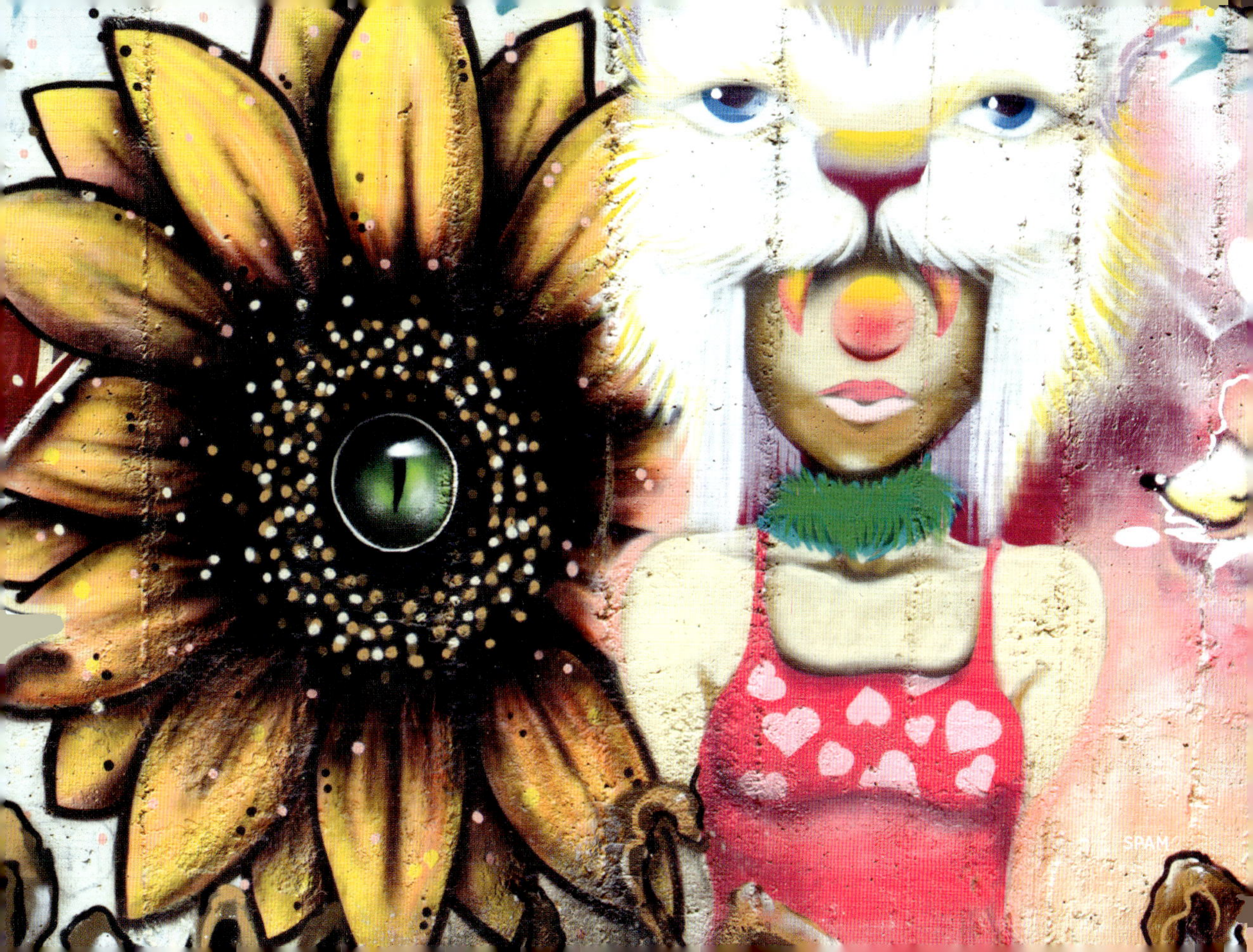
SPAM

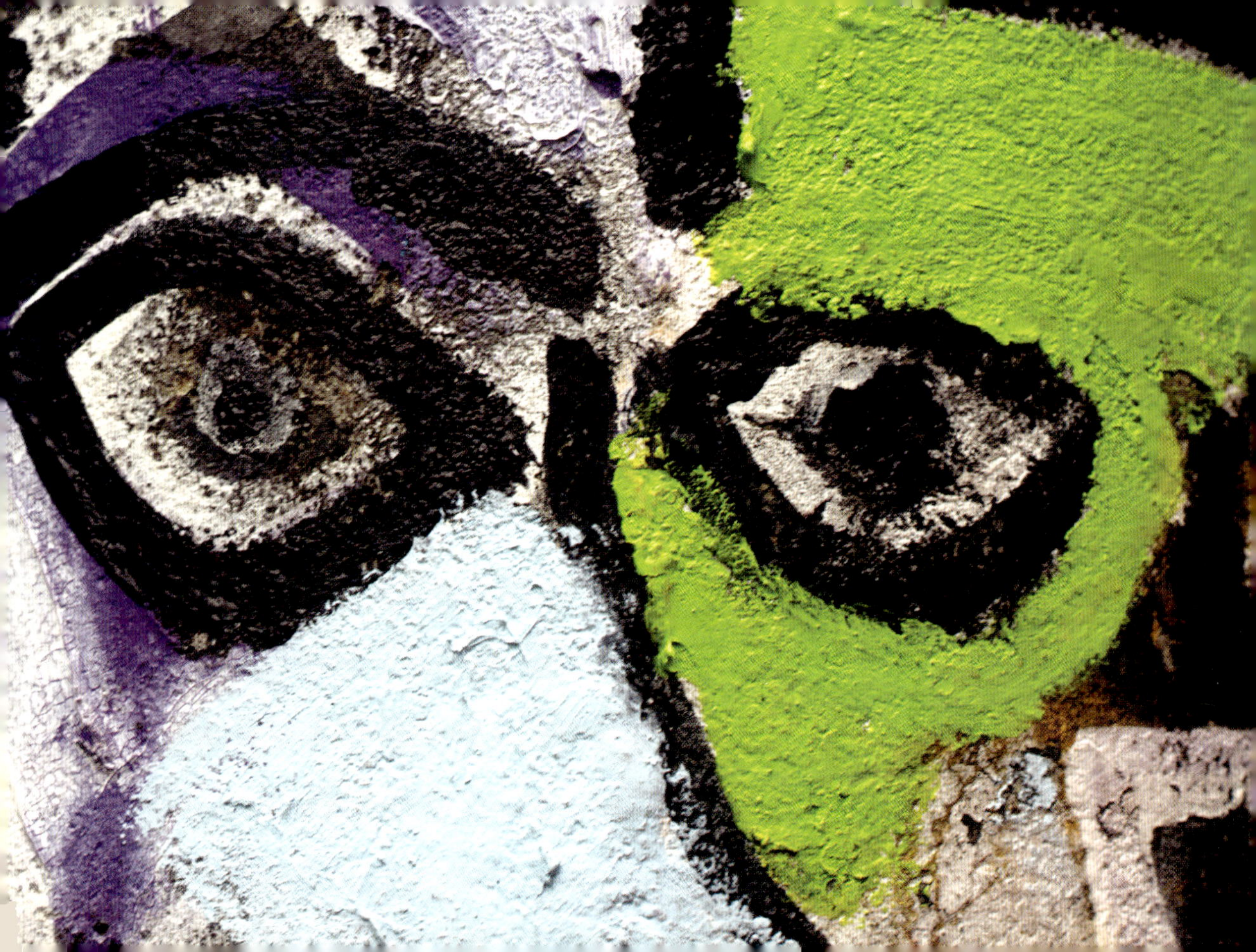

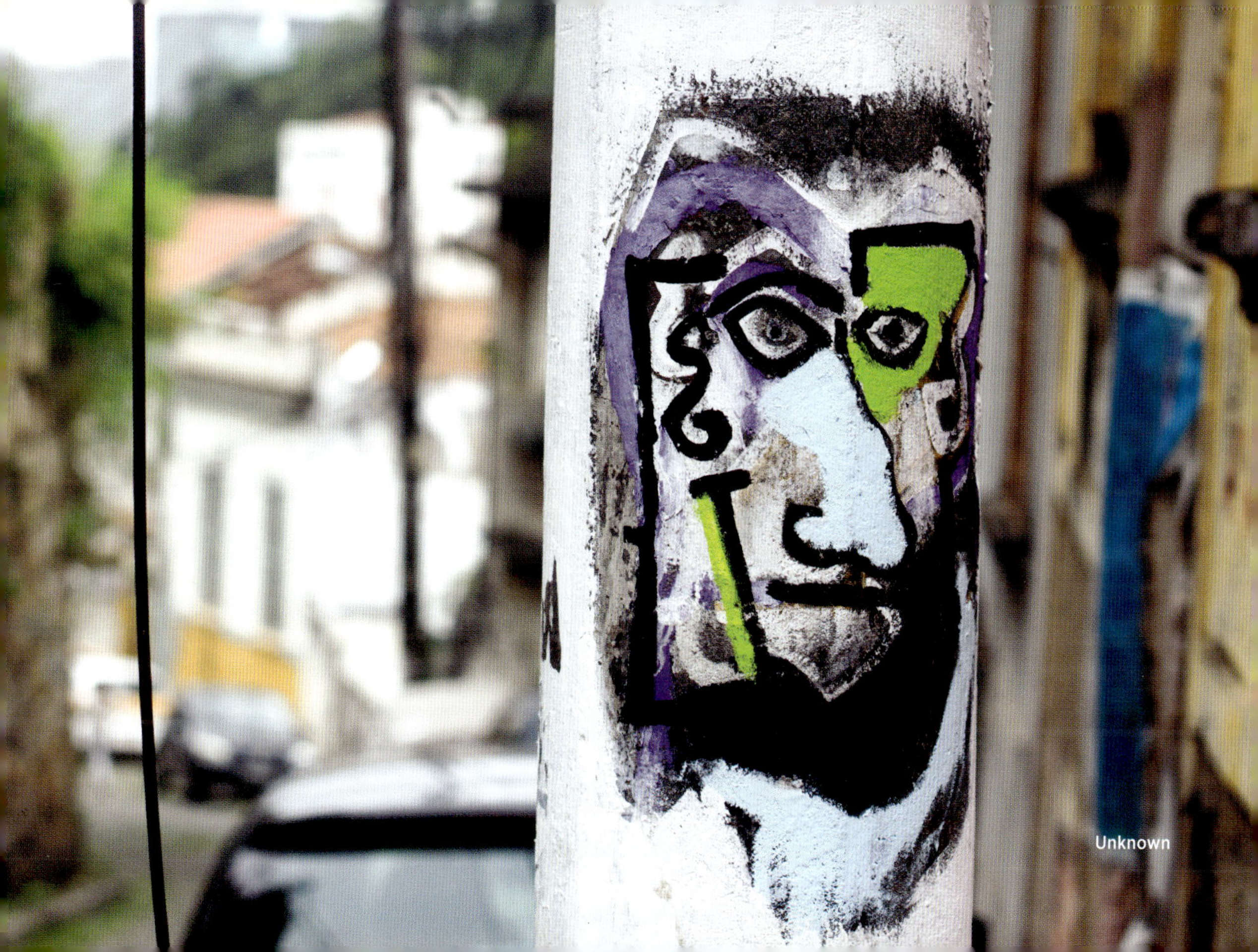

Unknown

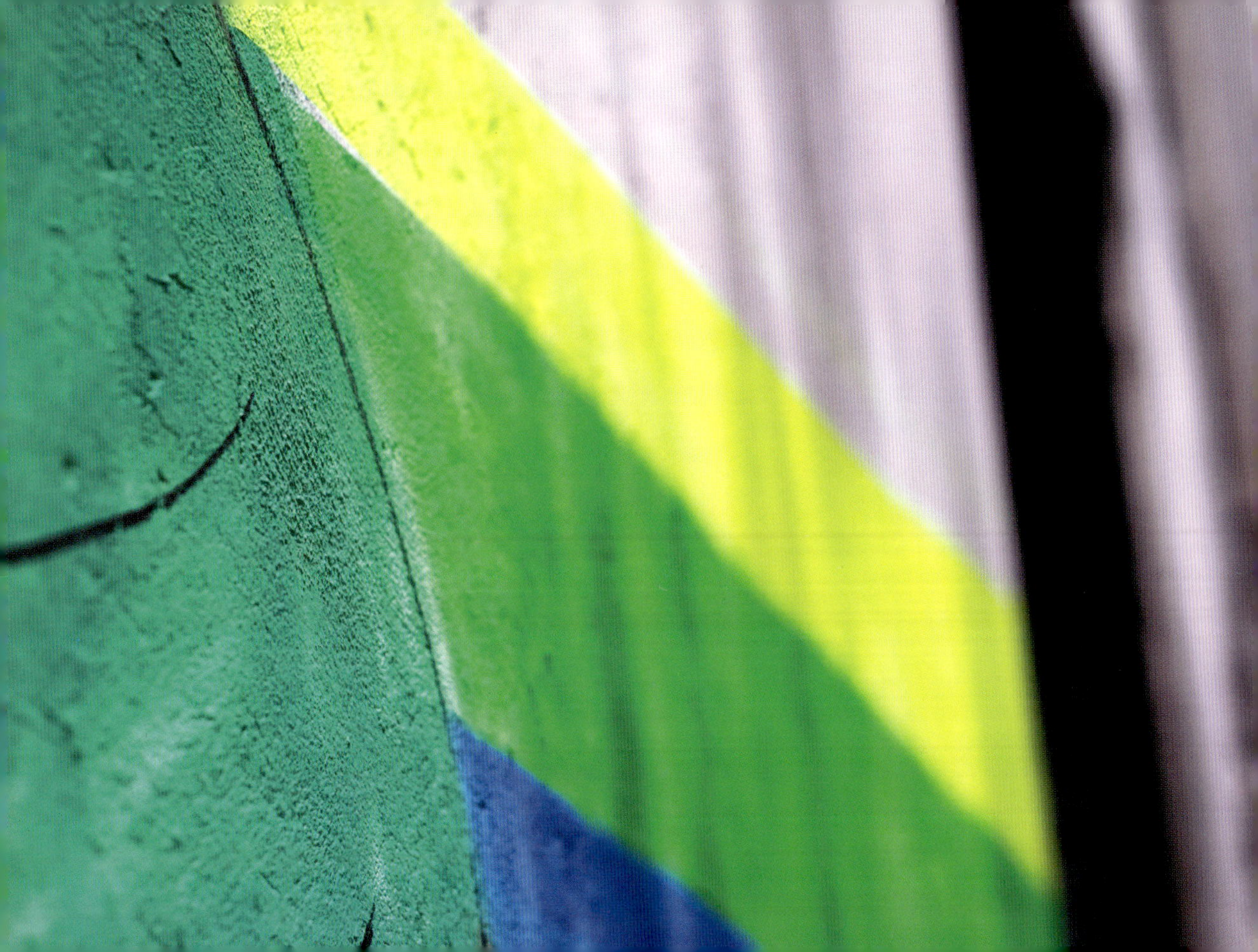

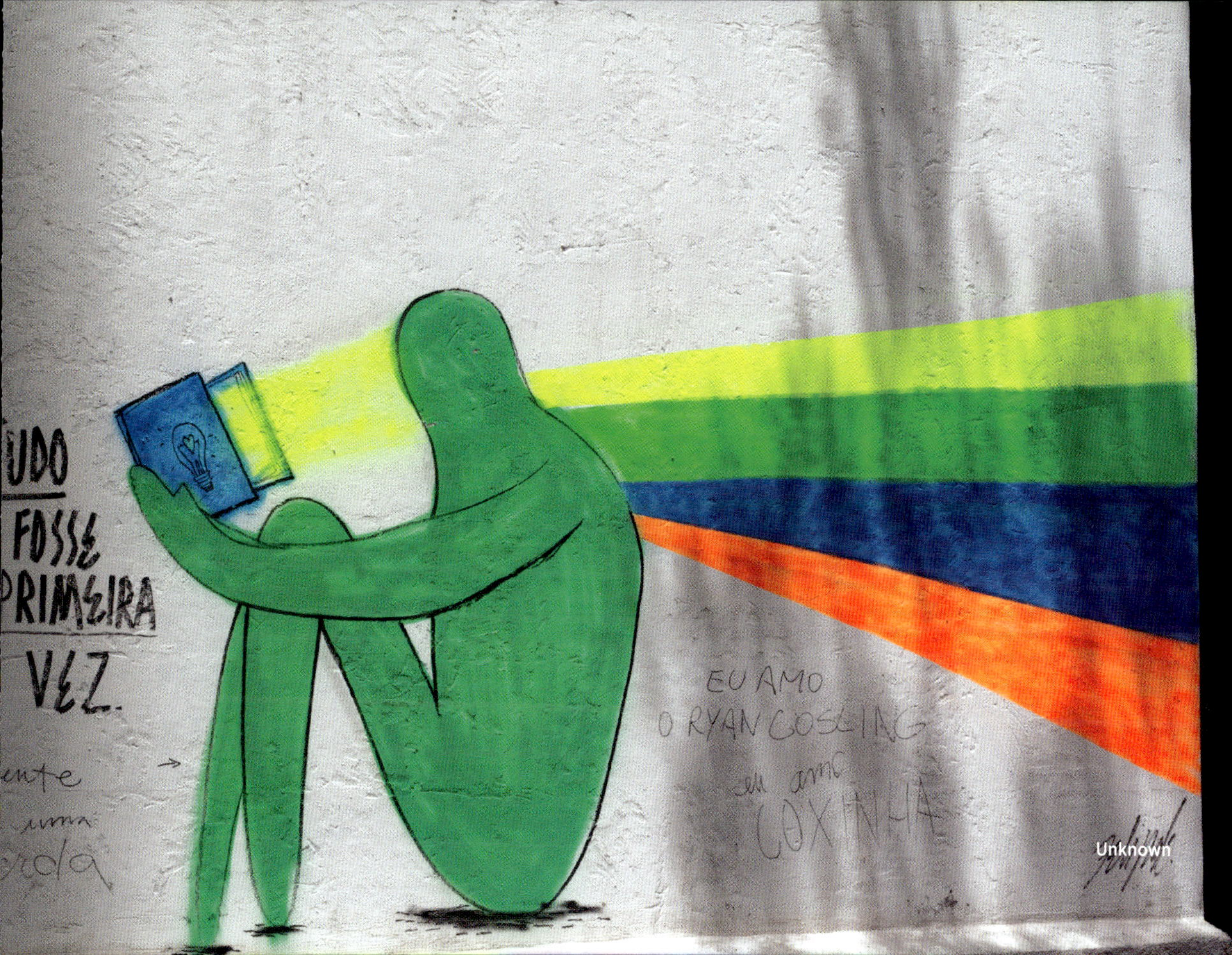

Unknown

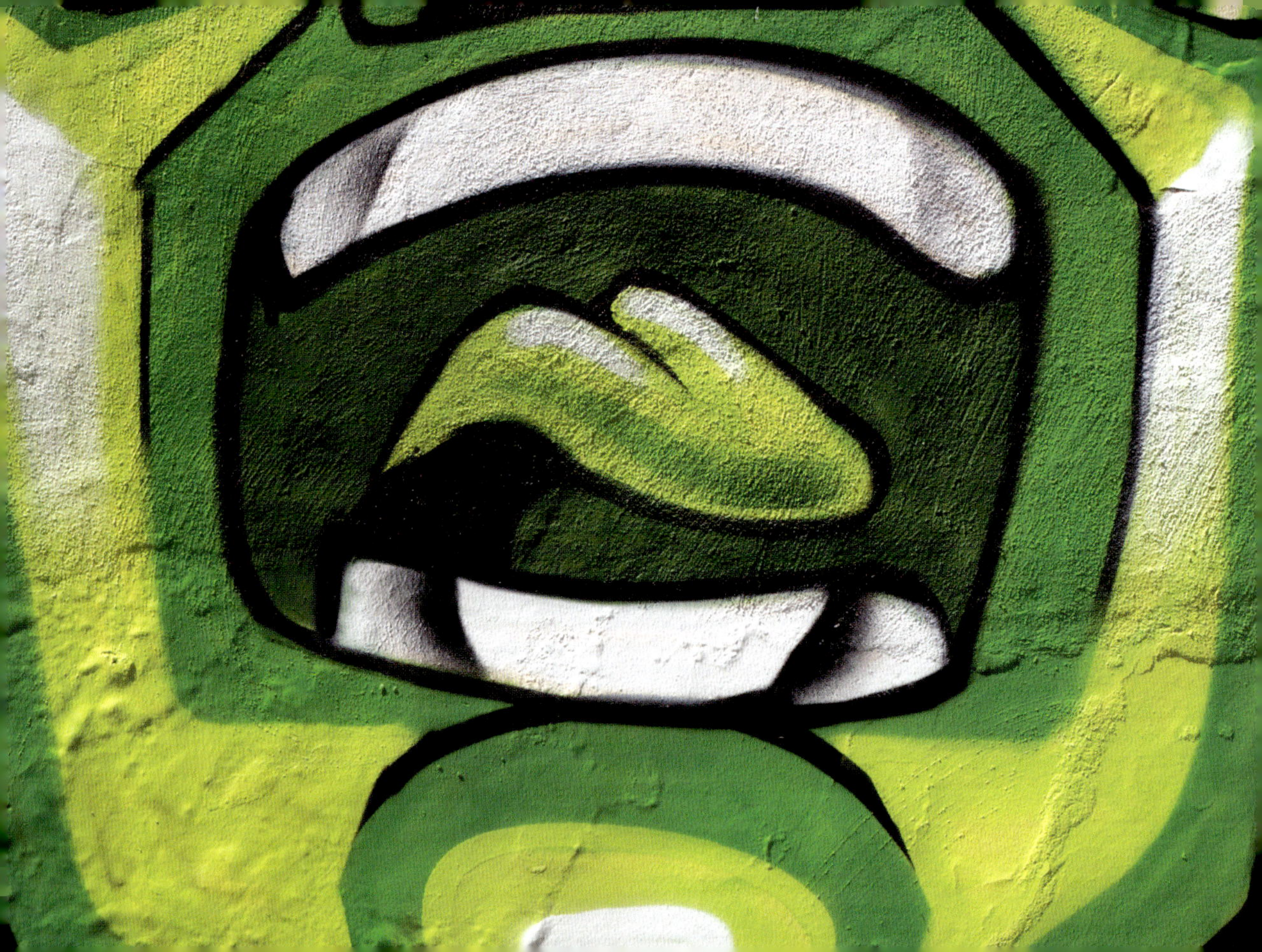

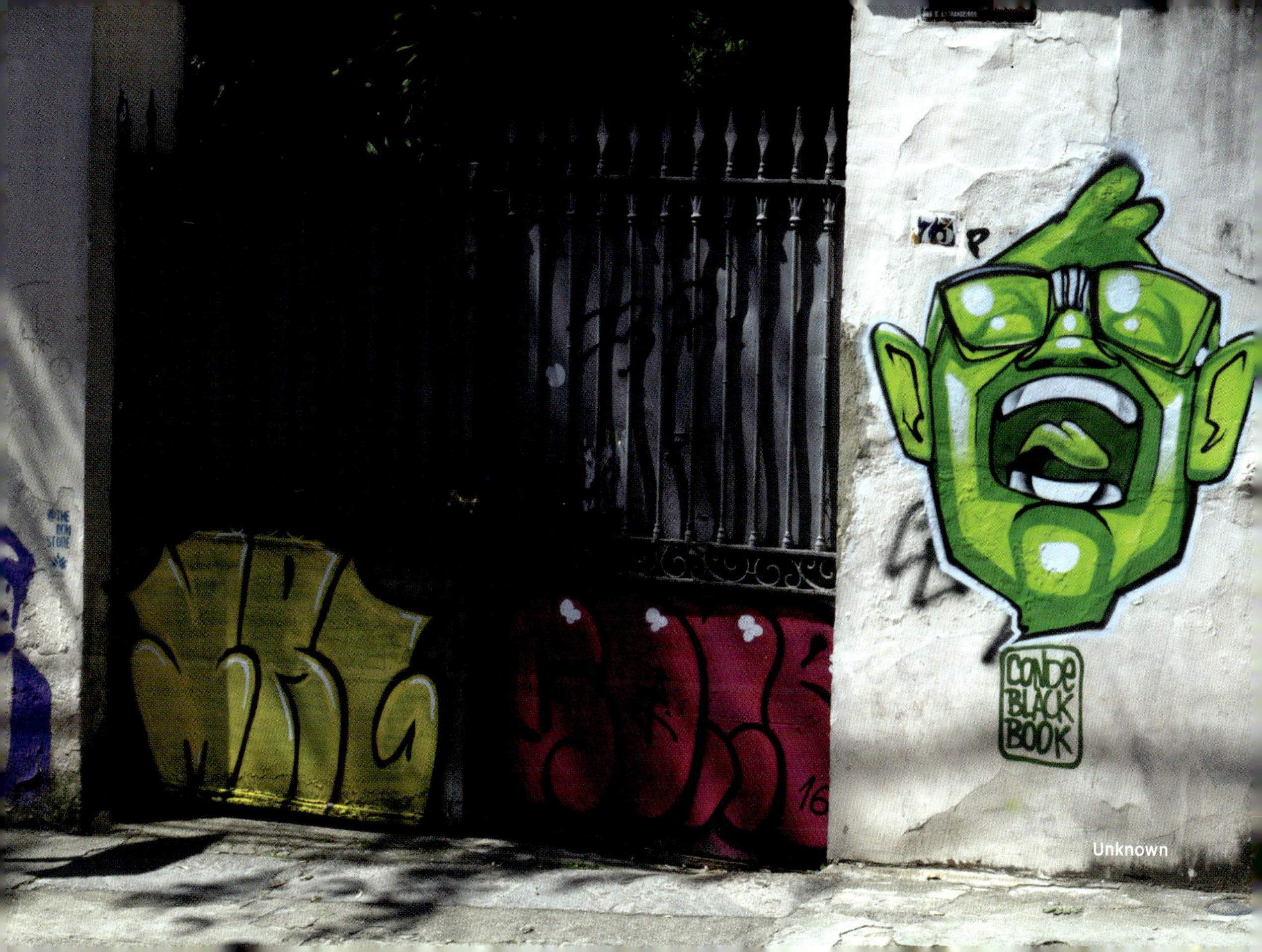

Unknown

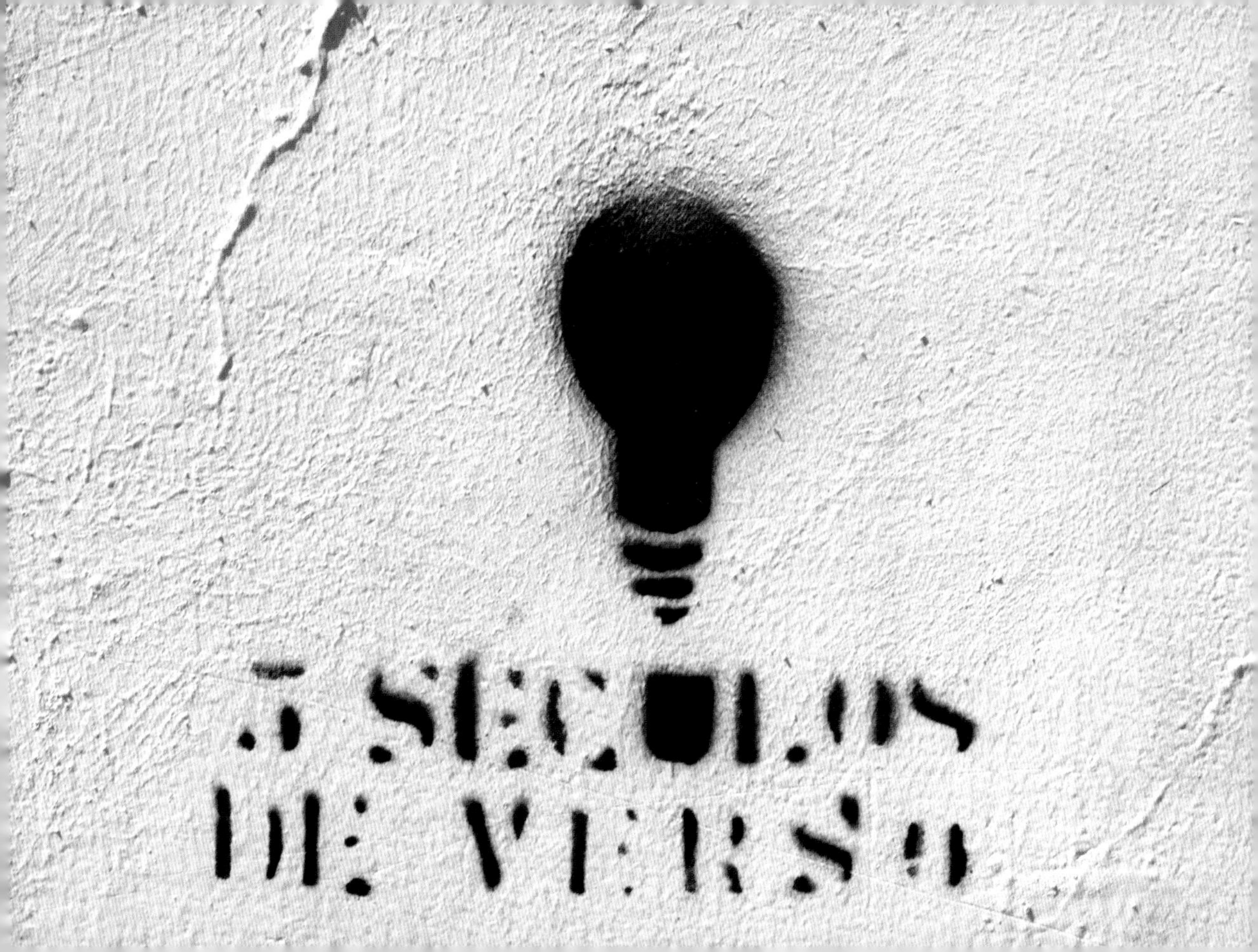
5 SECULOS
DE VERSO

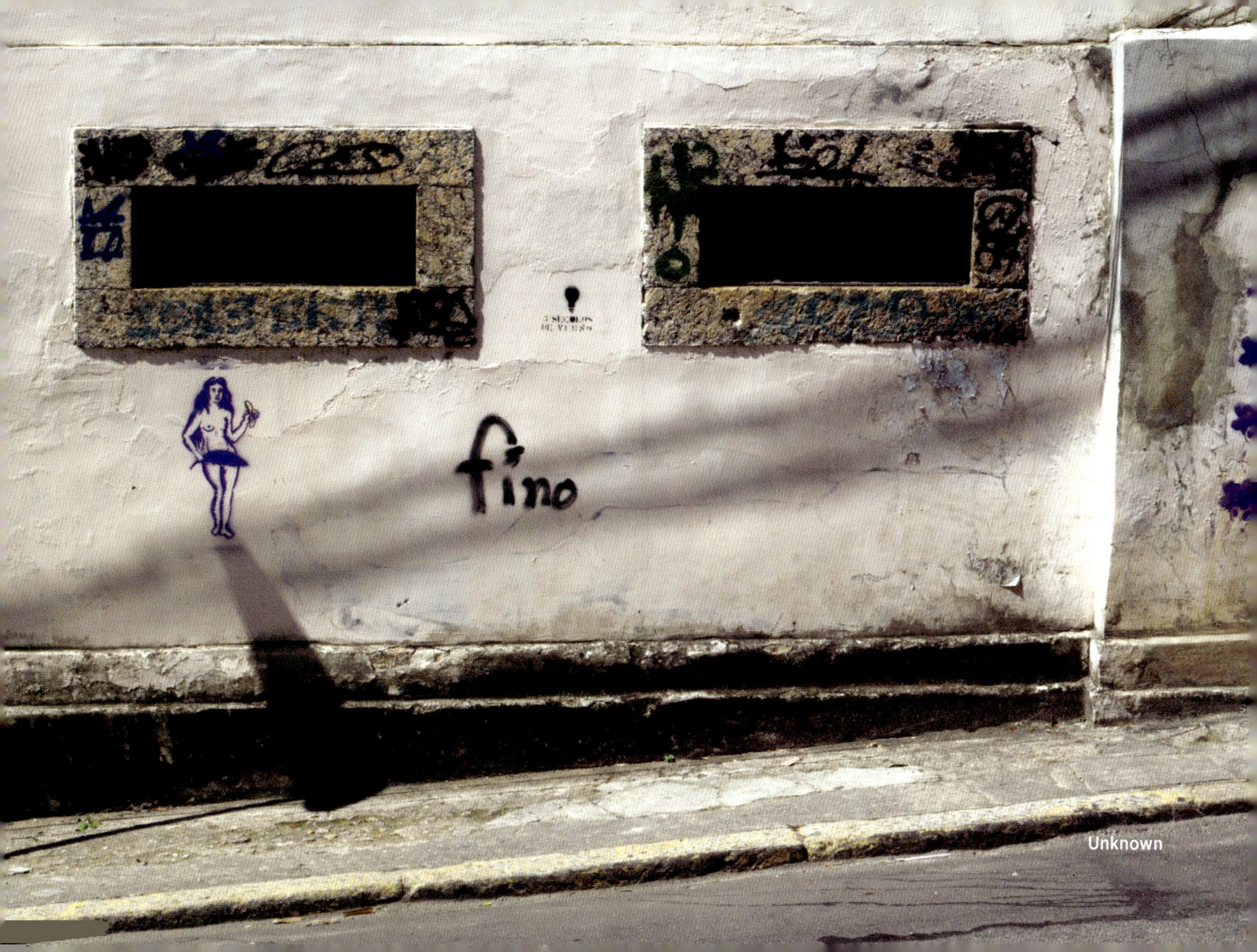

Unknown

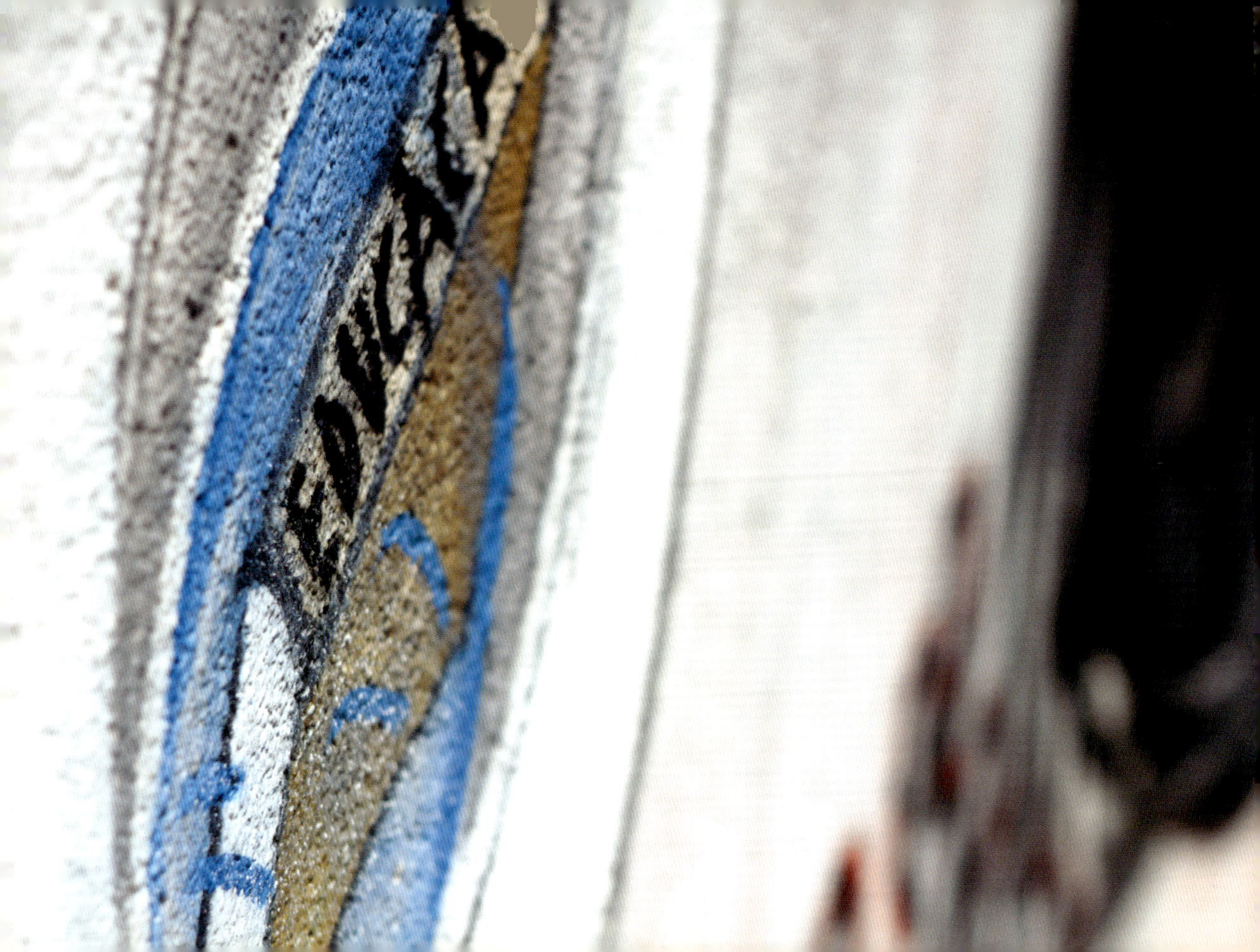

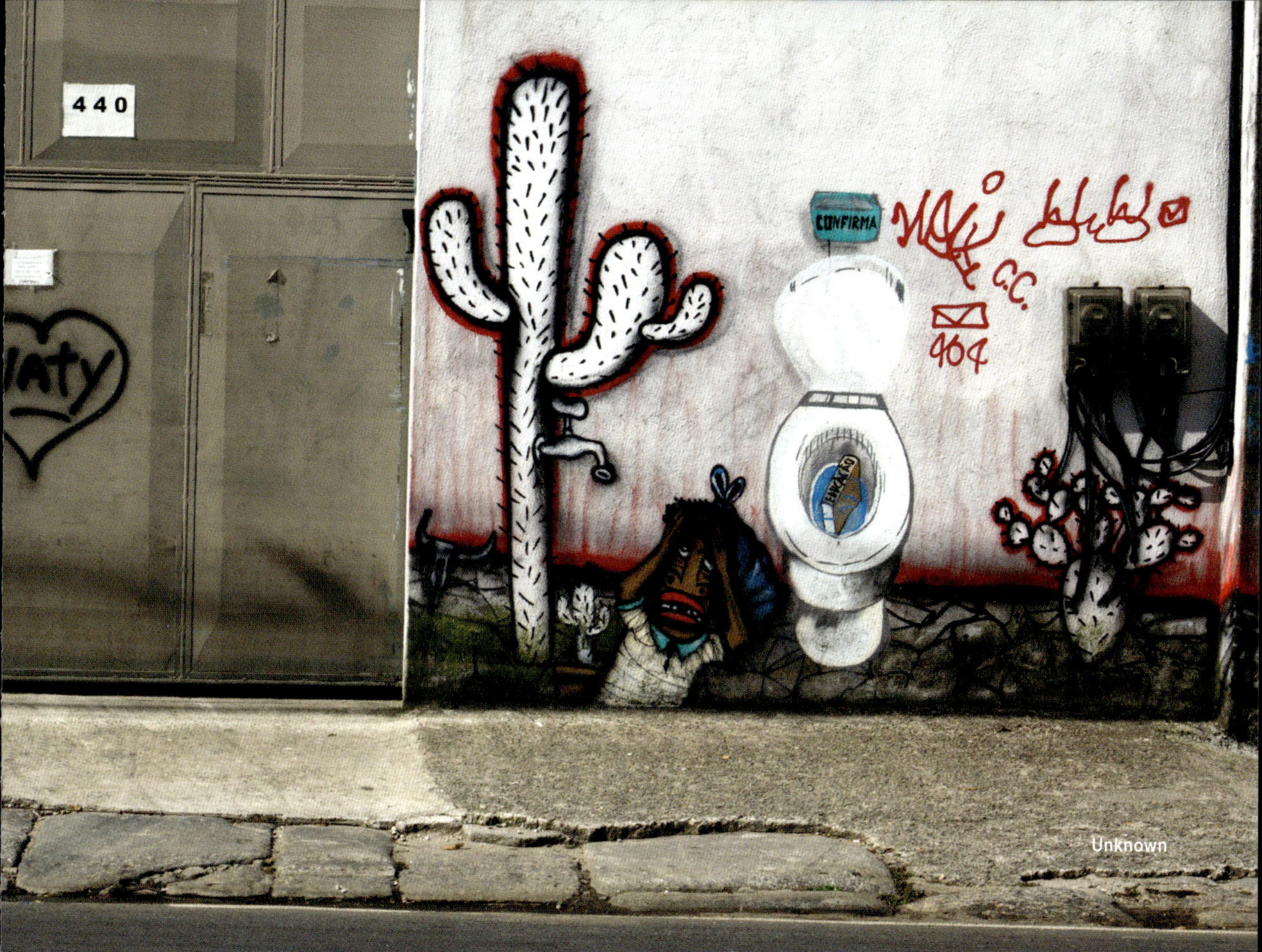

Unknown

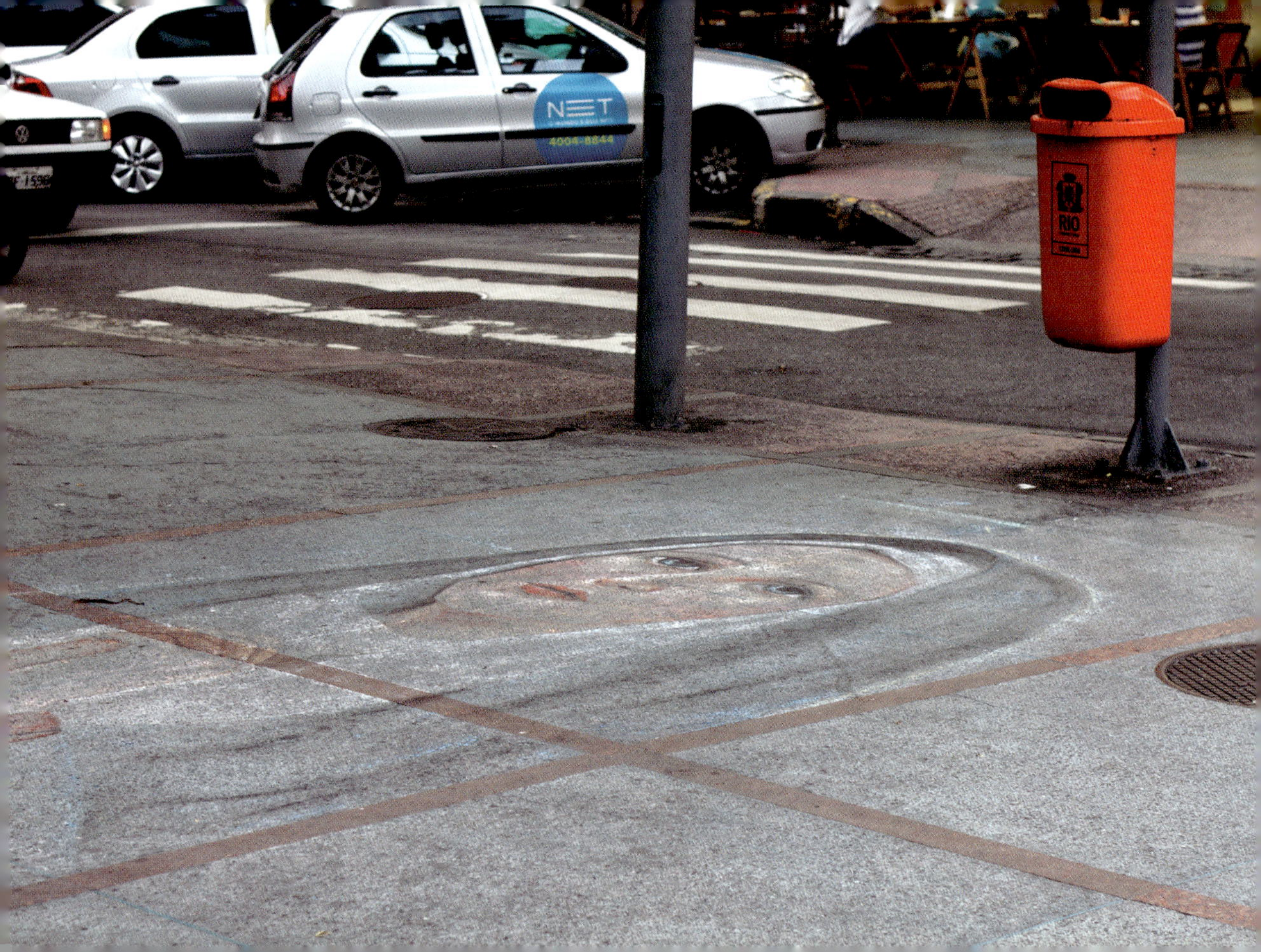
NET
4004-8844
RIO

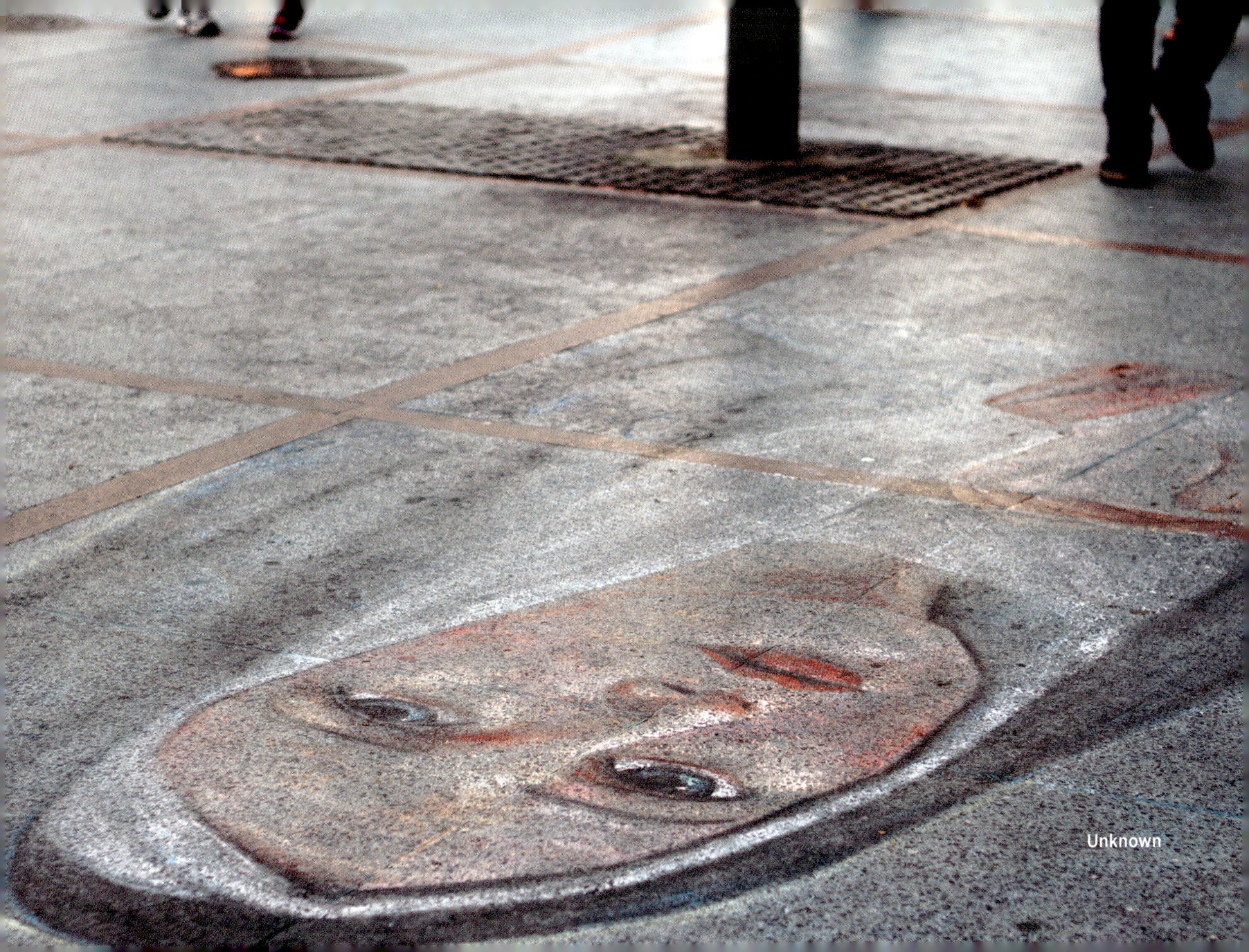

Unknown

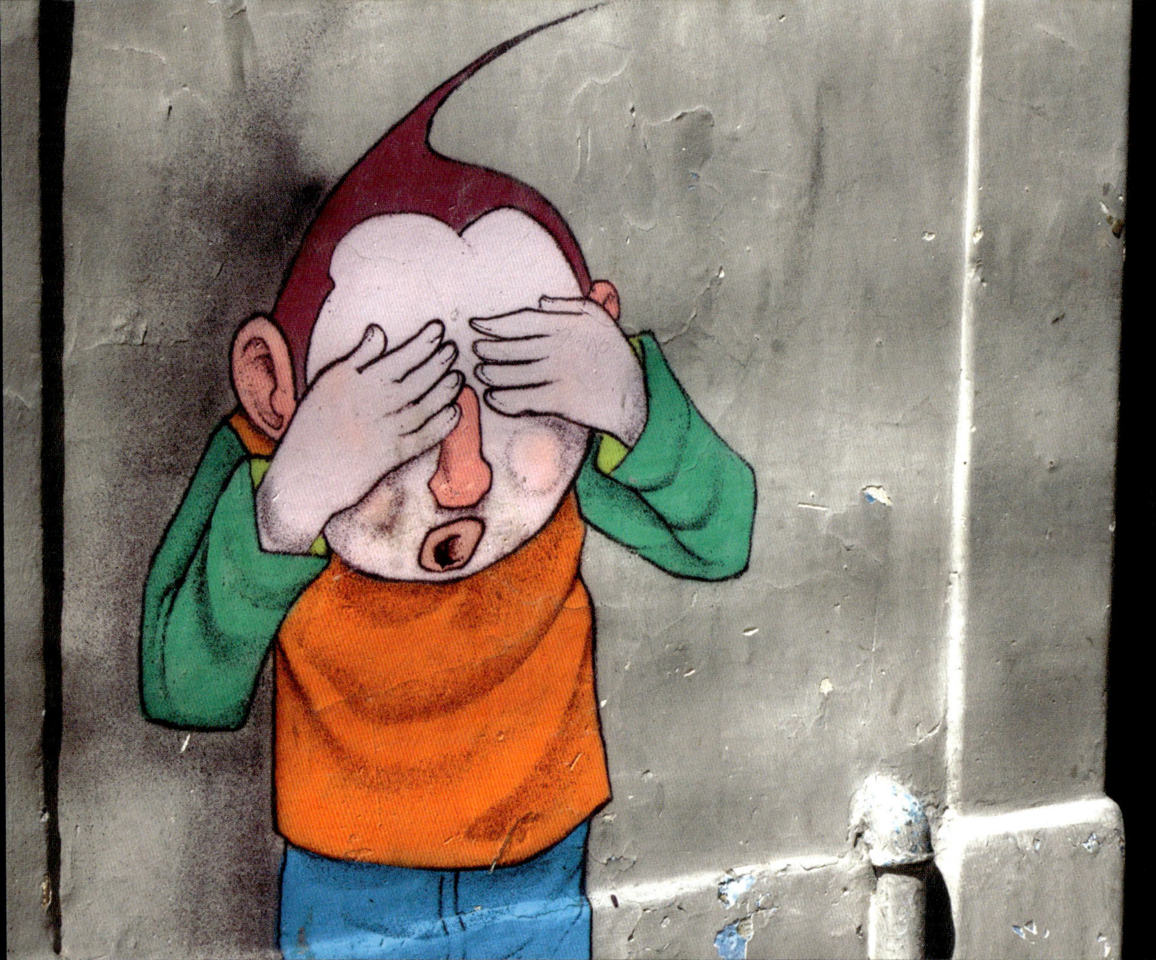

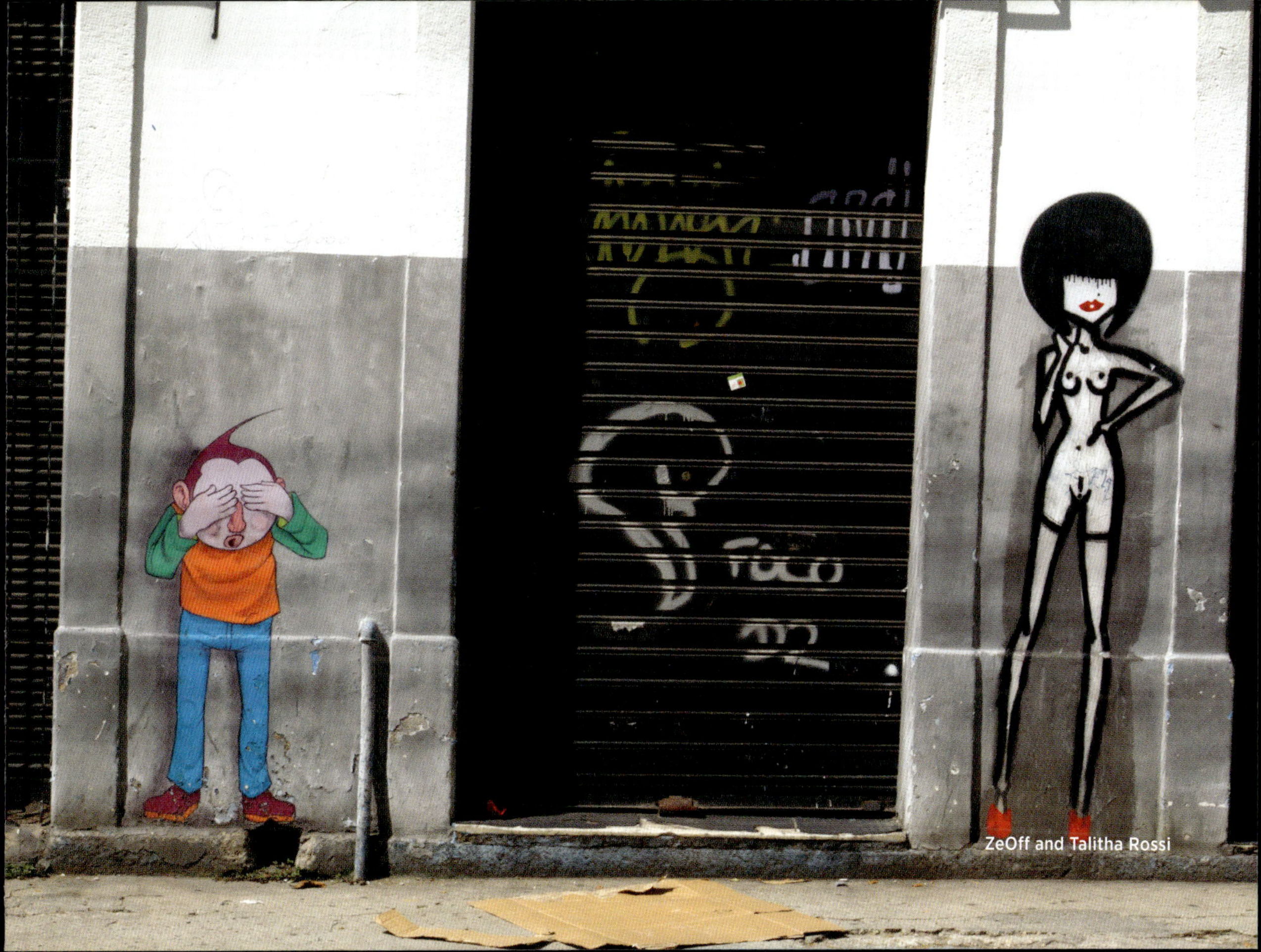

ZeOff and Talitha Rossi

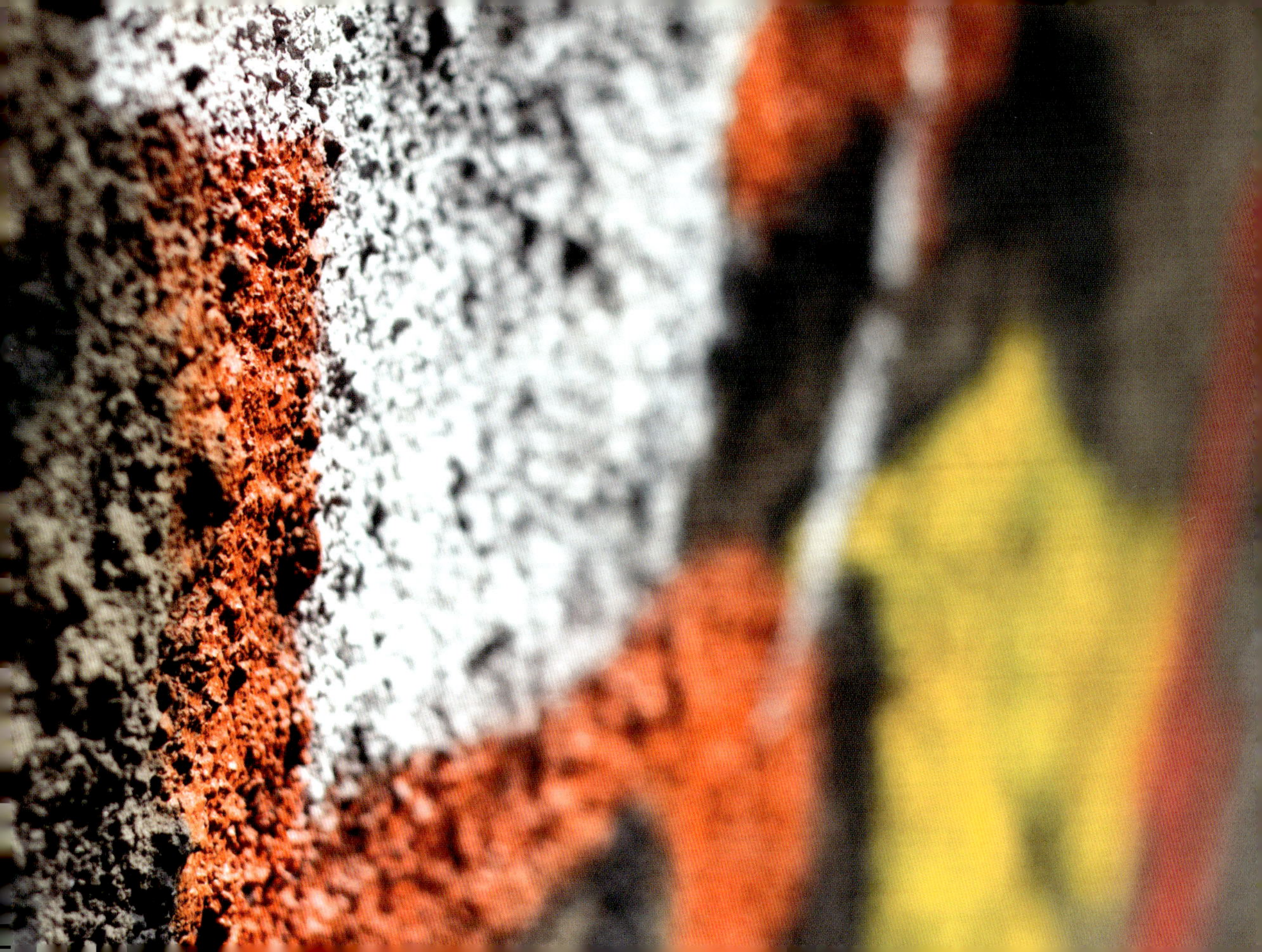

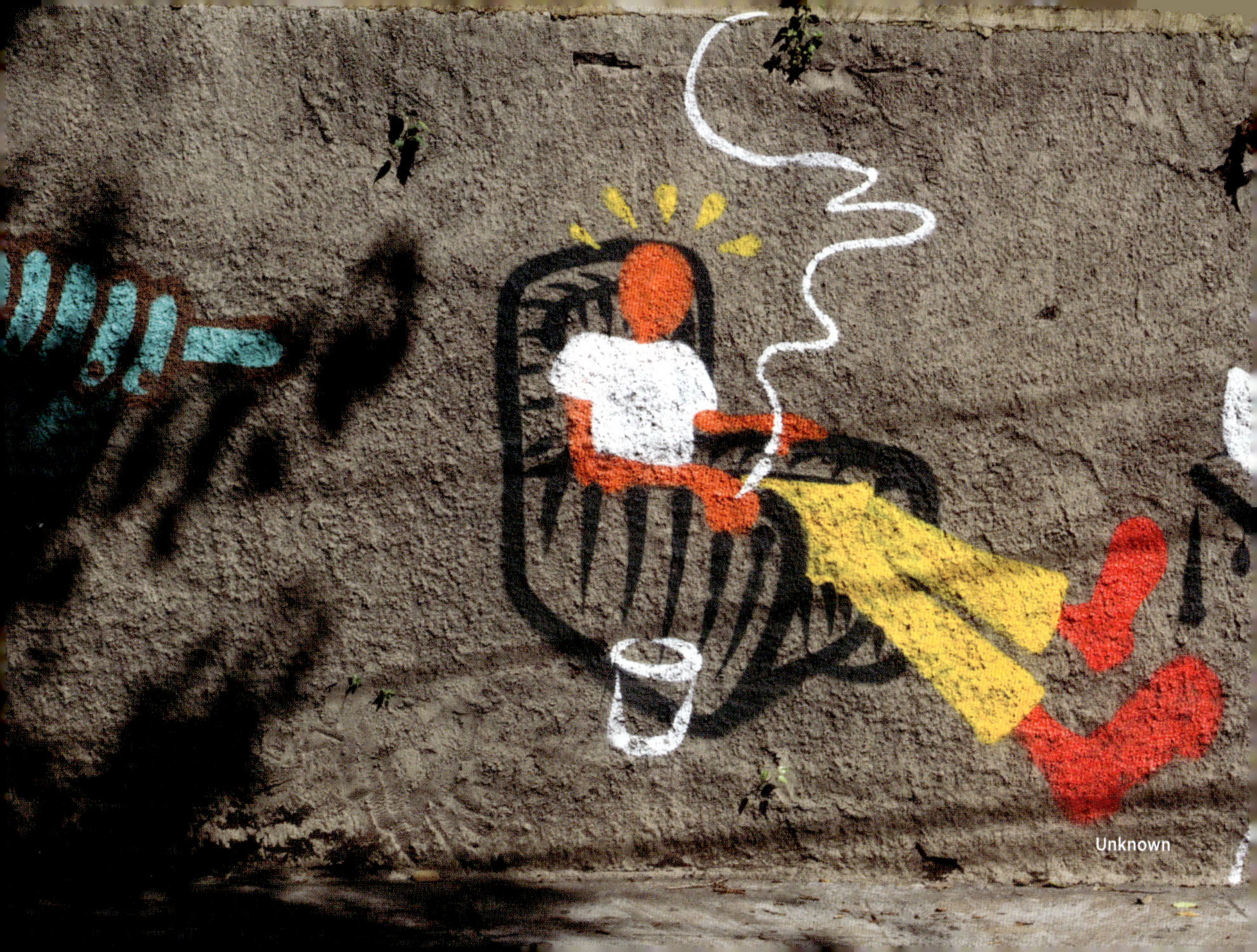

Unknown

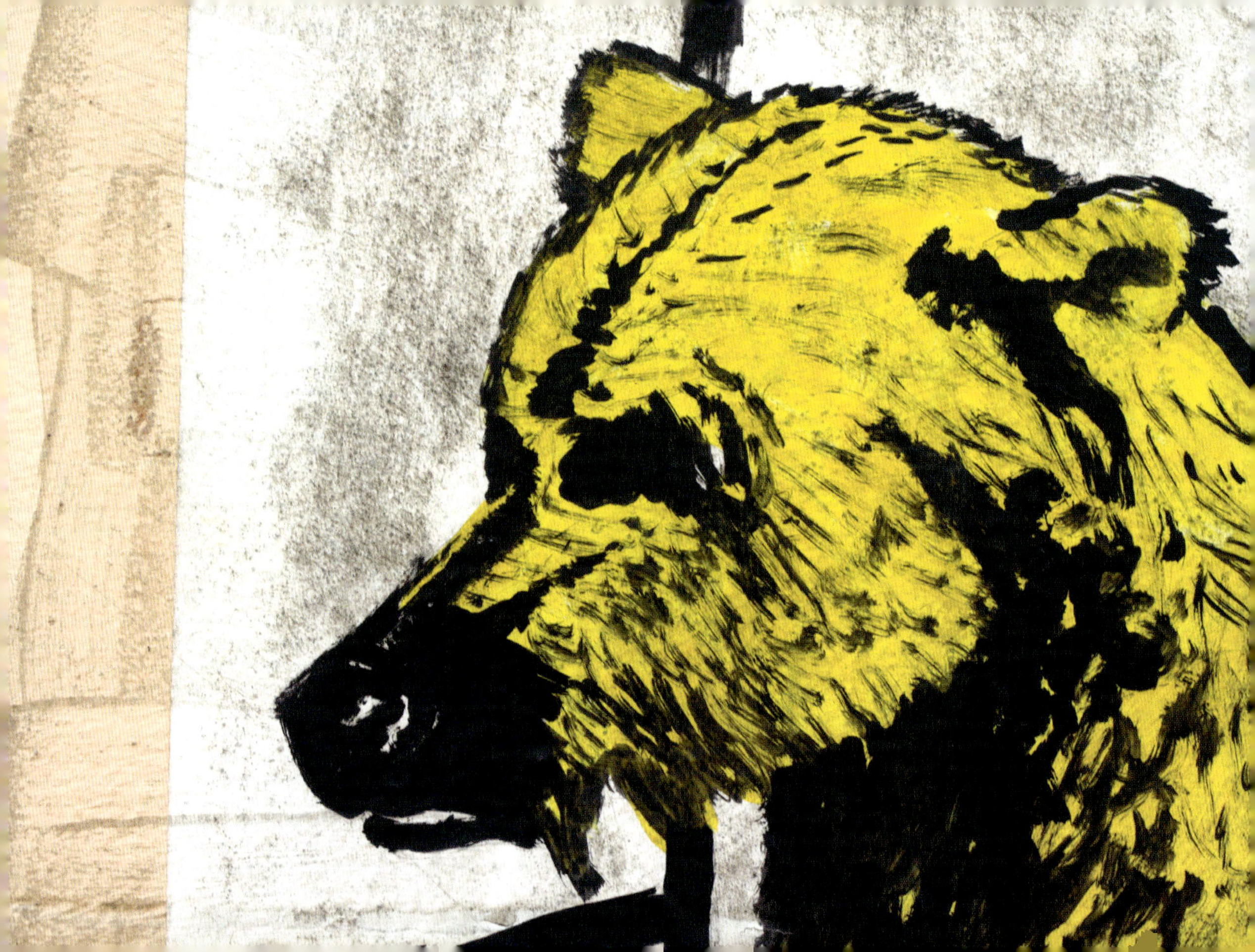

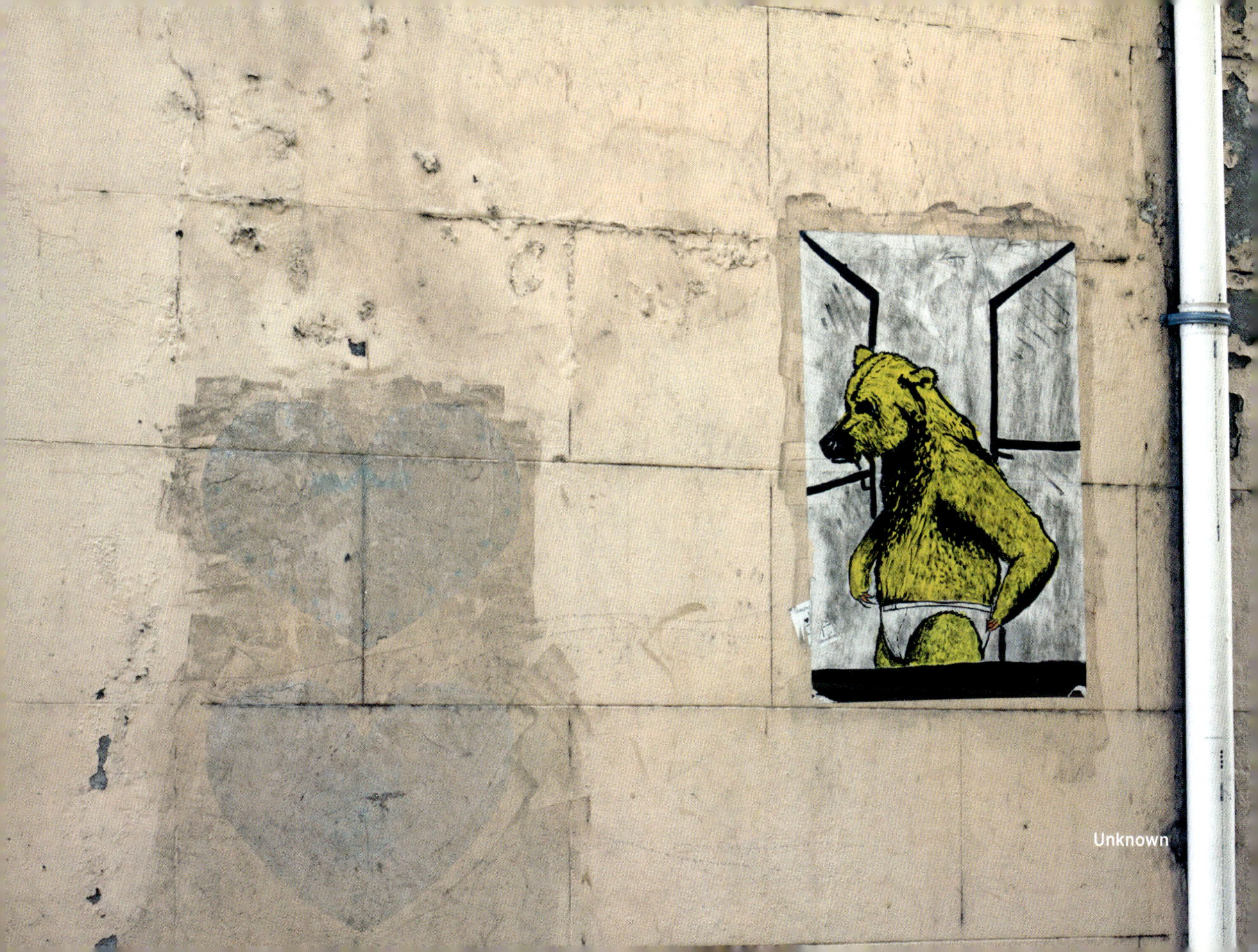

Unknown

VIDA ONE LOVE
2015
AMOR INFINITO
MAD.RJ.MUNDO
VIDA NO ALTO

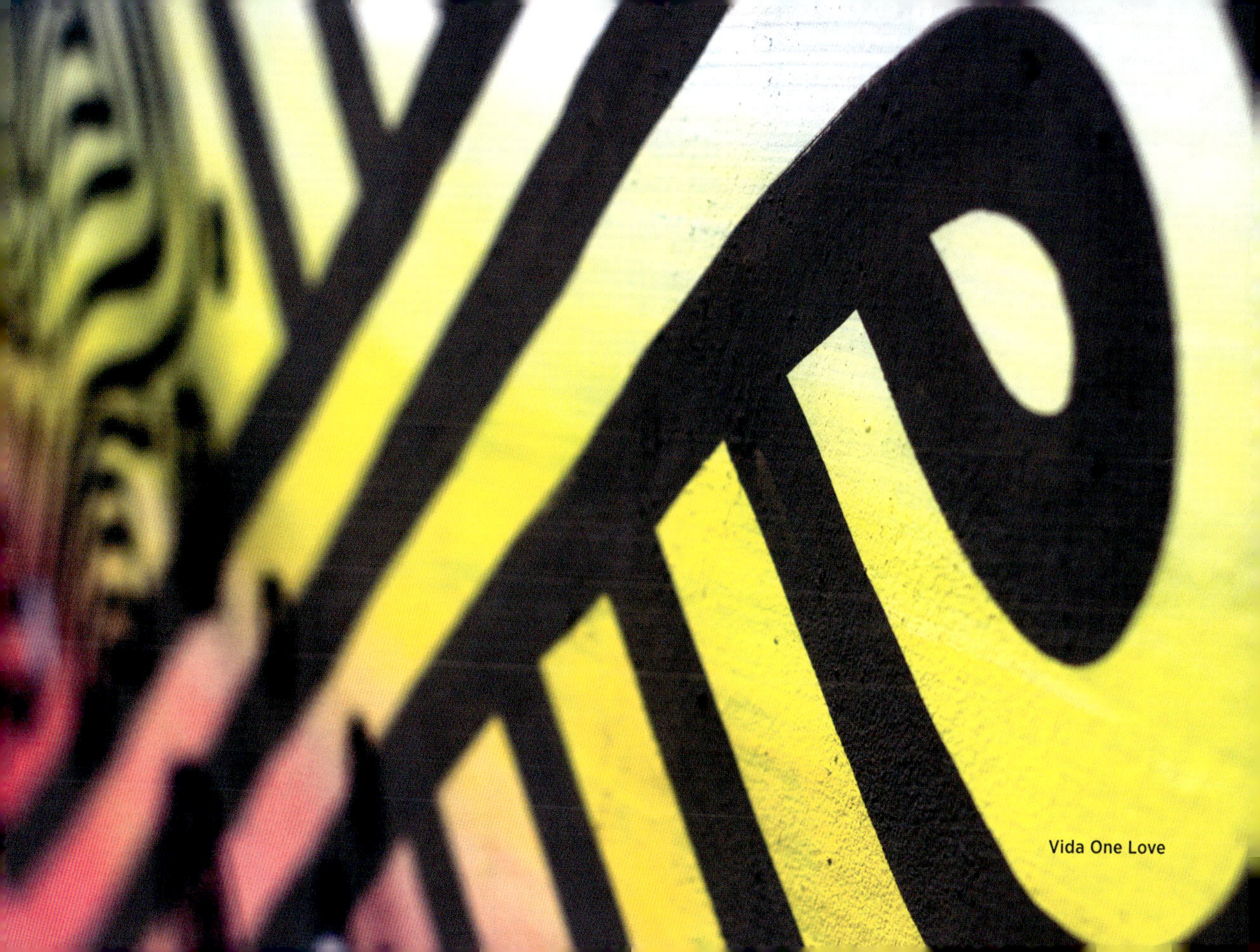

Vida One Love

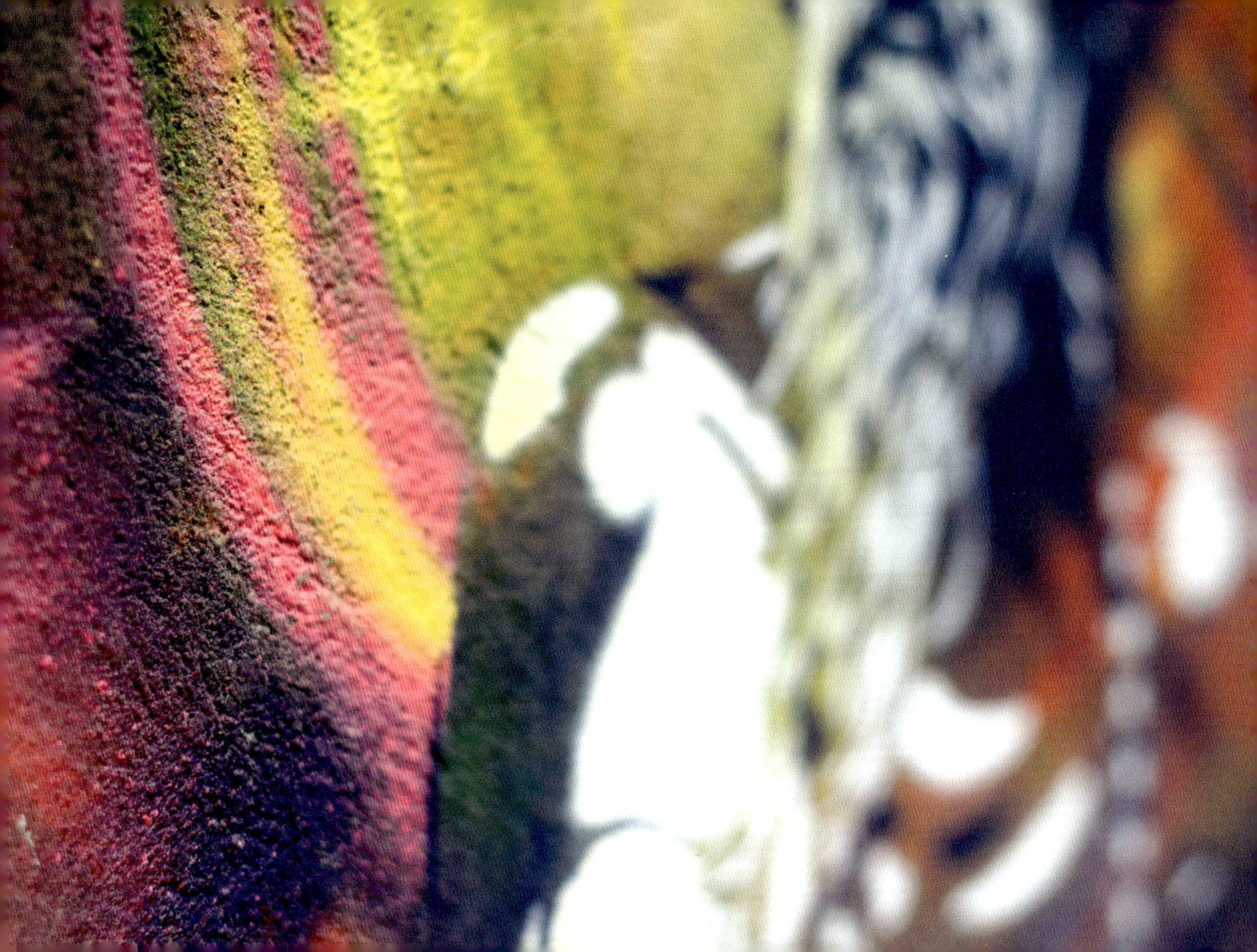

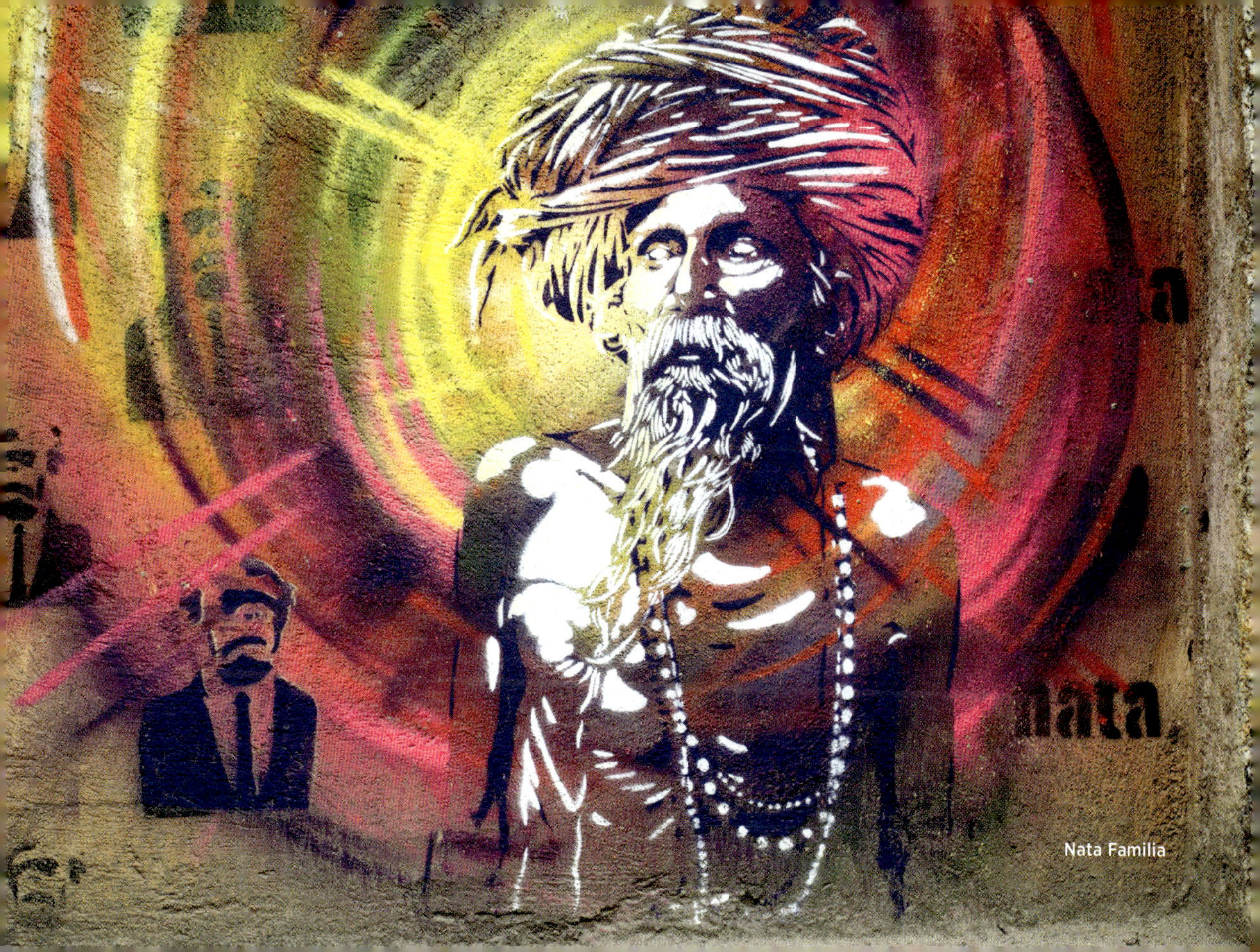

Nata Familia

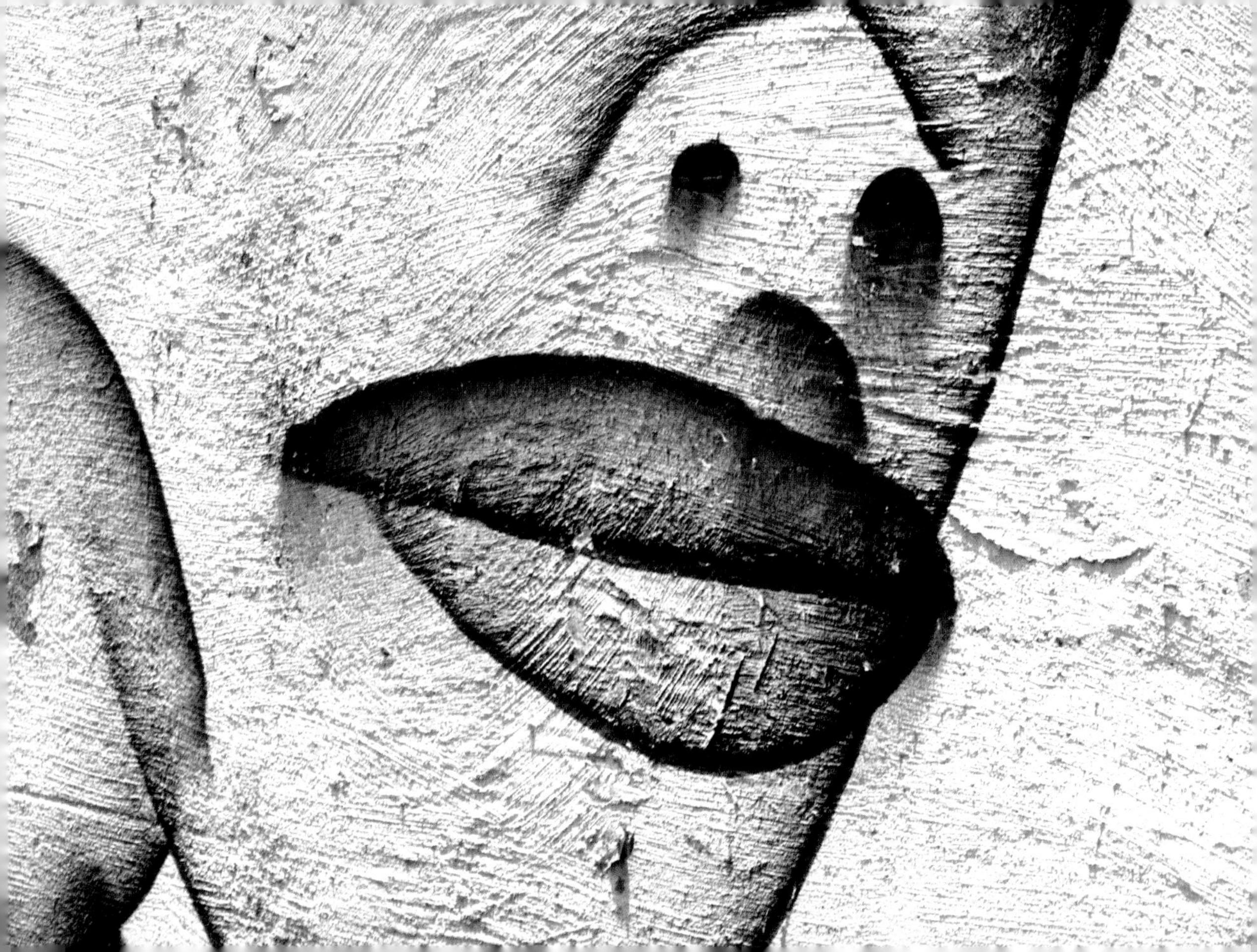

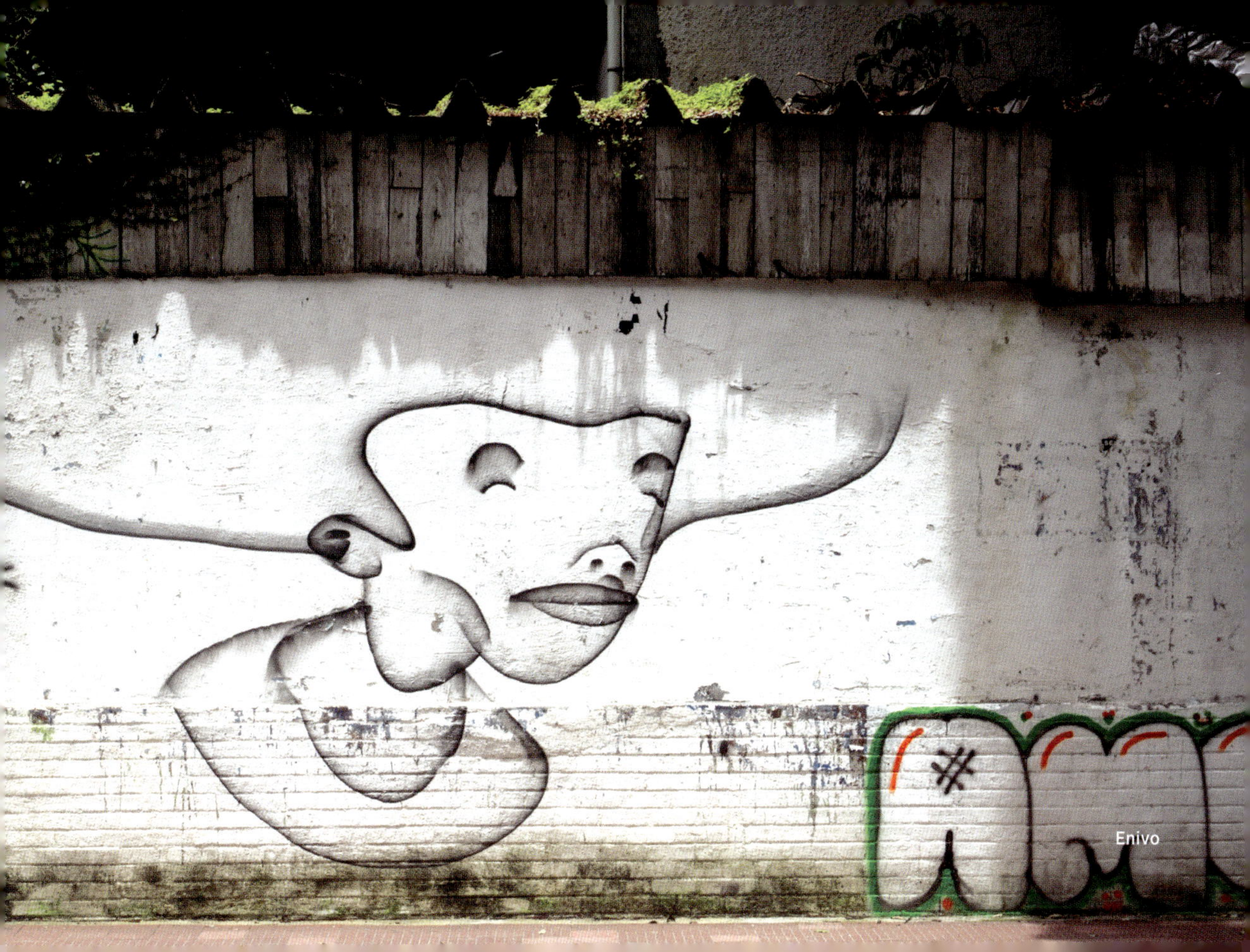

Enivo

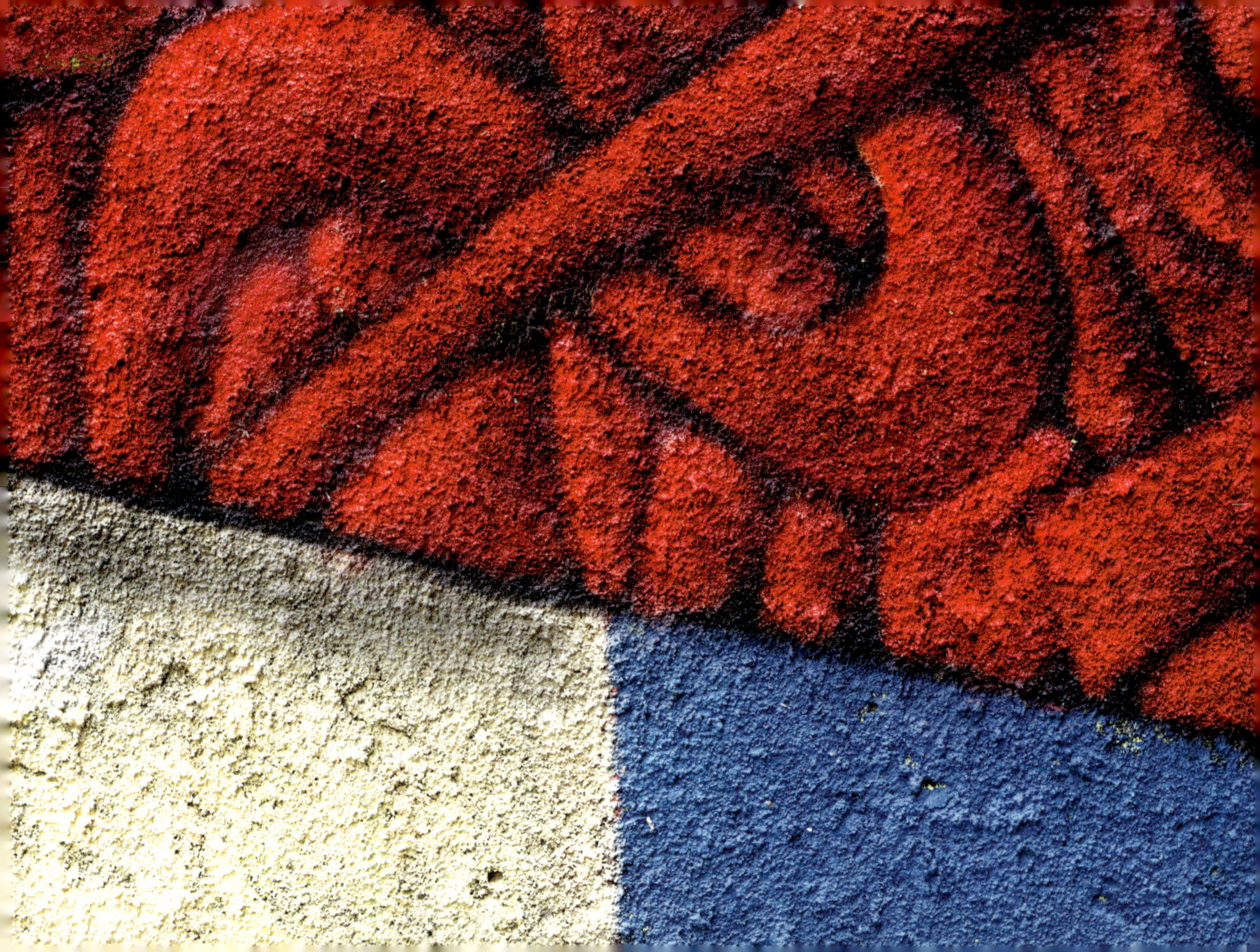

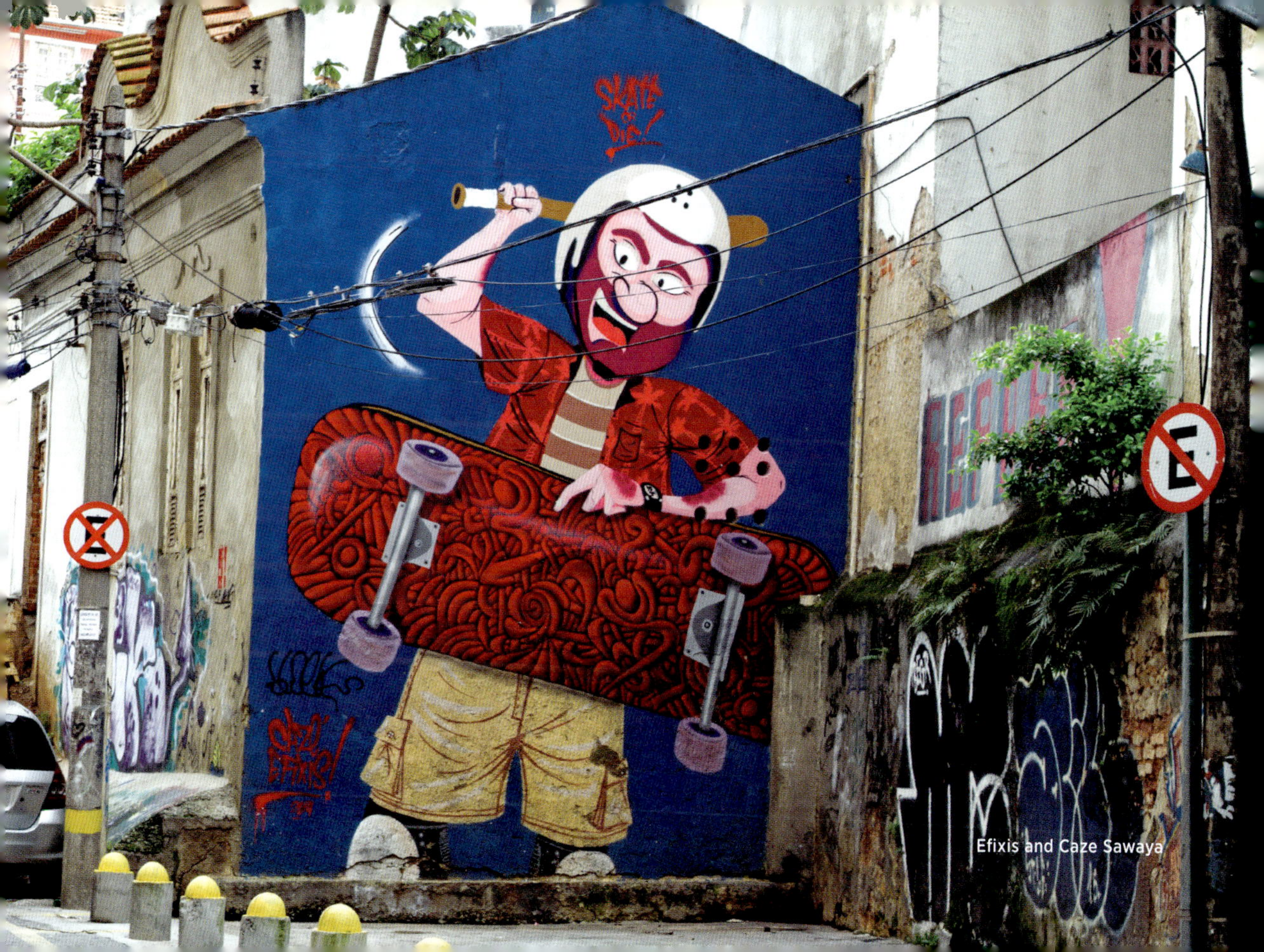

Efixis and Caze Sawaya

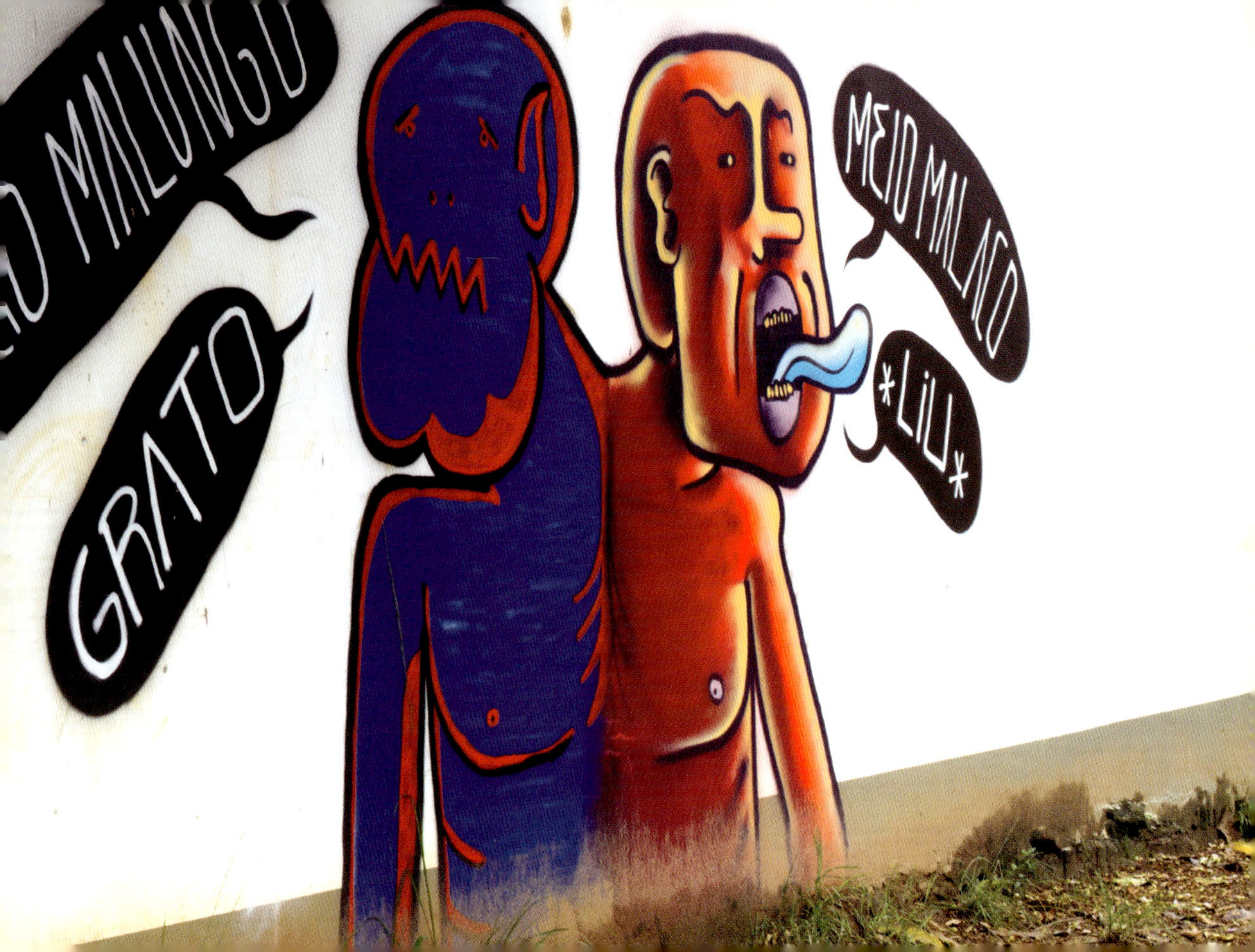
MALUNGO
GRATO
MEIO MALACO
LiU

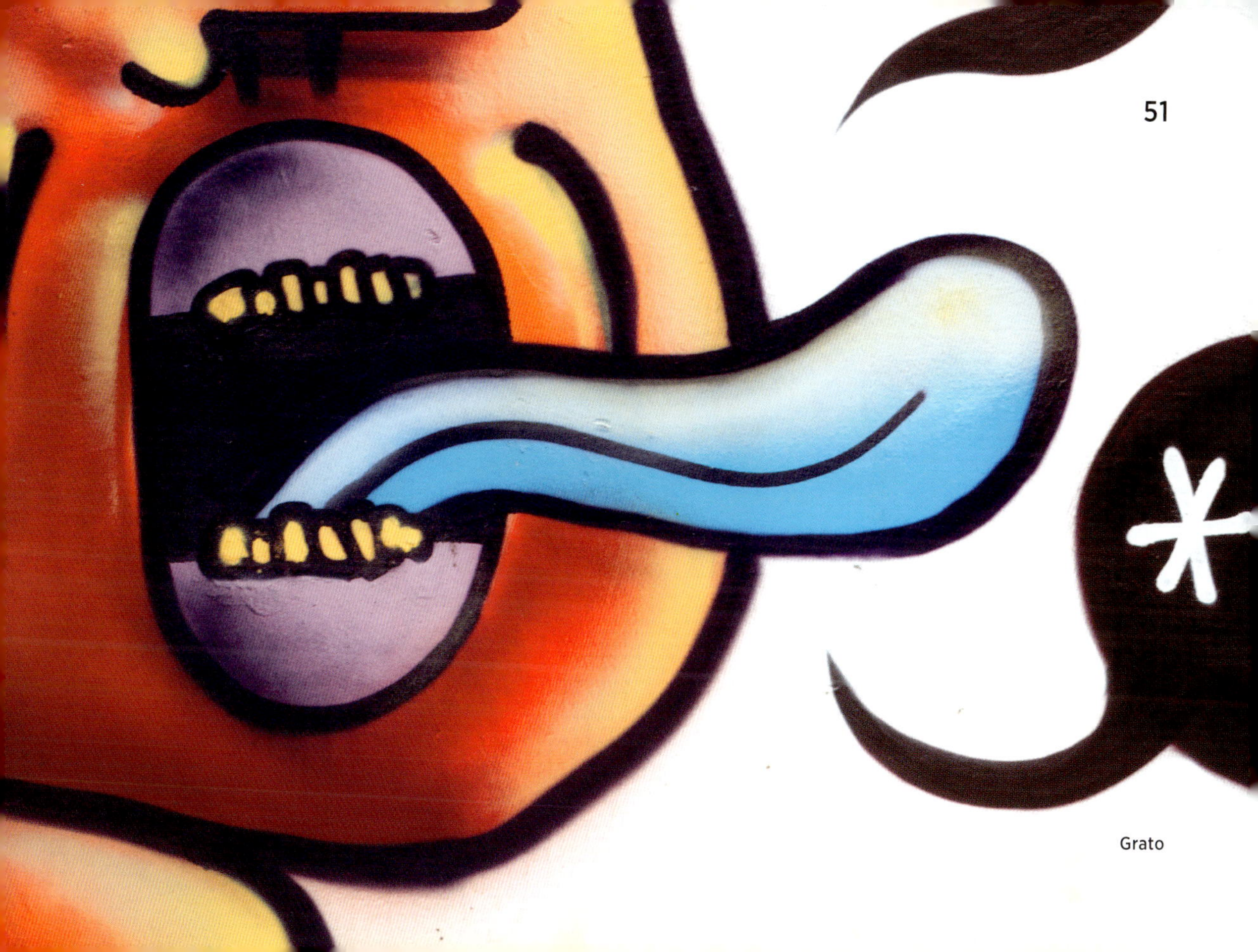

Grato

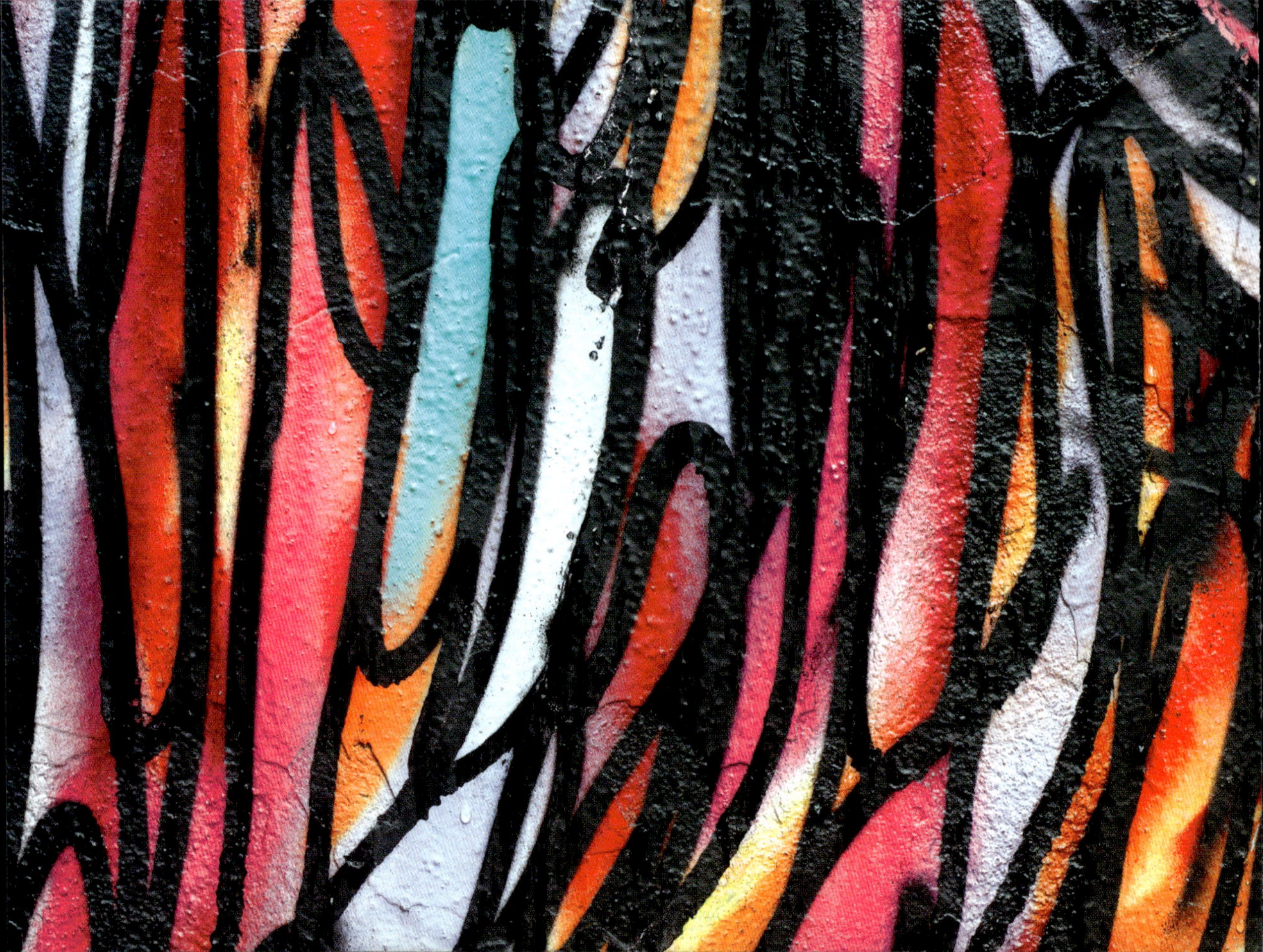

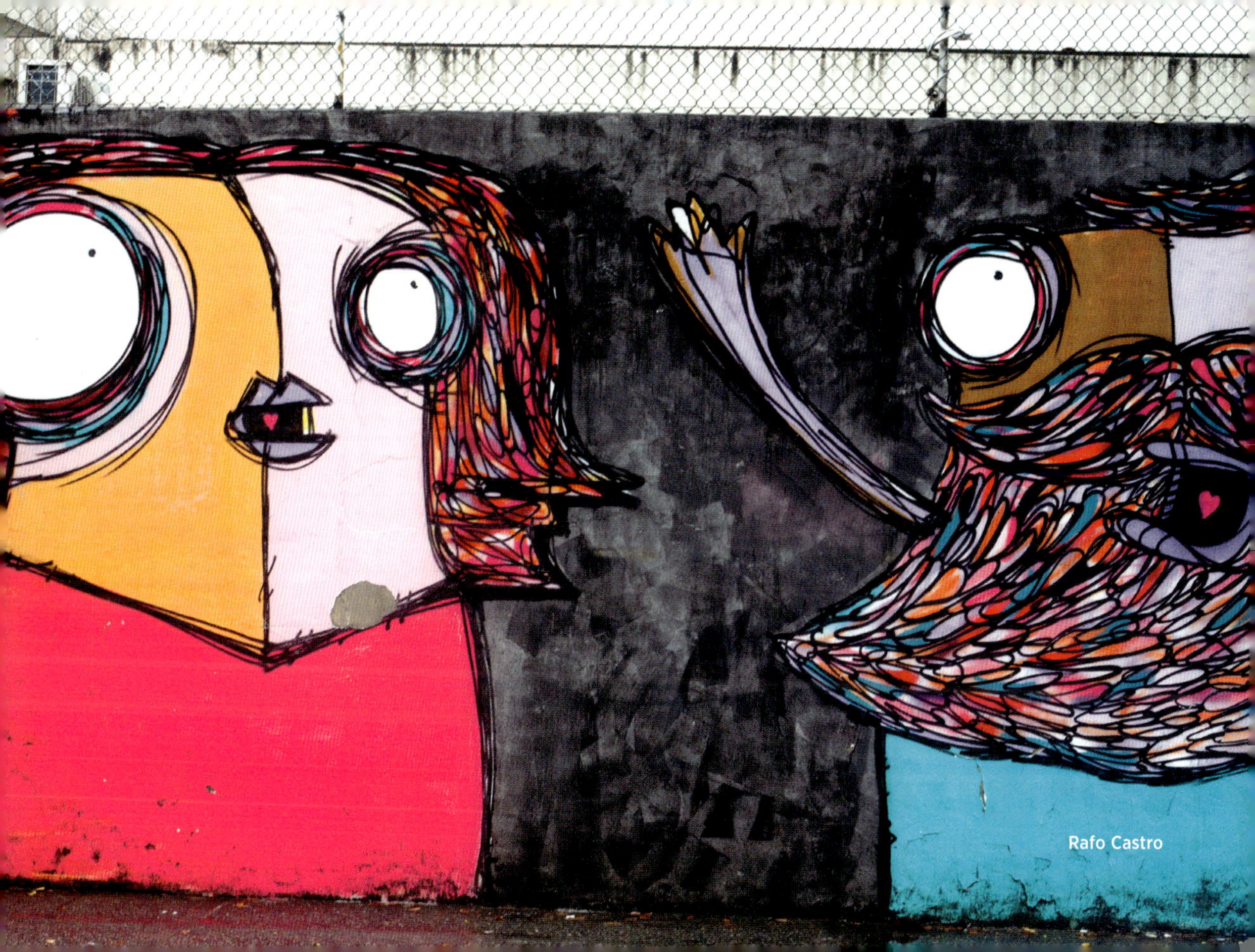

Rafo Castro

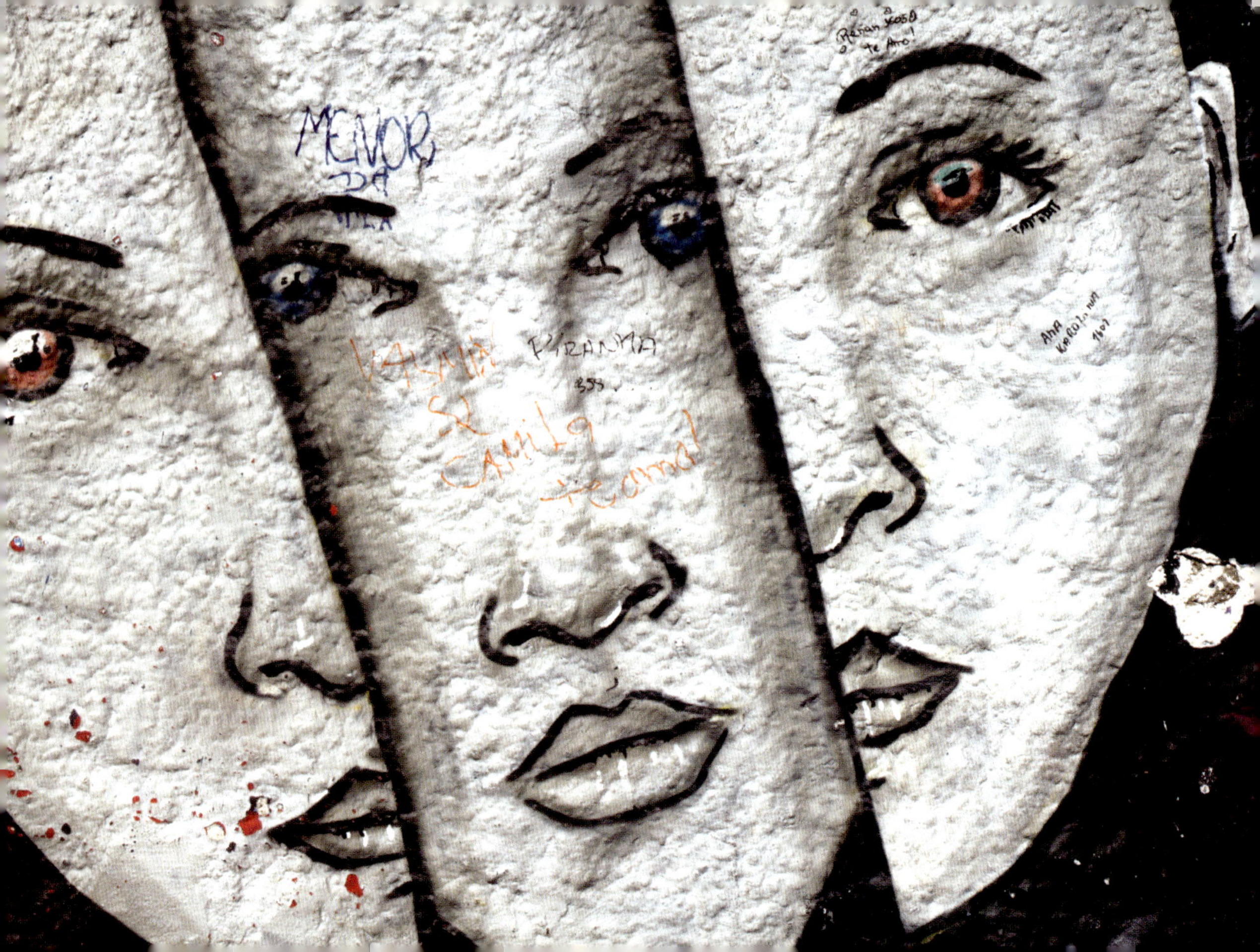
MENOR
PIRANHA

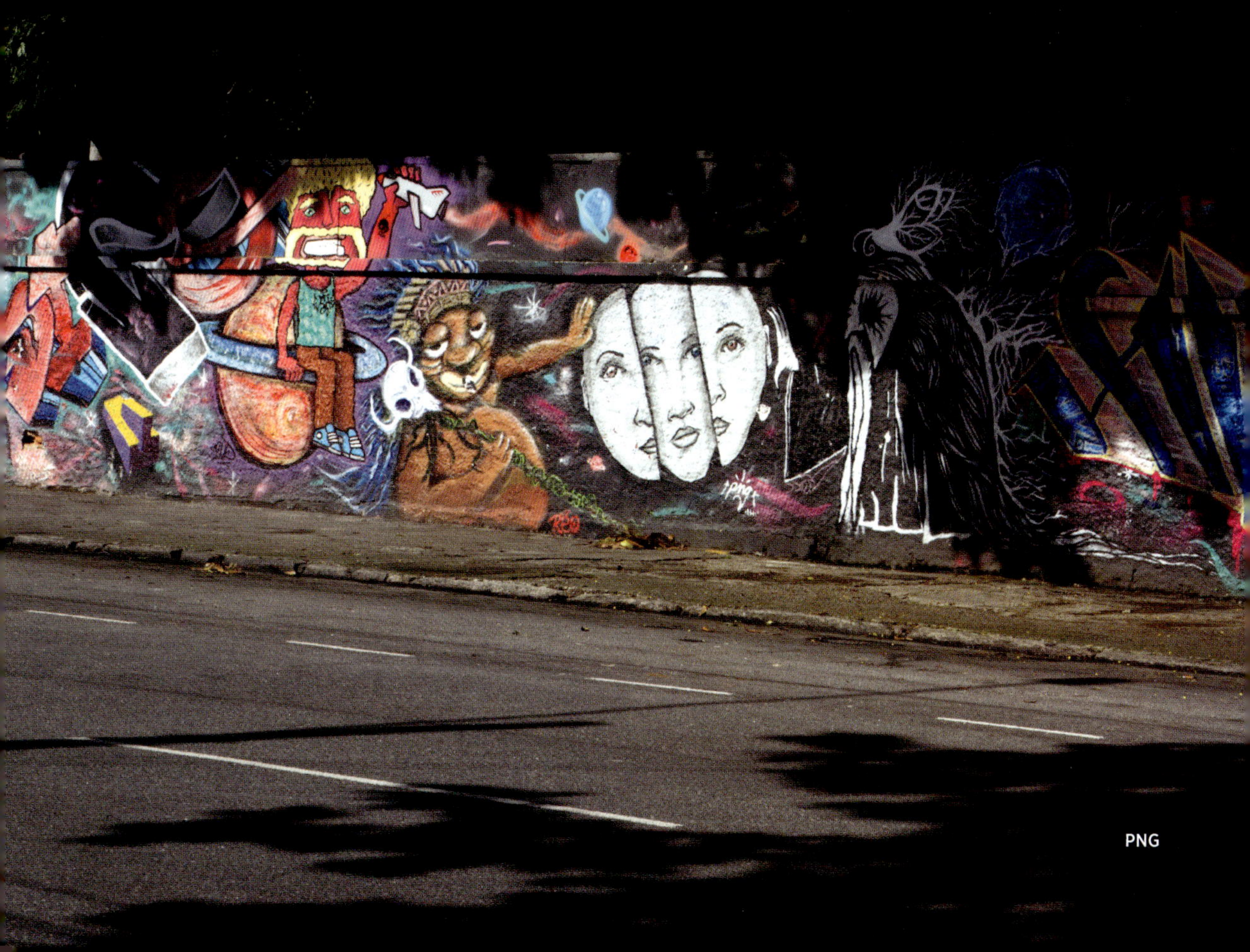

PNG

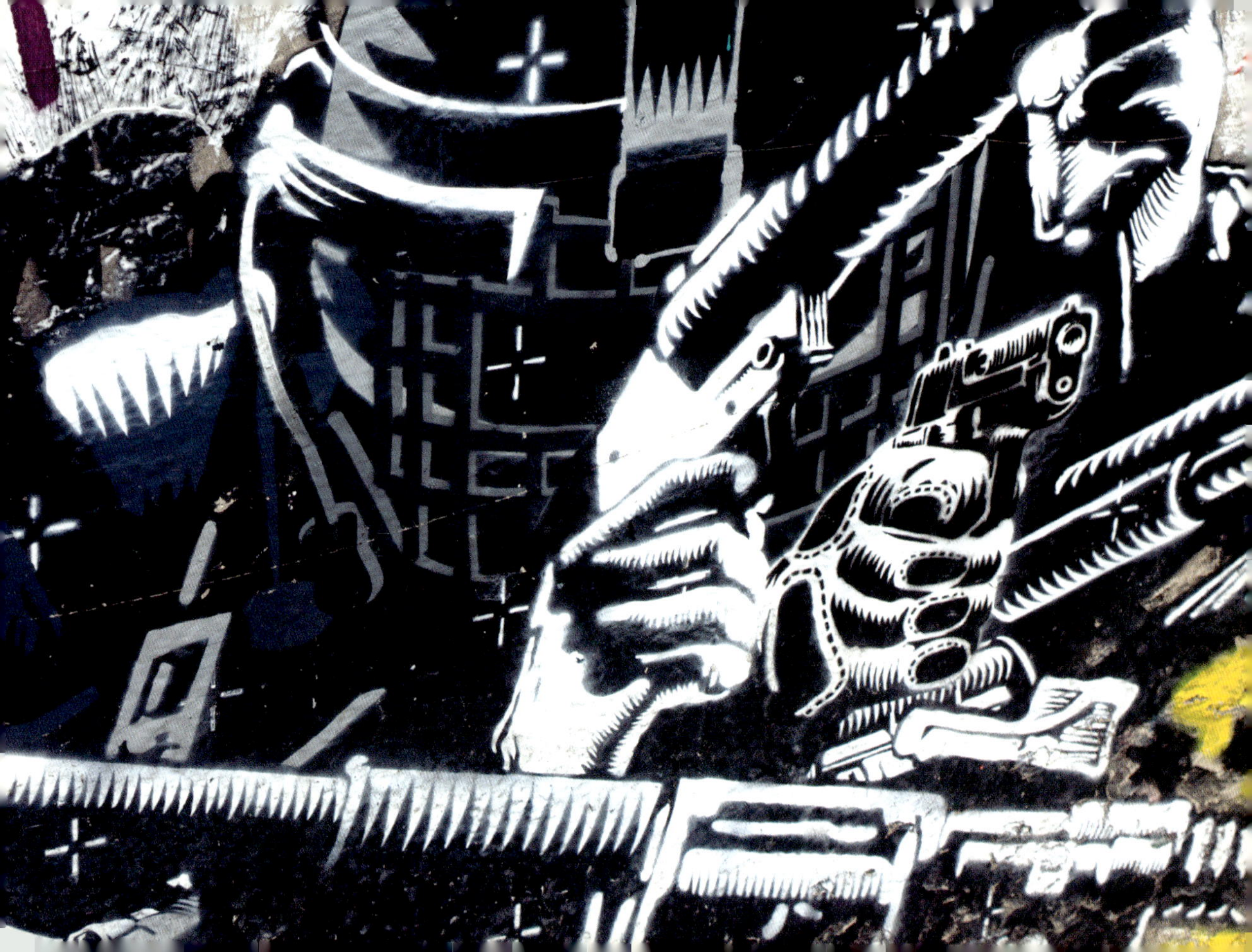

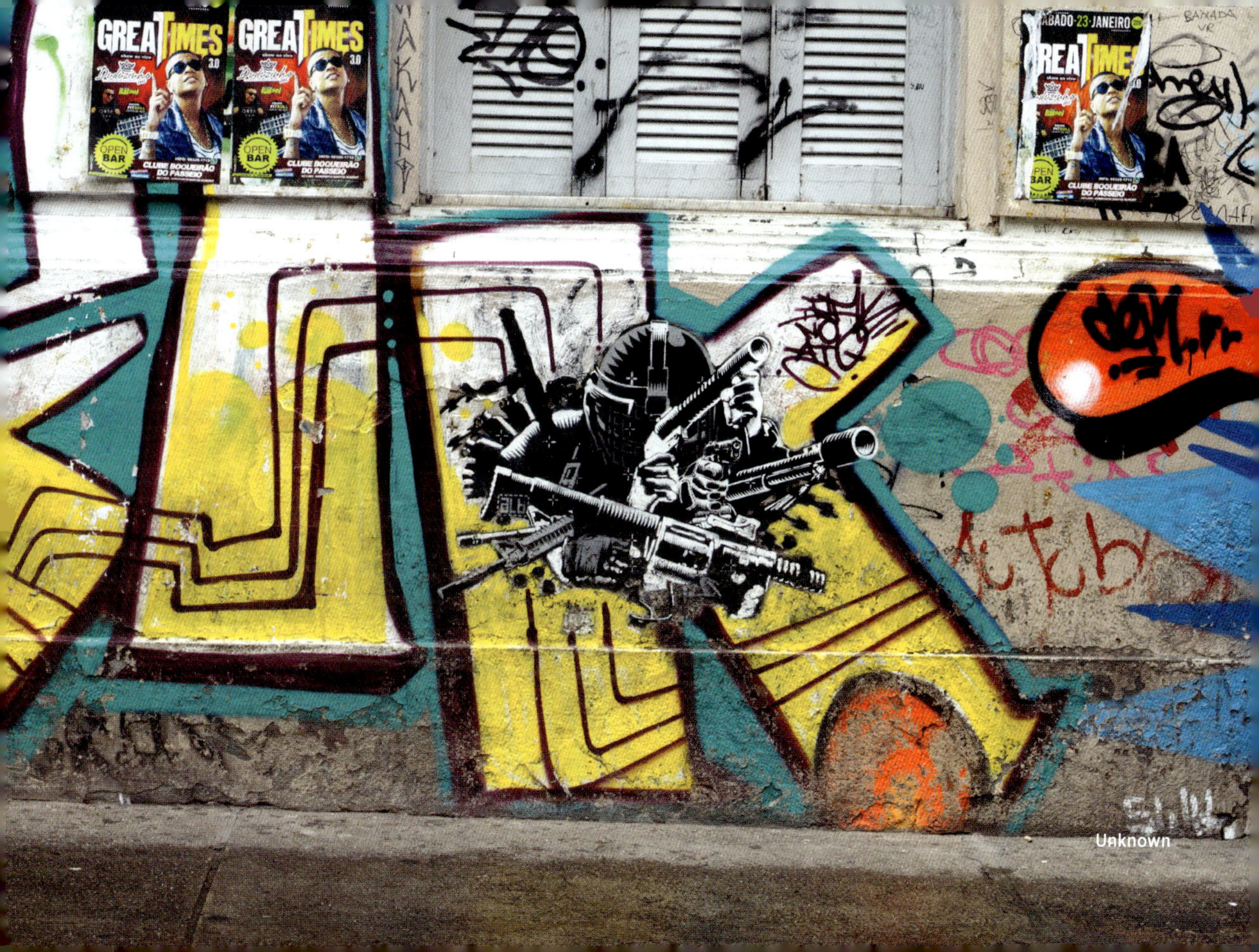
GREAT TIMES
OPEN BAR
CLUBE BOQUEIRÃO DO PASSEIO
GREAT TIMES
OPEN BAR
CLUBE BOQUEIRÃO DO PASSEIO
SÁBADO·23·JANEIRO
OPEN BAR
CLUBE BOQUEIRÃO DO PASSEIO

Unknown

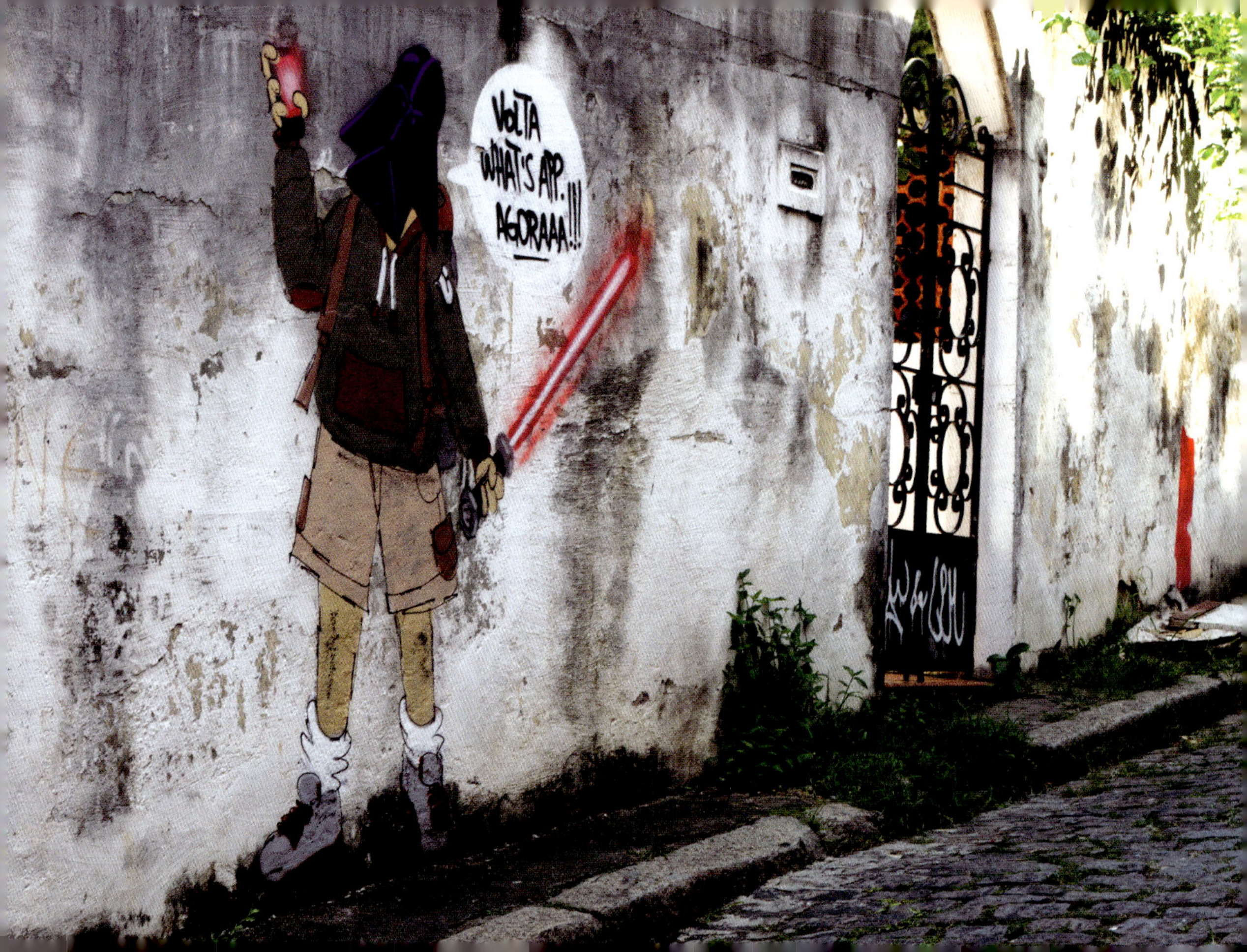
VOLTA WHAT'S APP. AGORAAA!!!

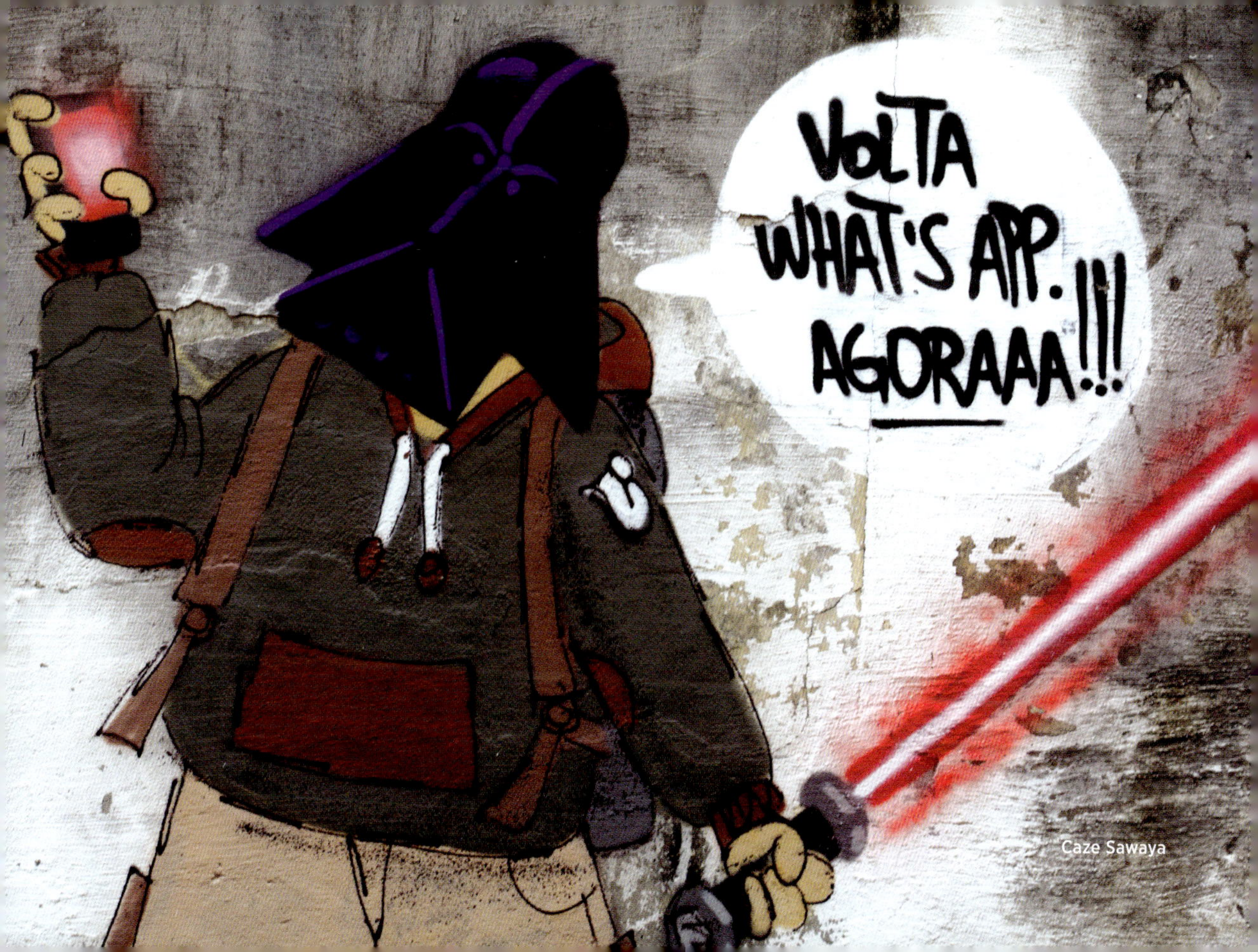

Caze Sawaya

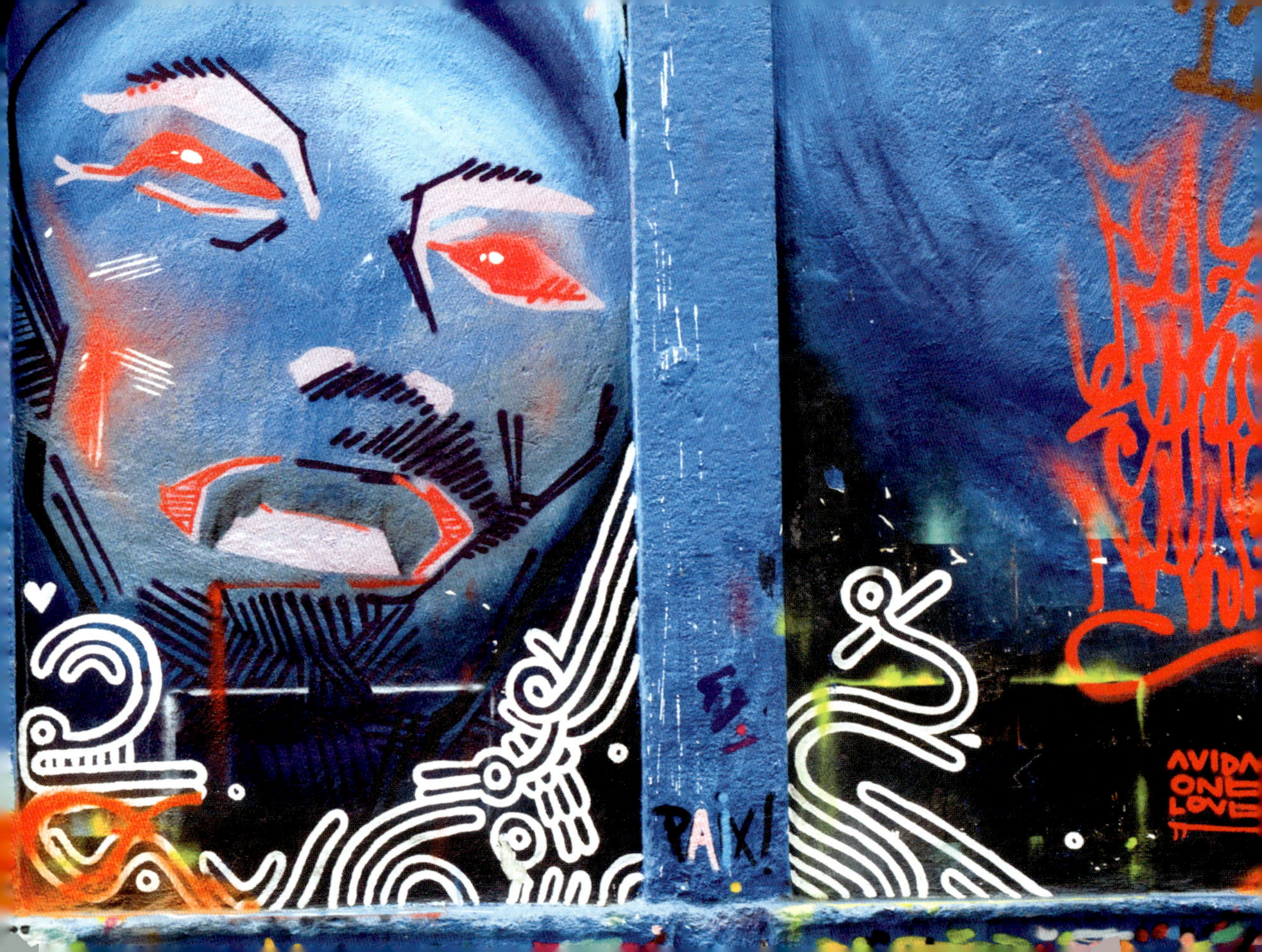
PAIX!
AVIDA
ONE
LOVE

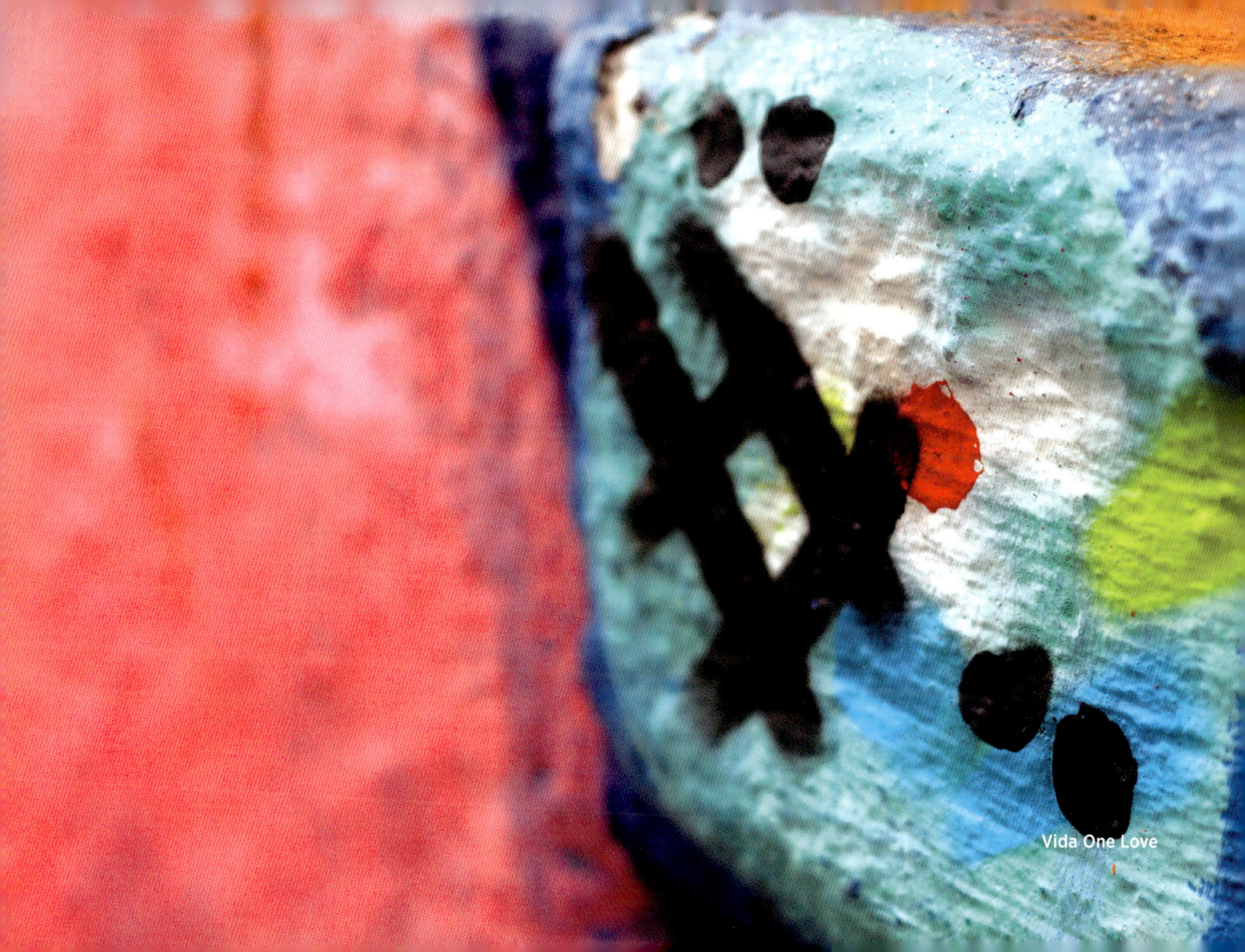

Vida One Love

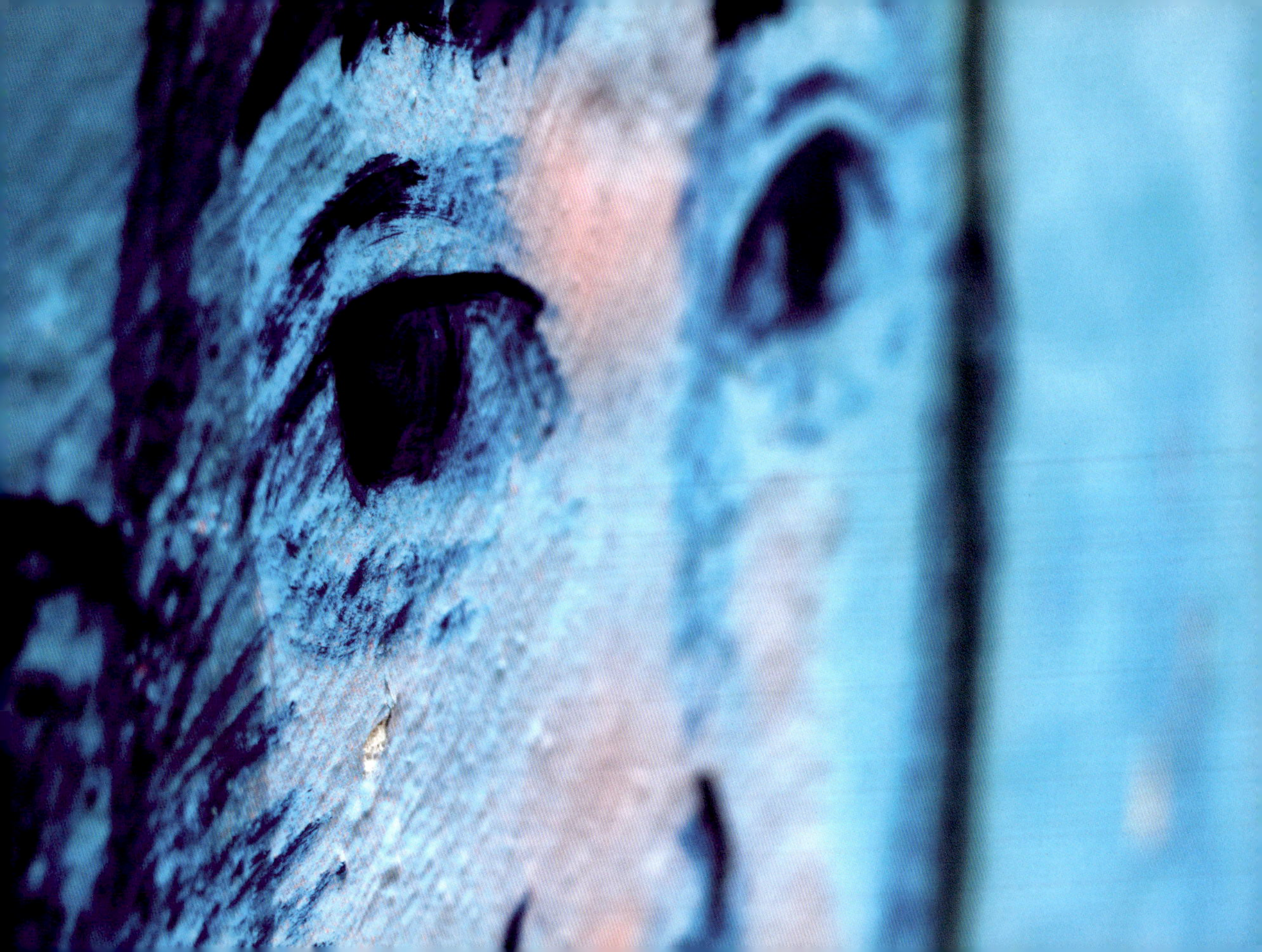

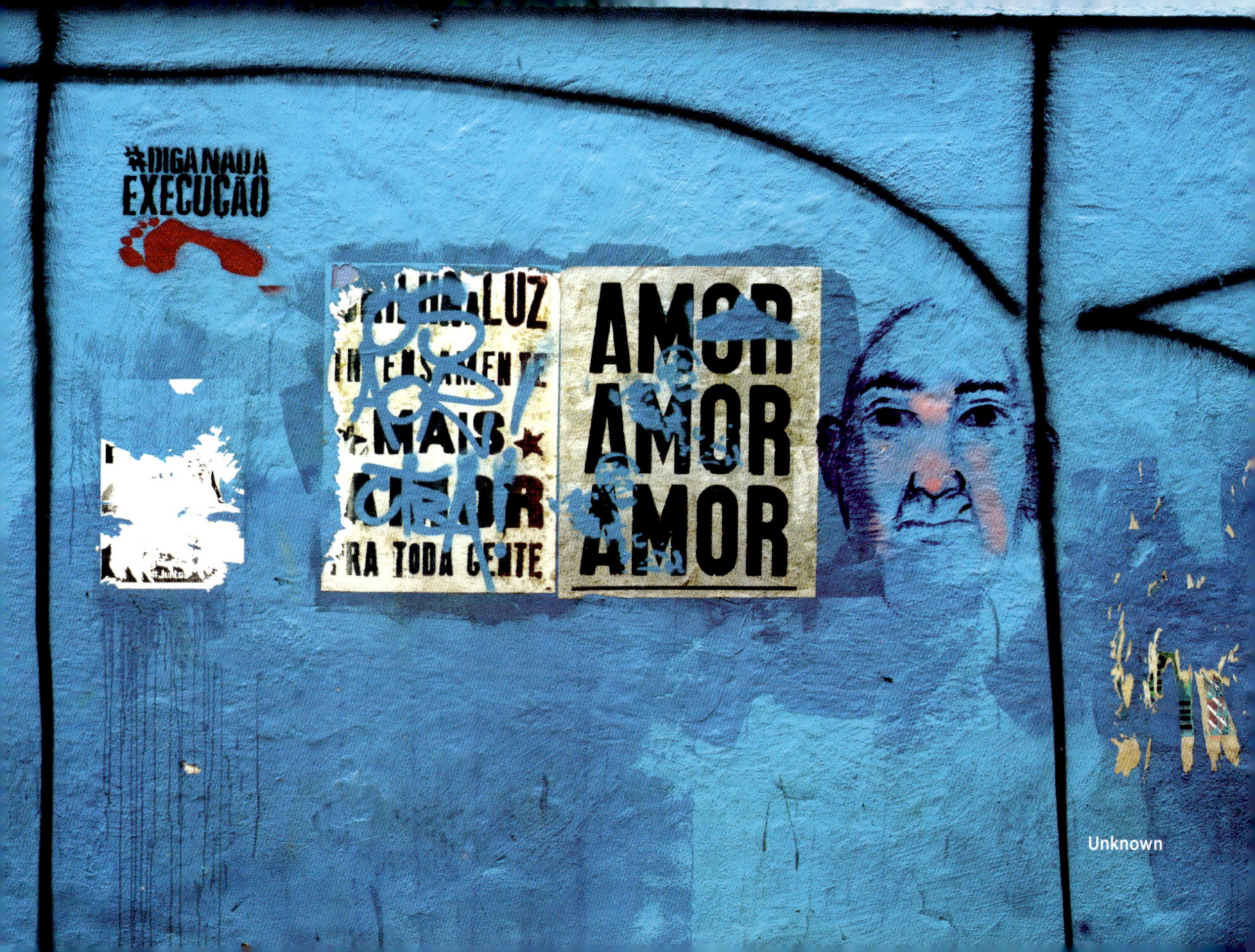

Unknown

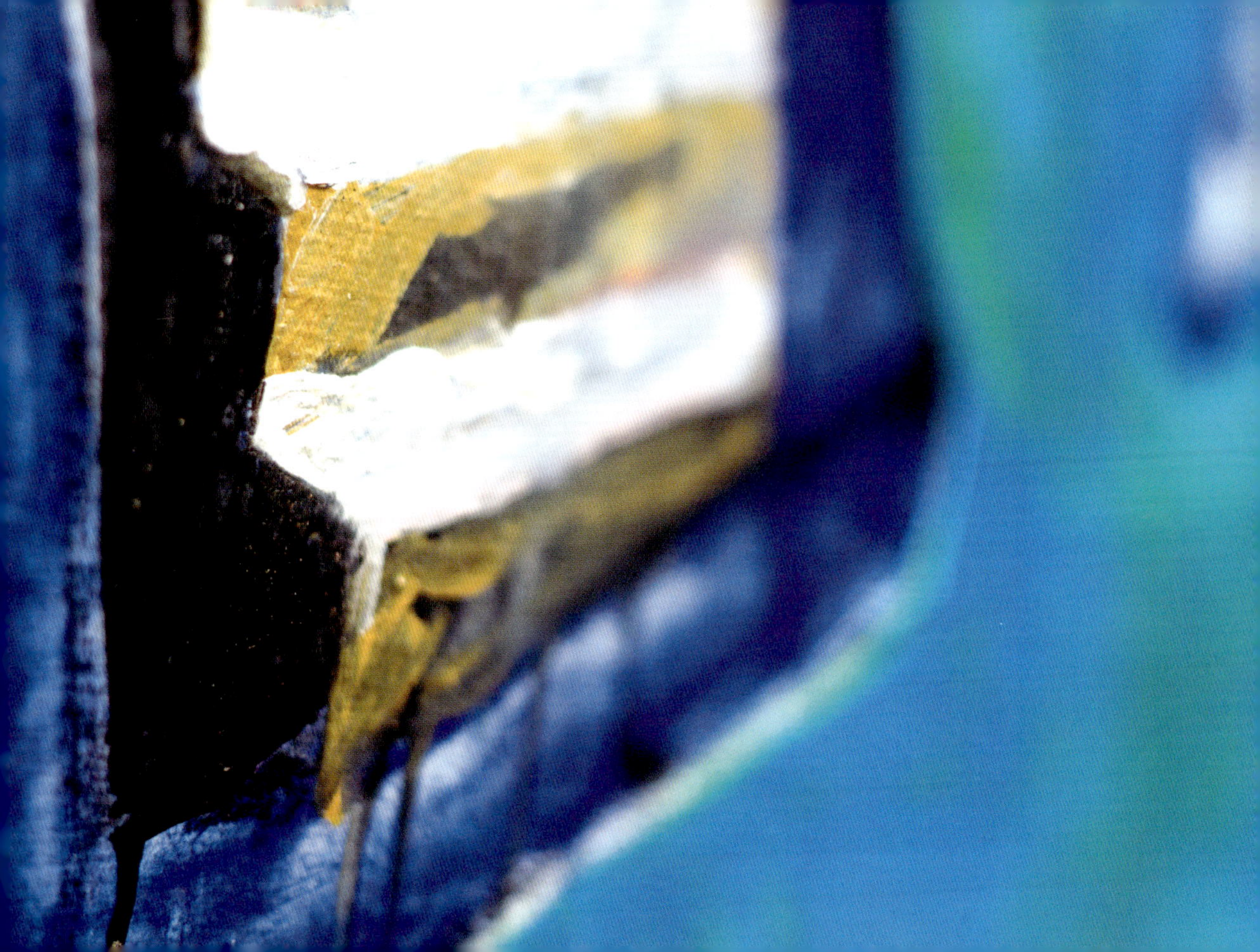

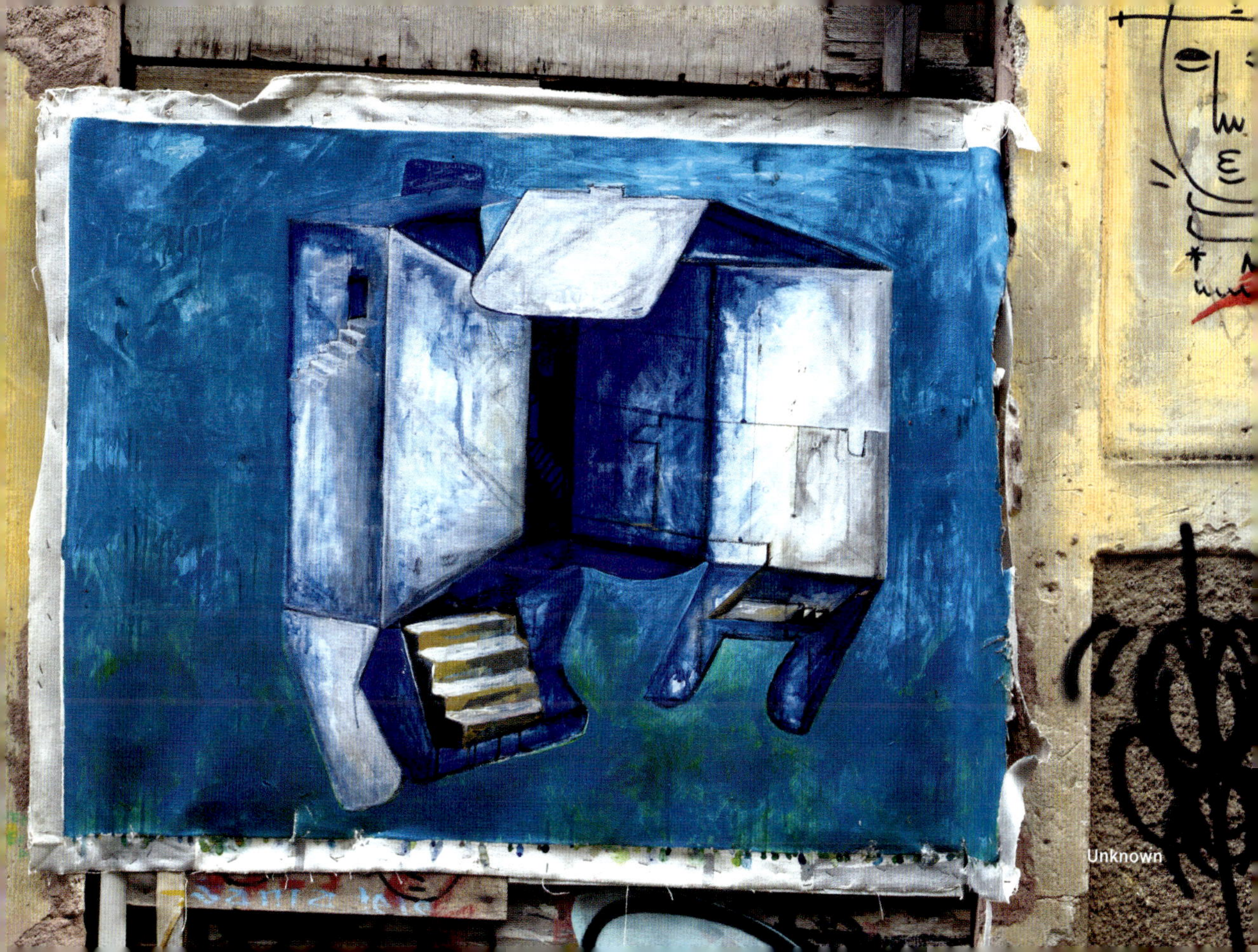

Unknown

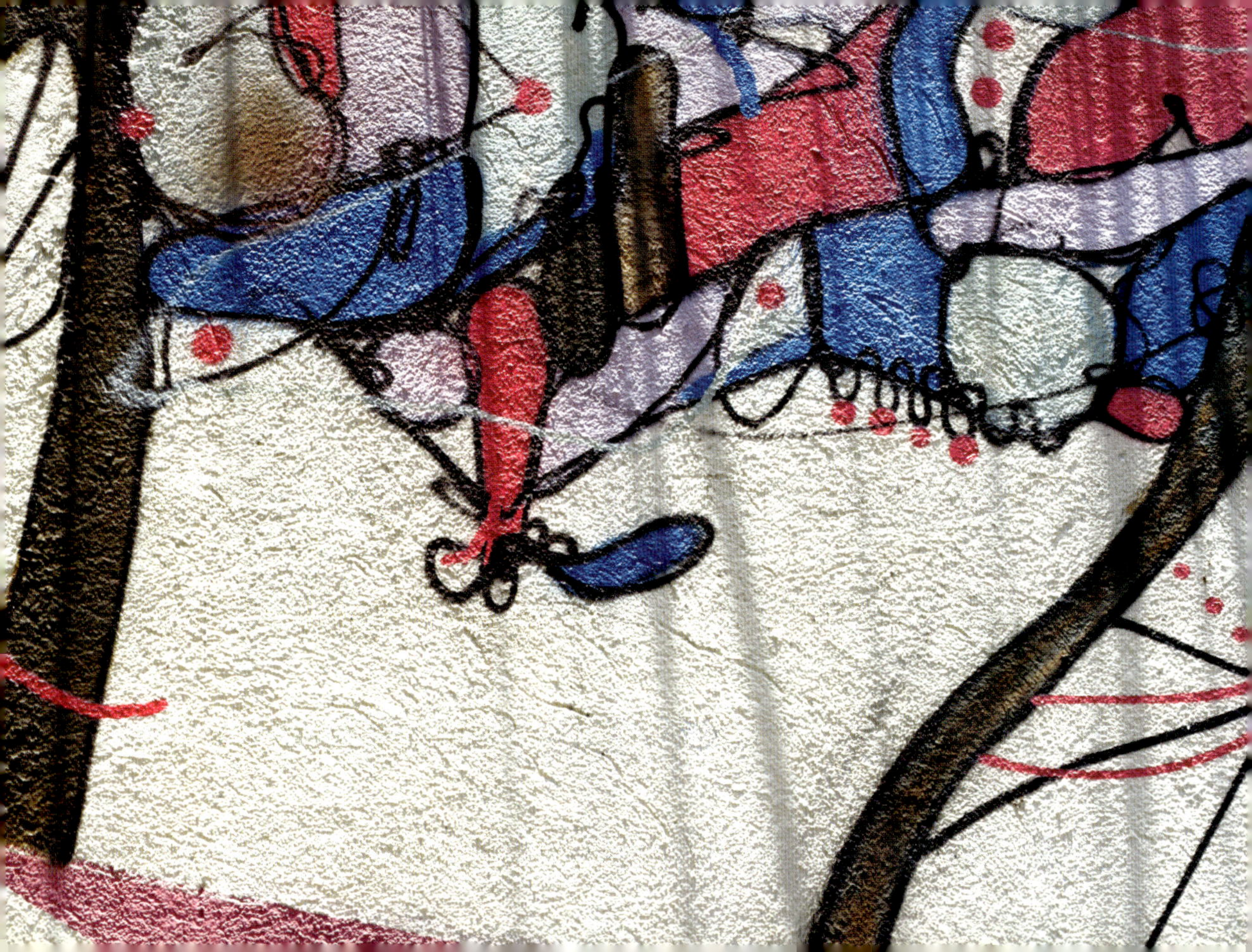

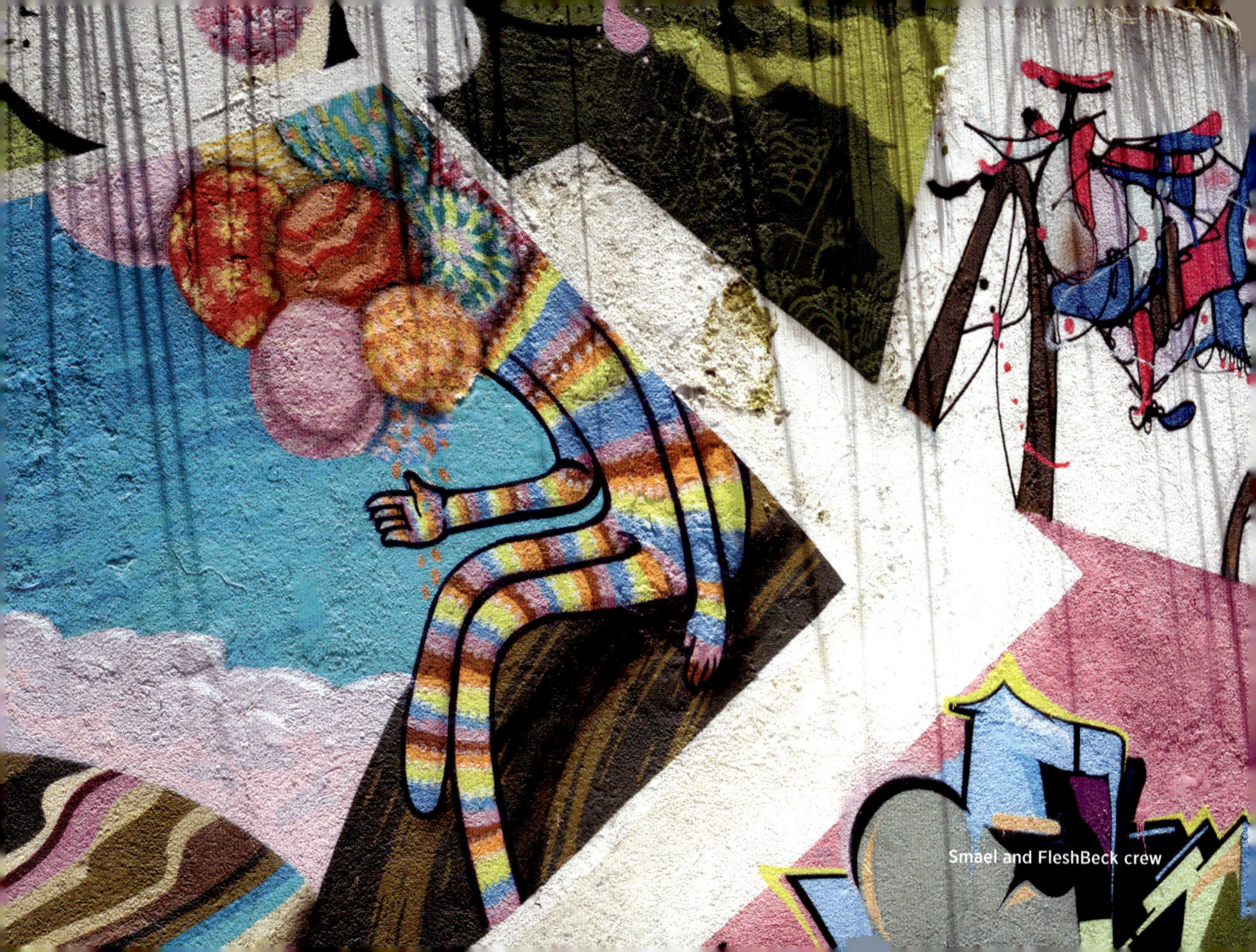

Smael and FleshBeck crew

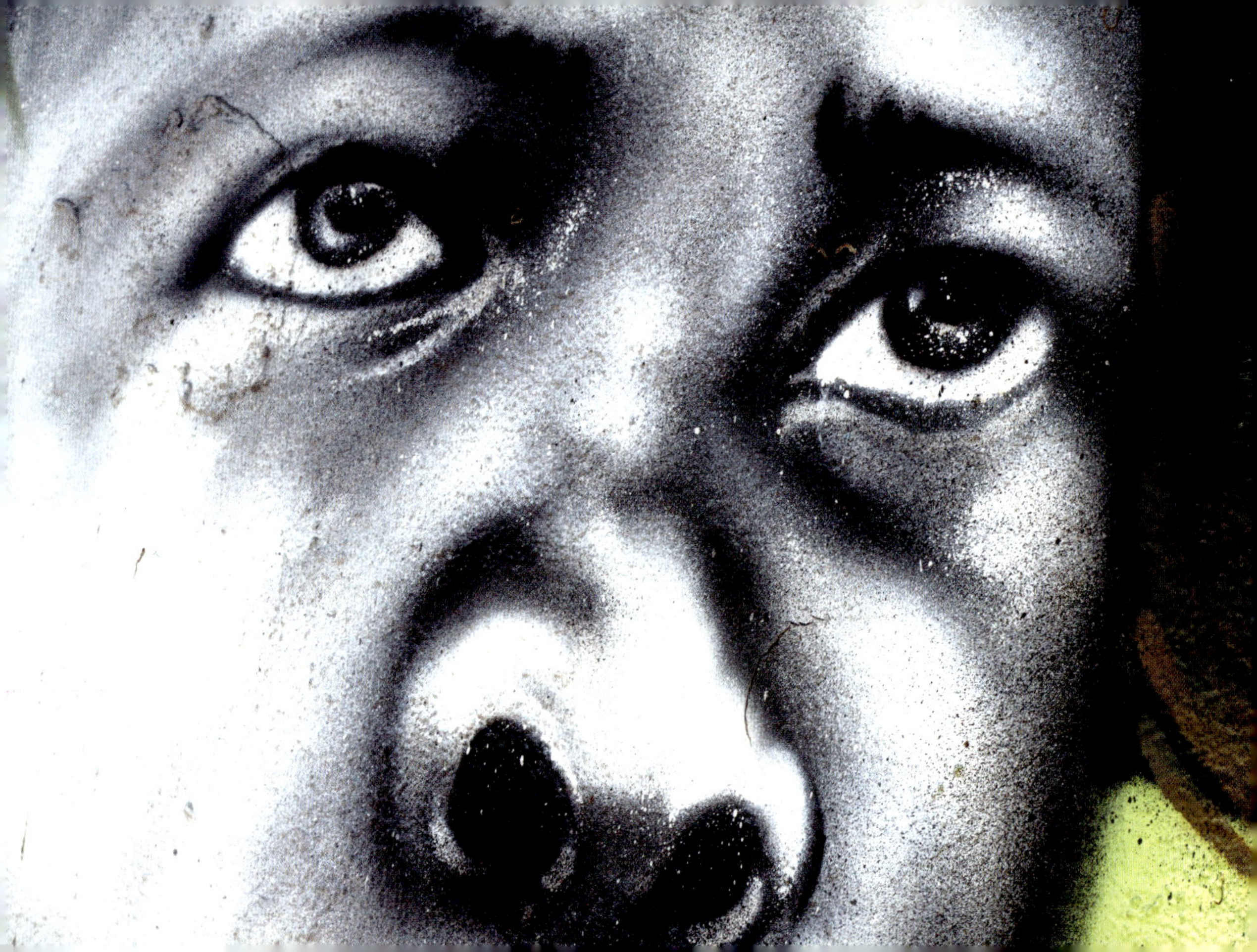

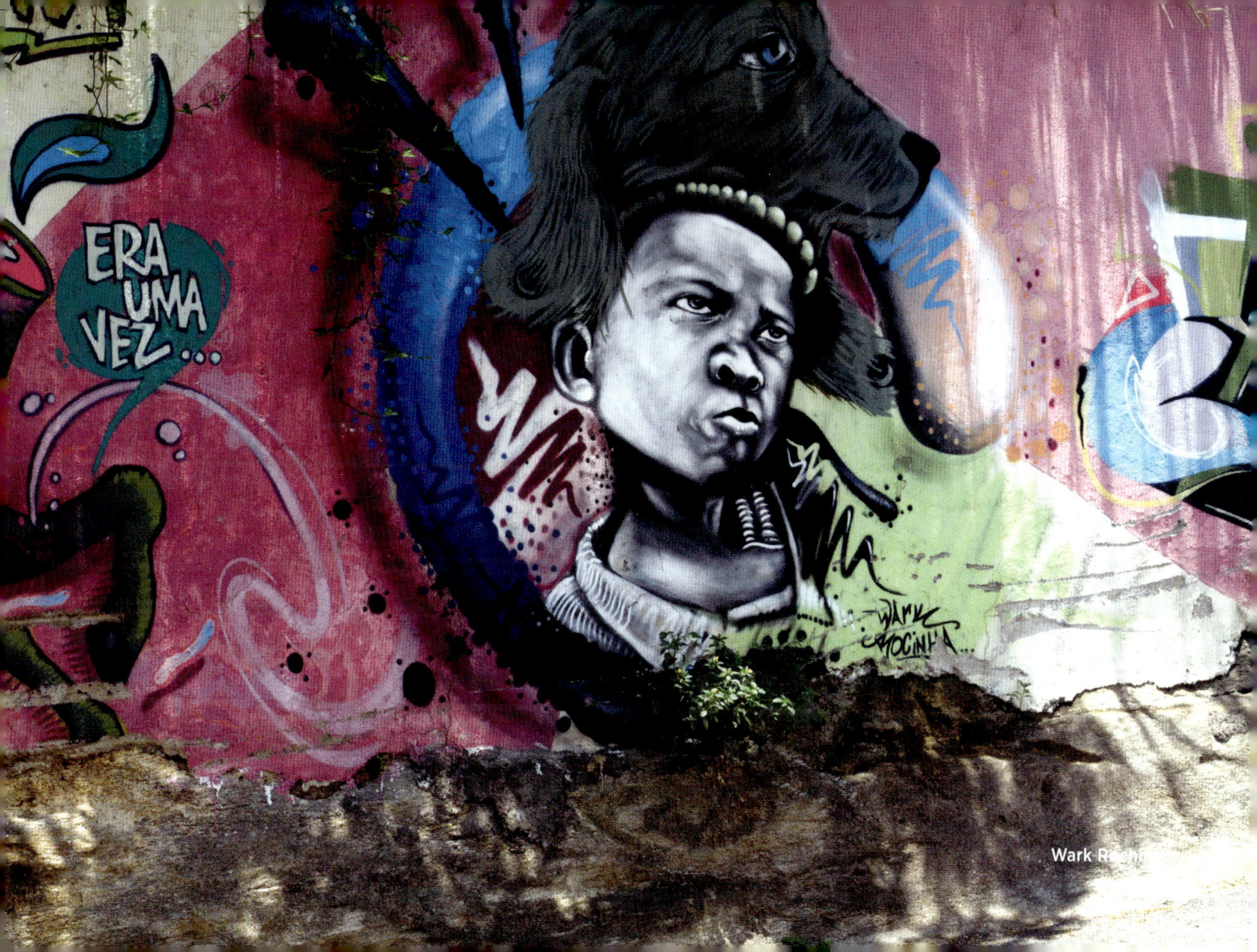

Wark R

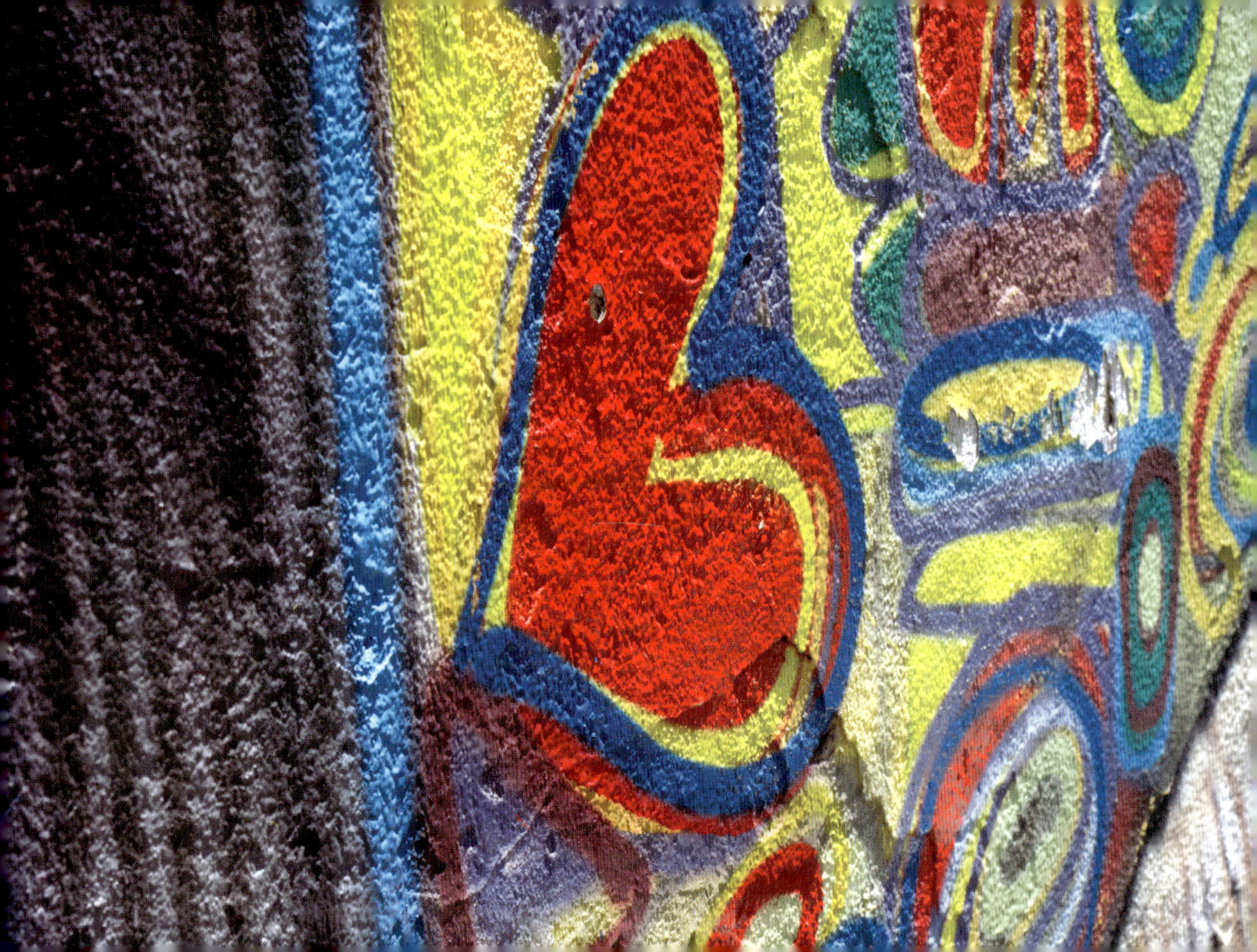

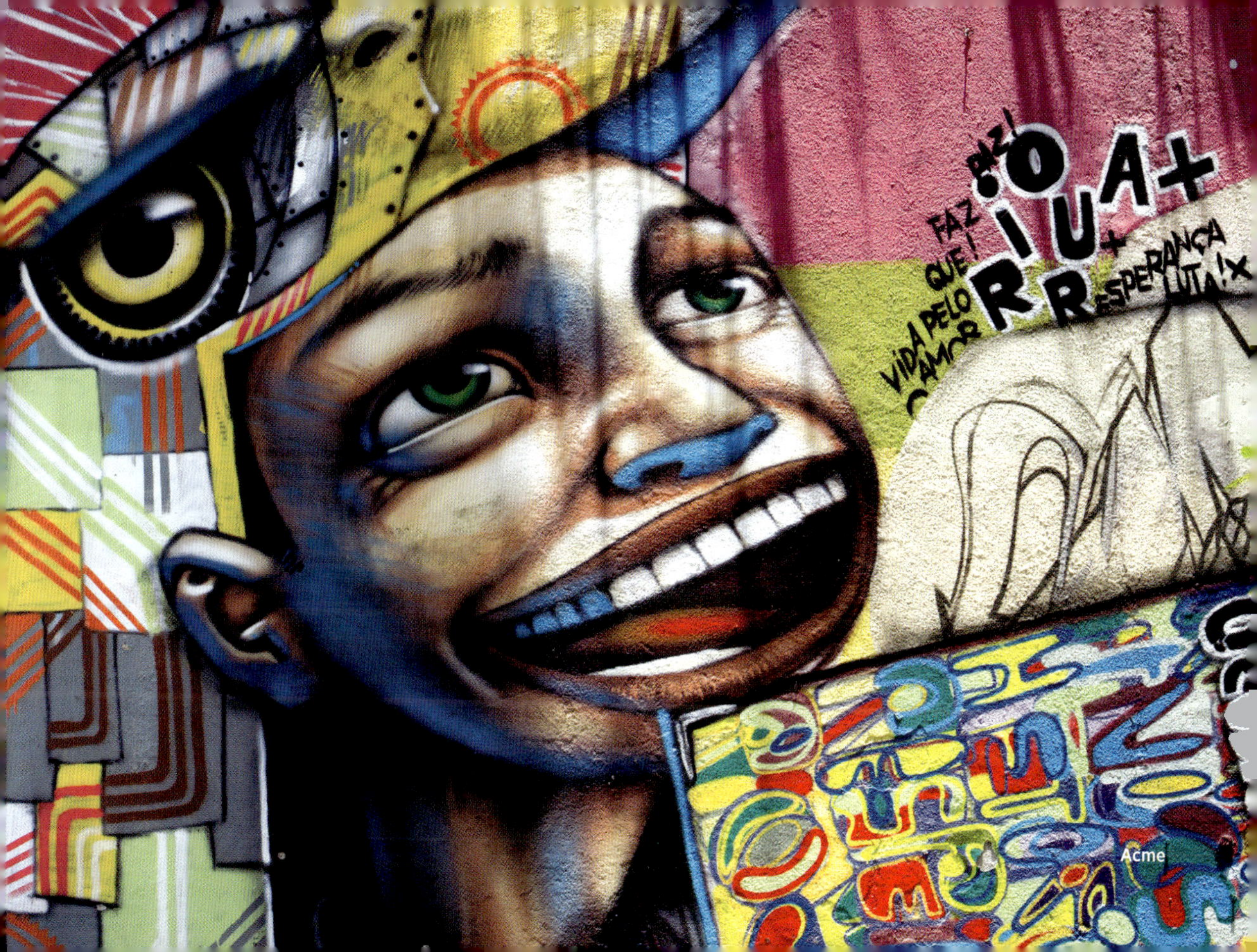
PAZ!
FAZ
QUE!
VIDA PELO
AMOR
ESPERANÇA
LUTA!
Acme

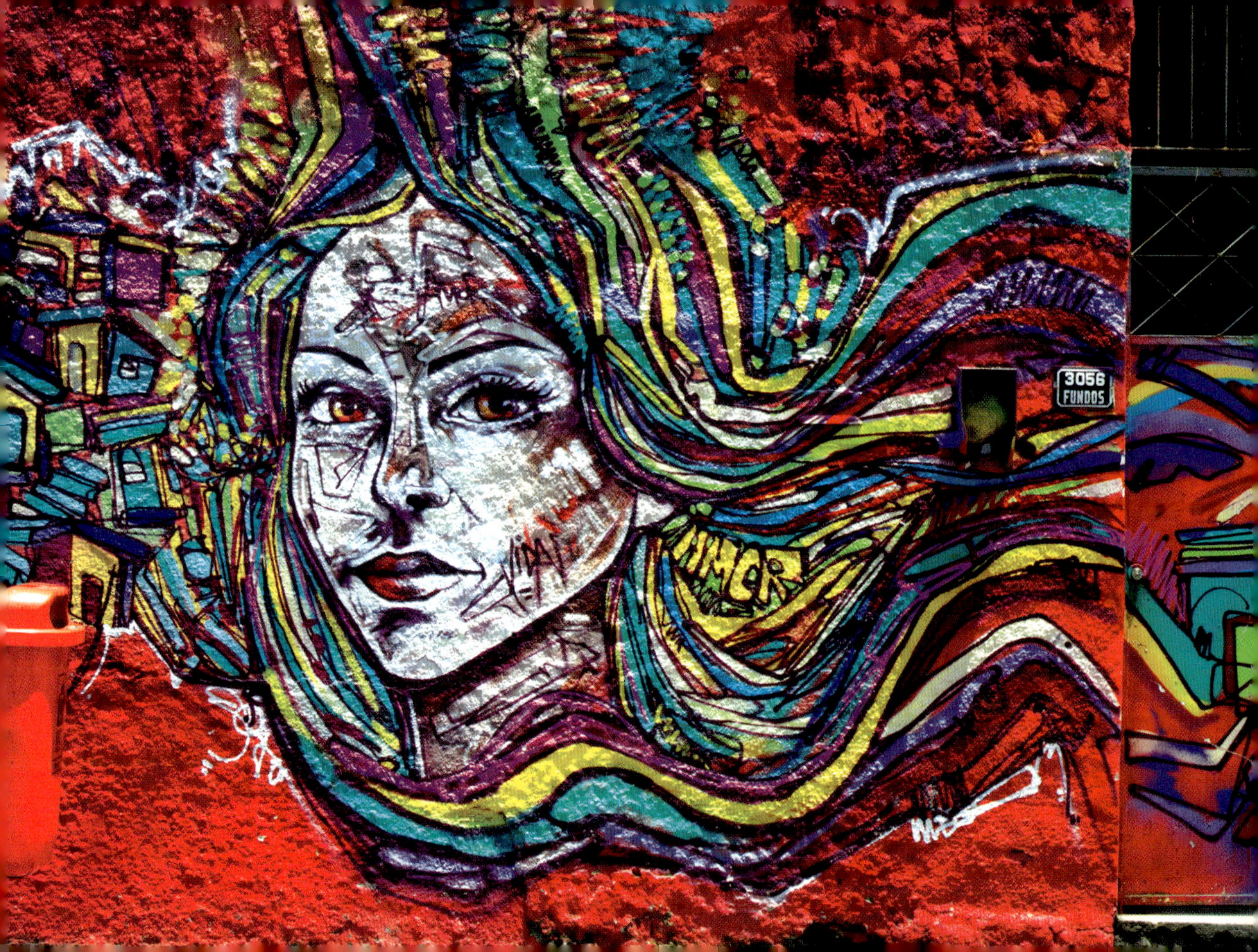
3056
FUNDOS

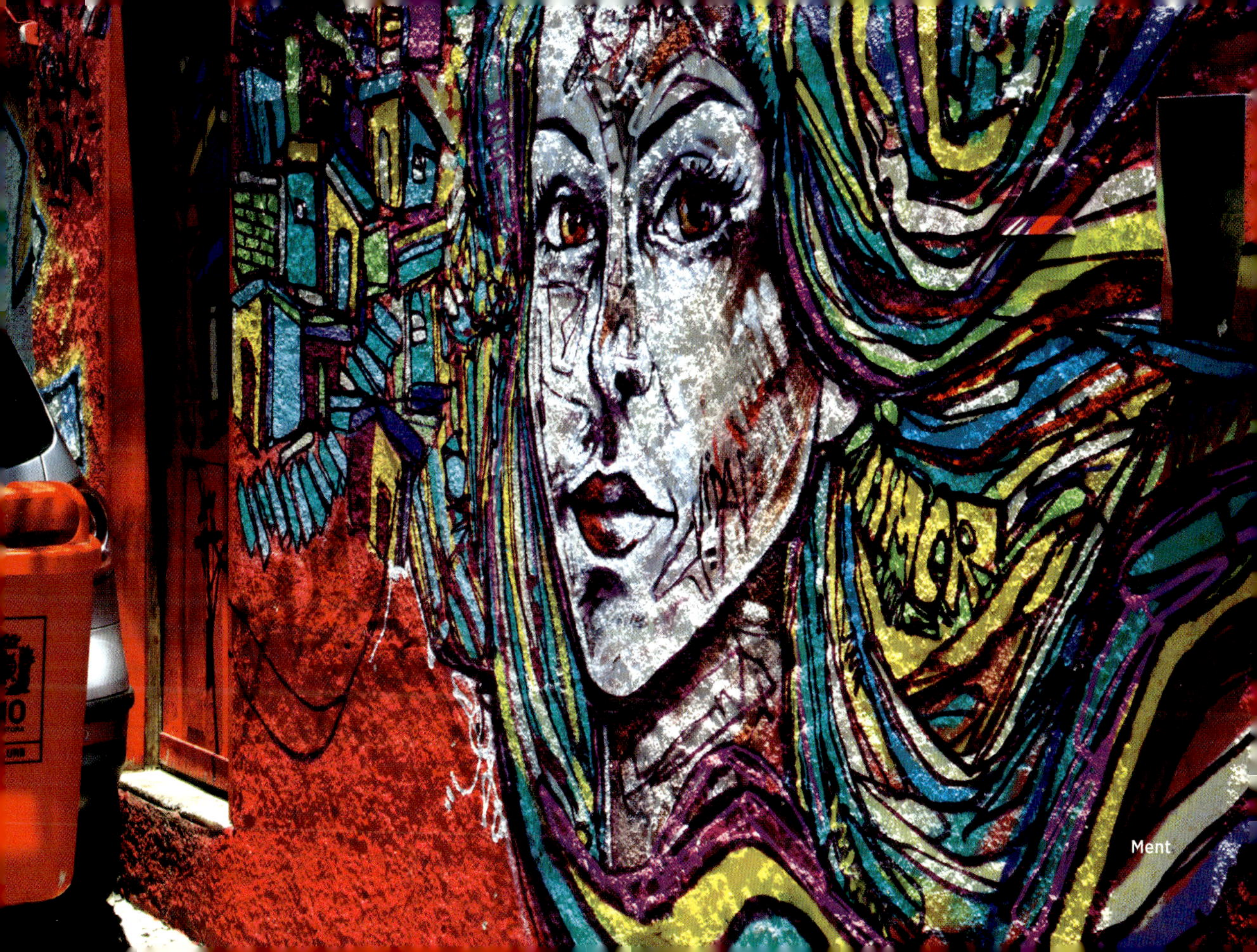
Ment

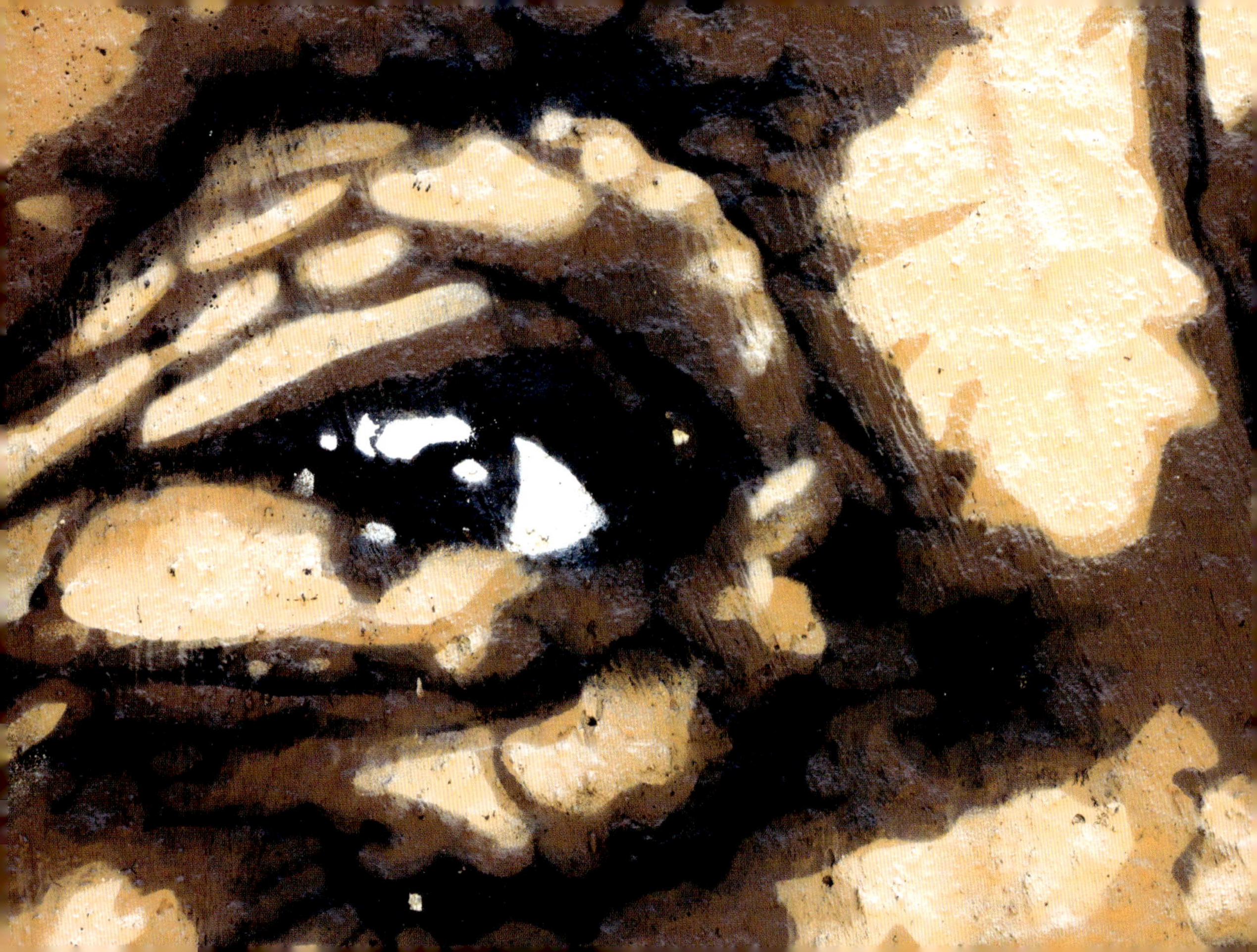

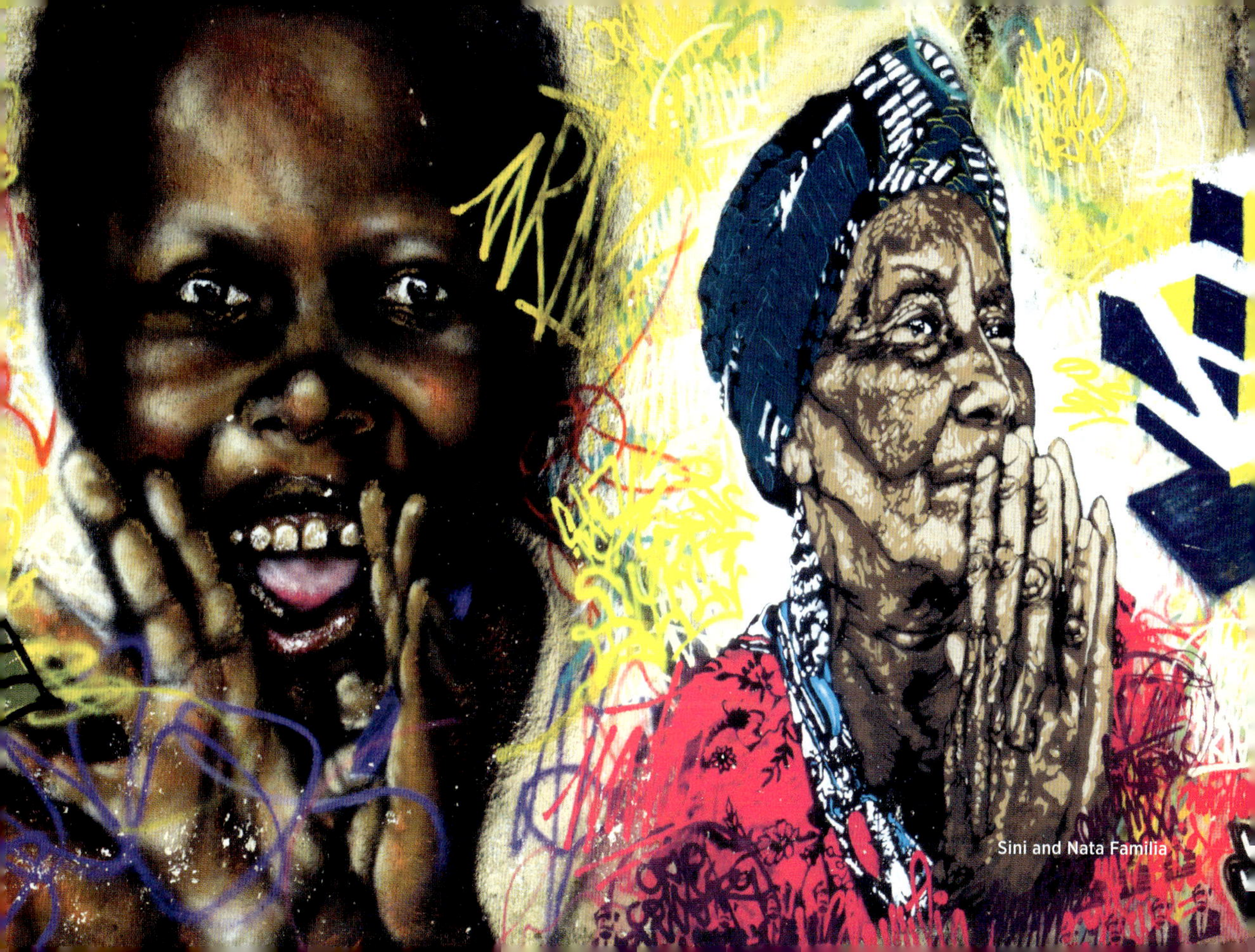

Sini and Nata Familia

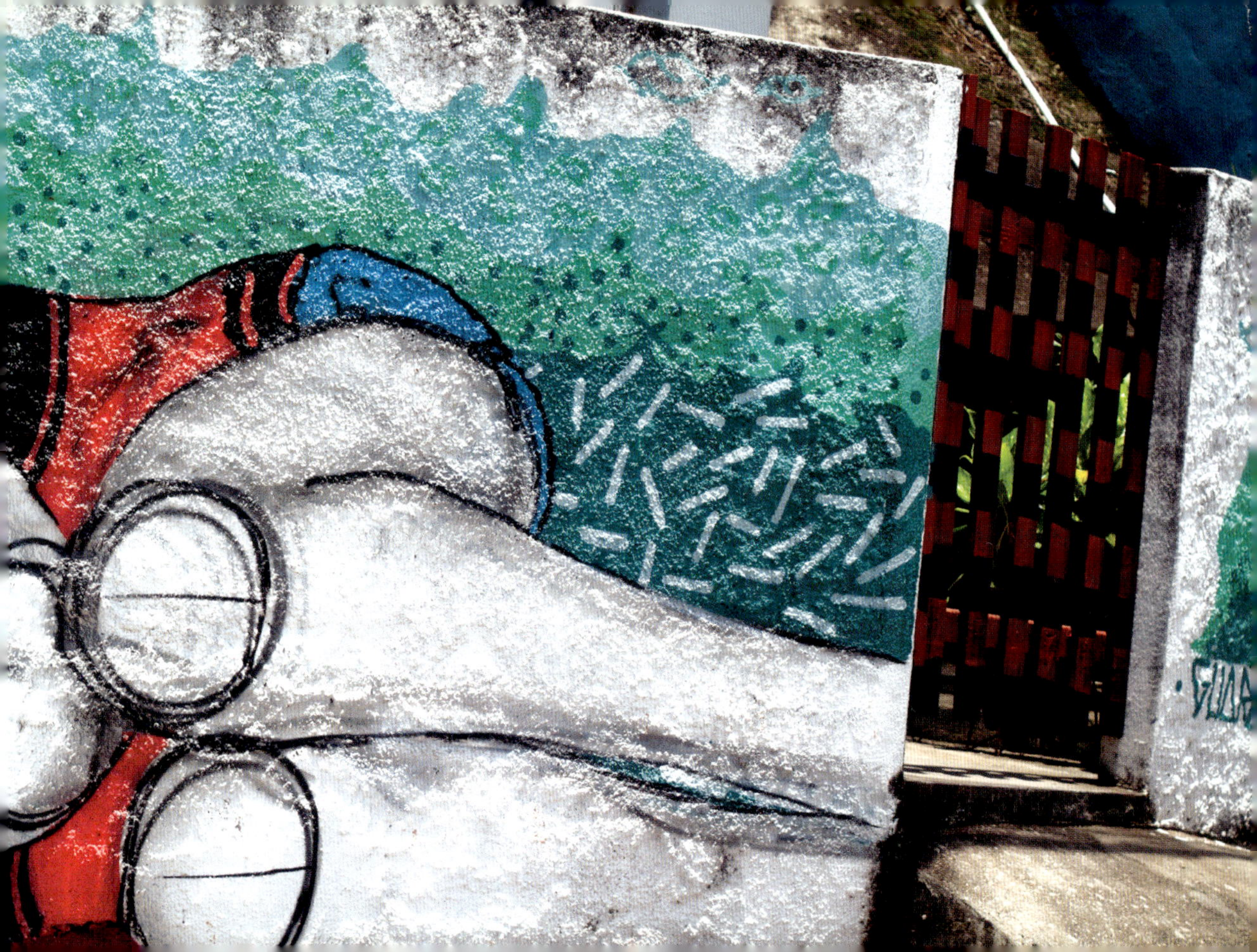

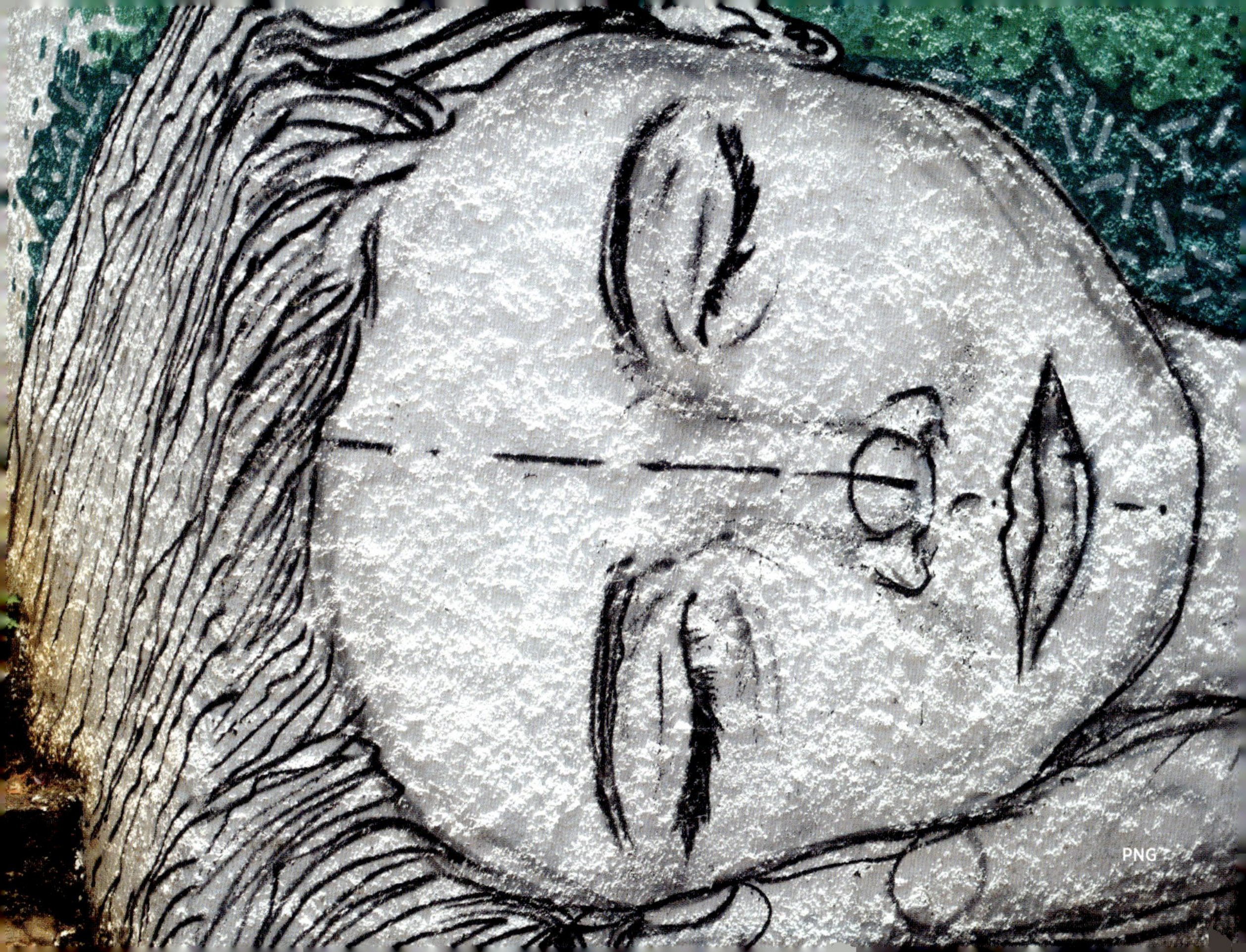
PNG

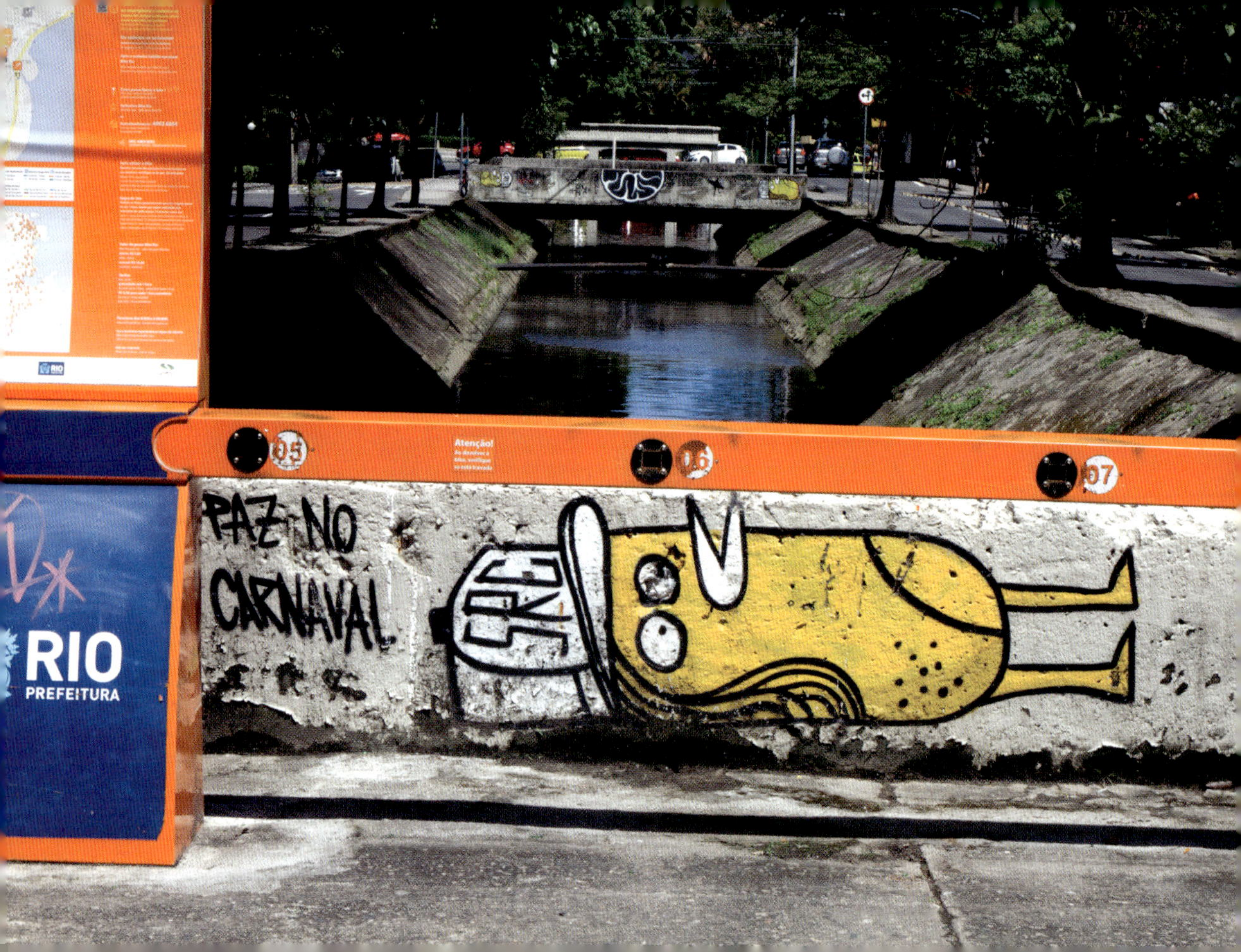
PAZ NO CARNAVAL
Atenção!
05
06
07
RIO
PREFEITURA

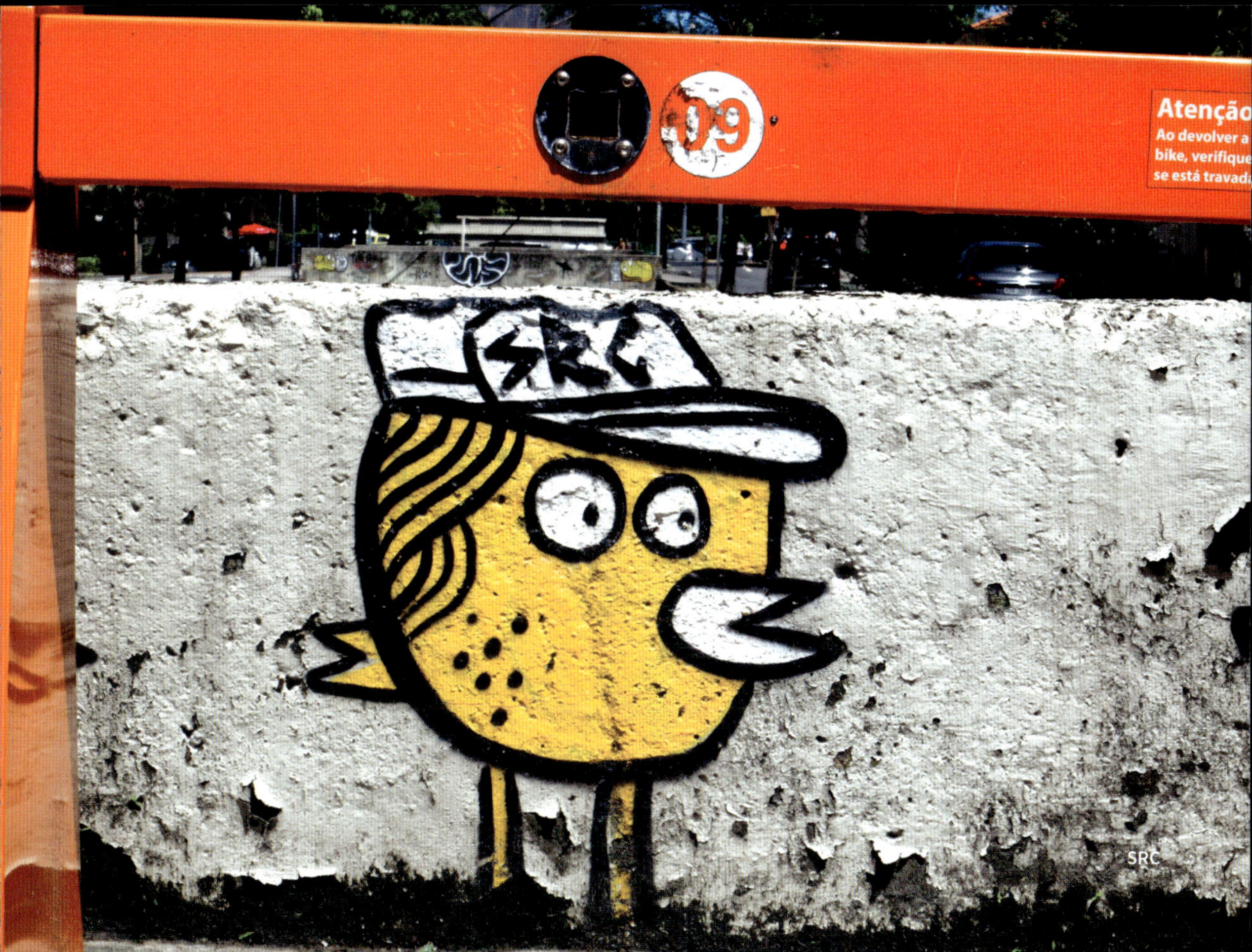

SRC

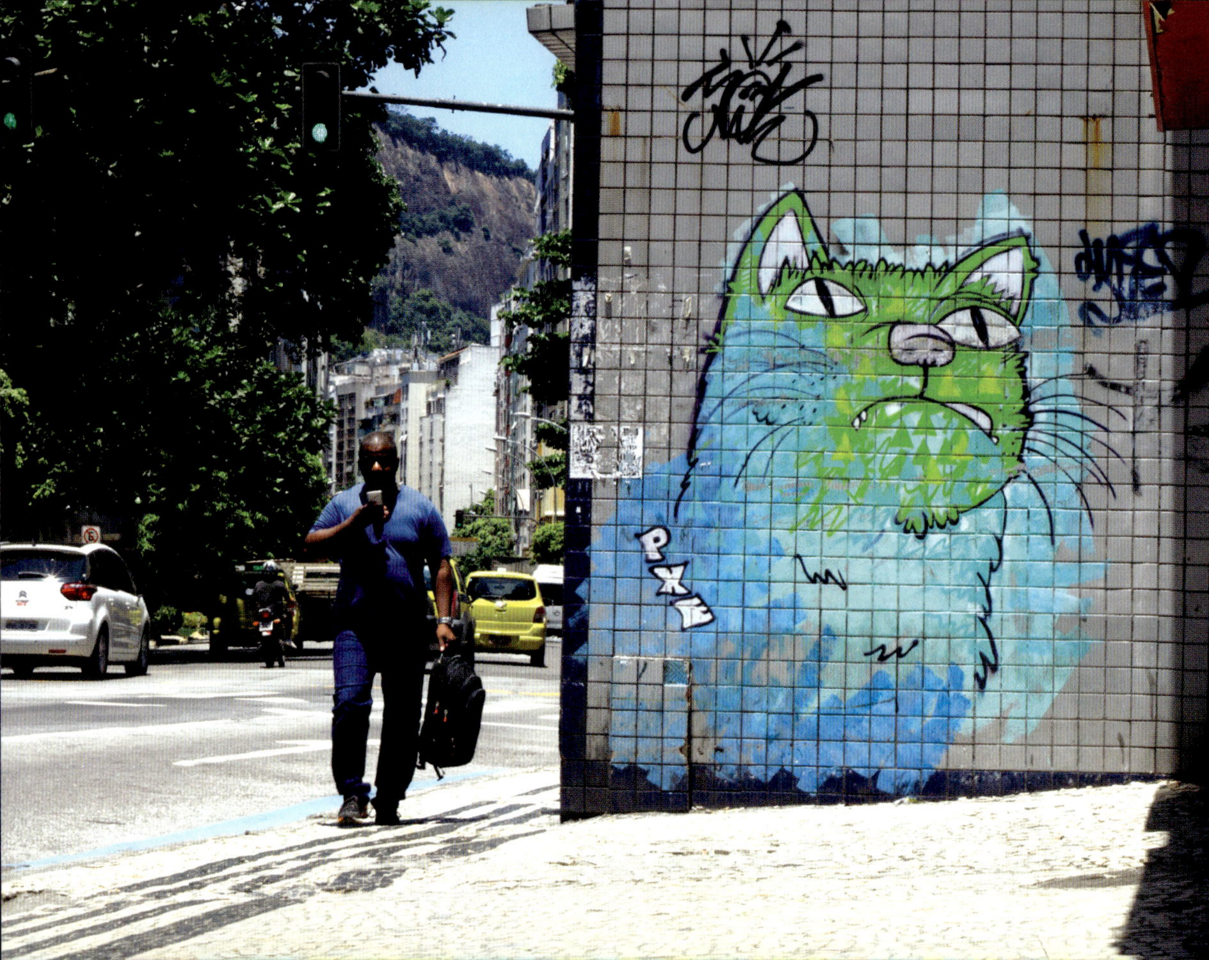
PXE

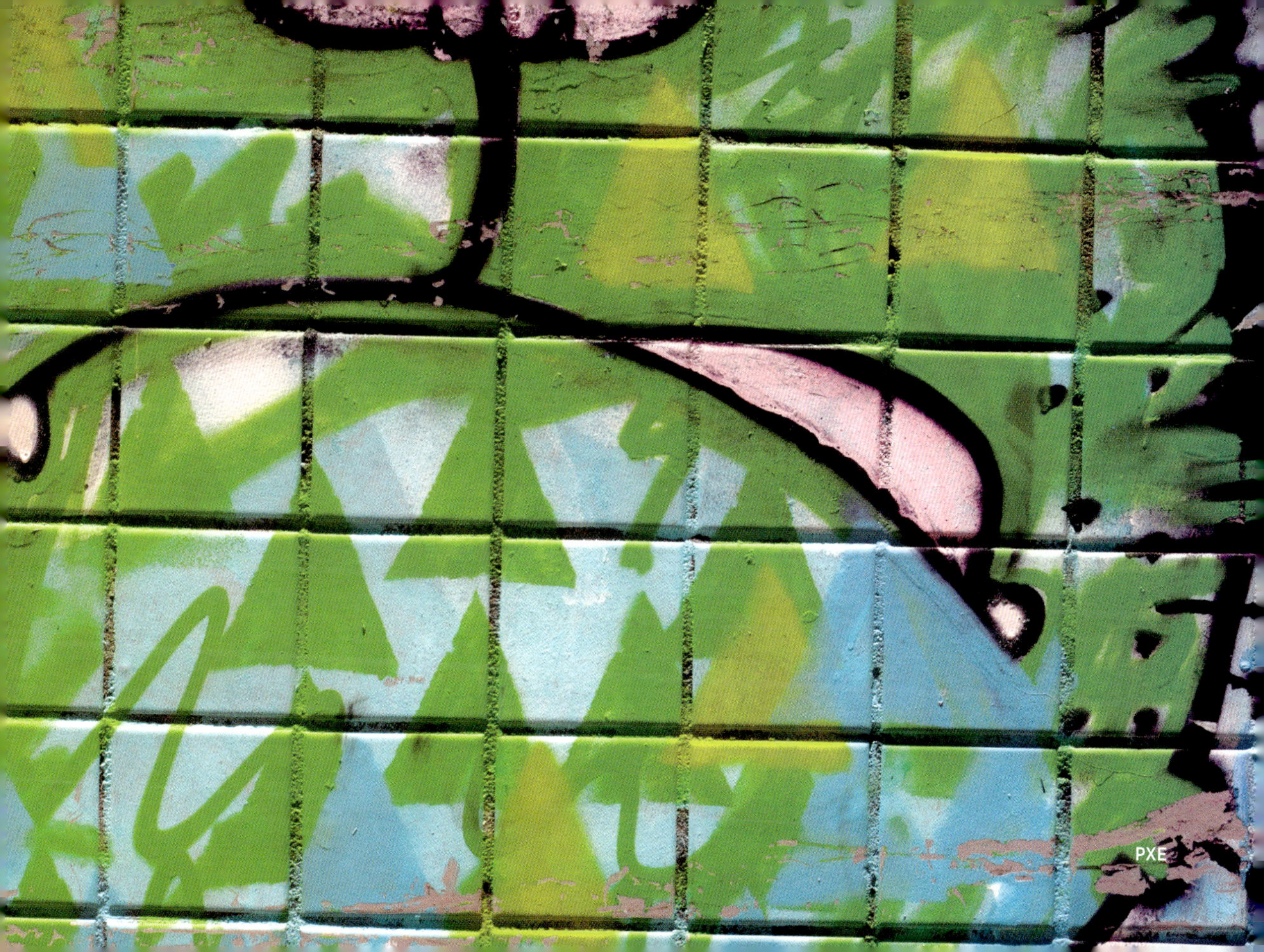
PXE

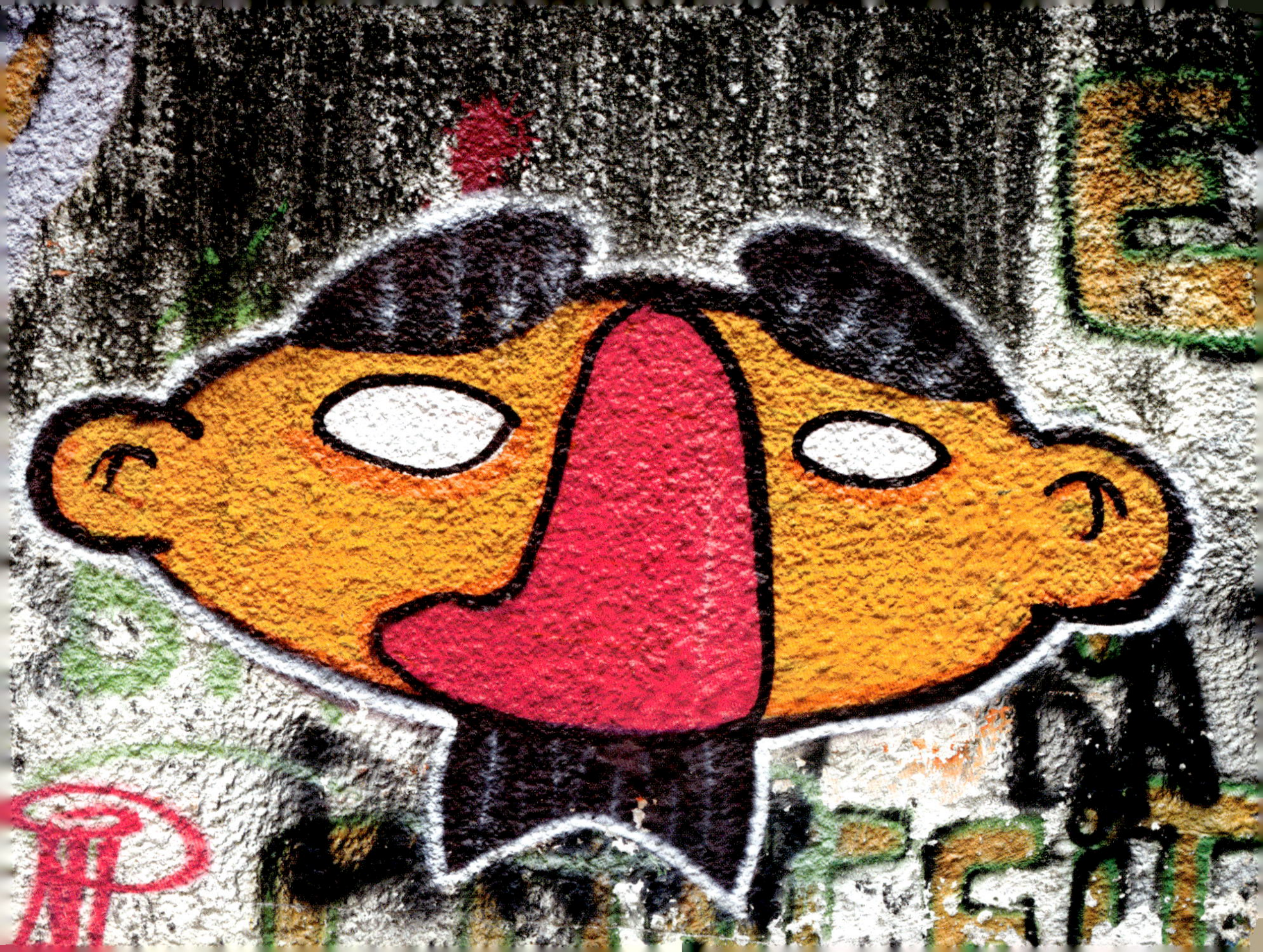
DA

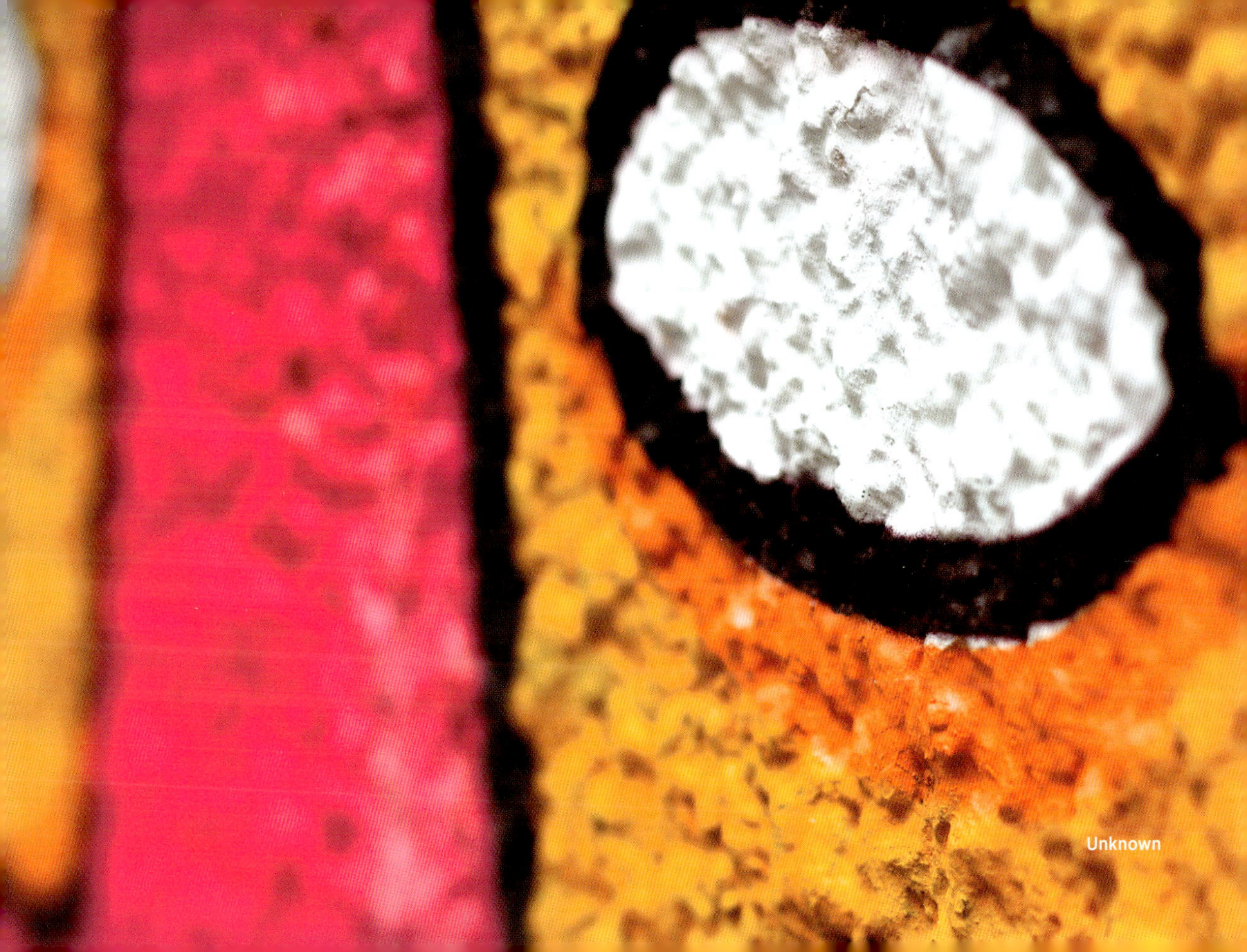

Unknown

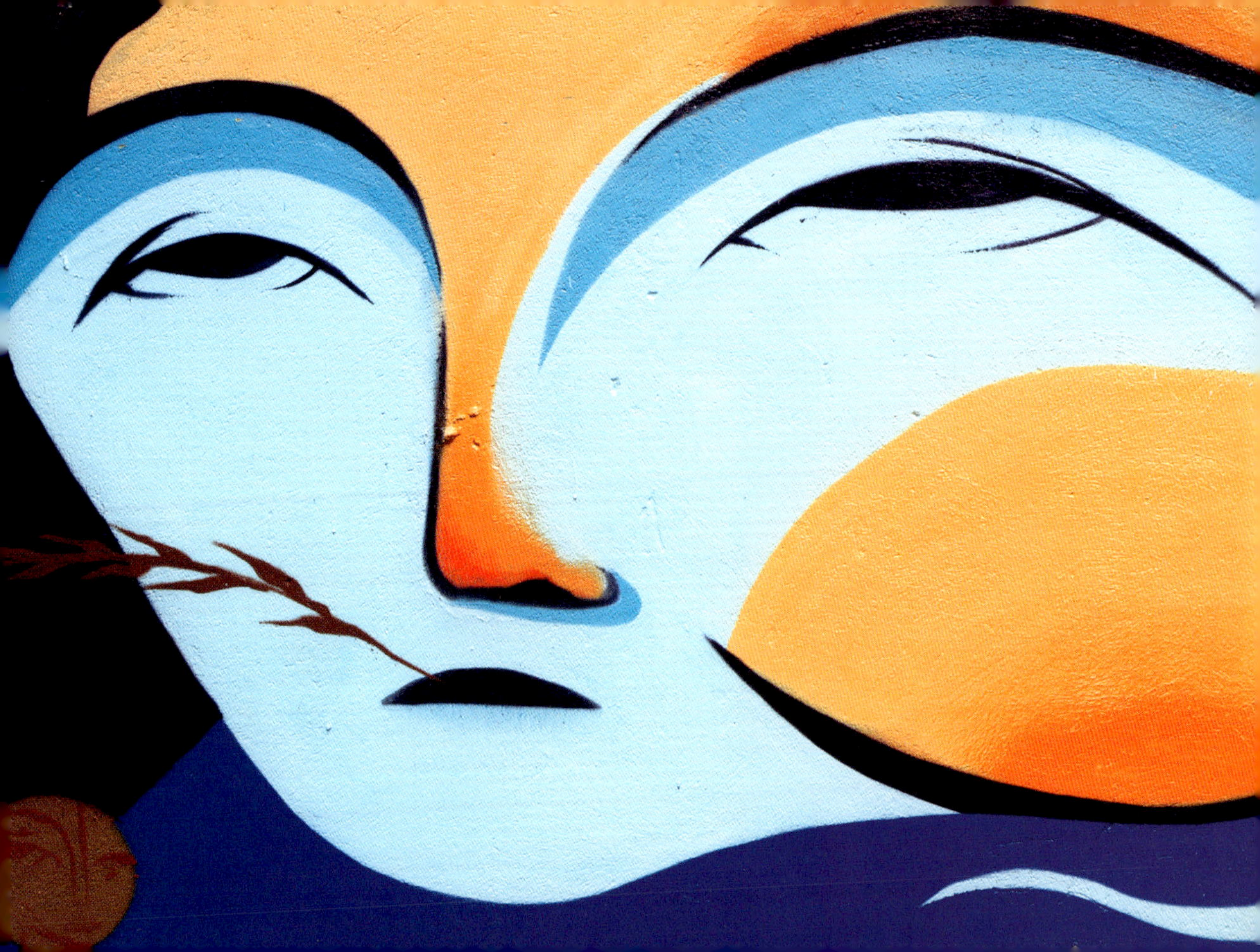

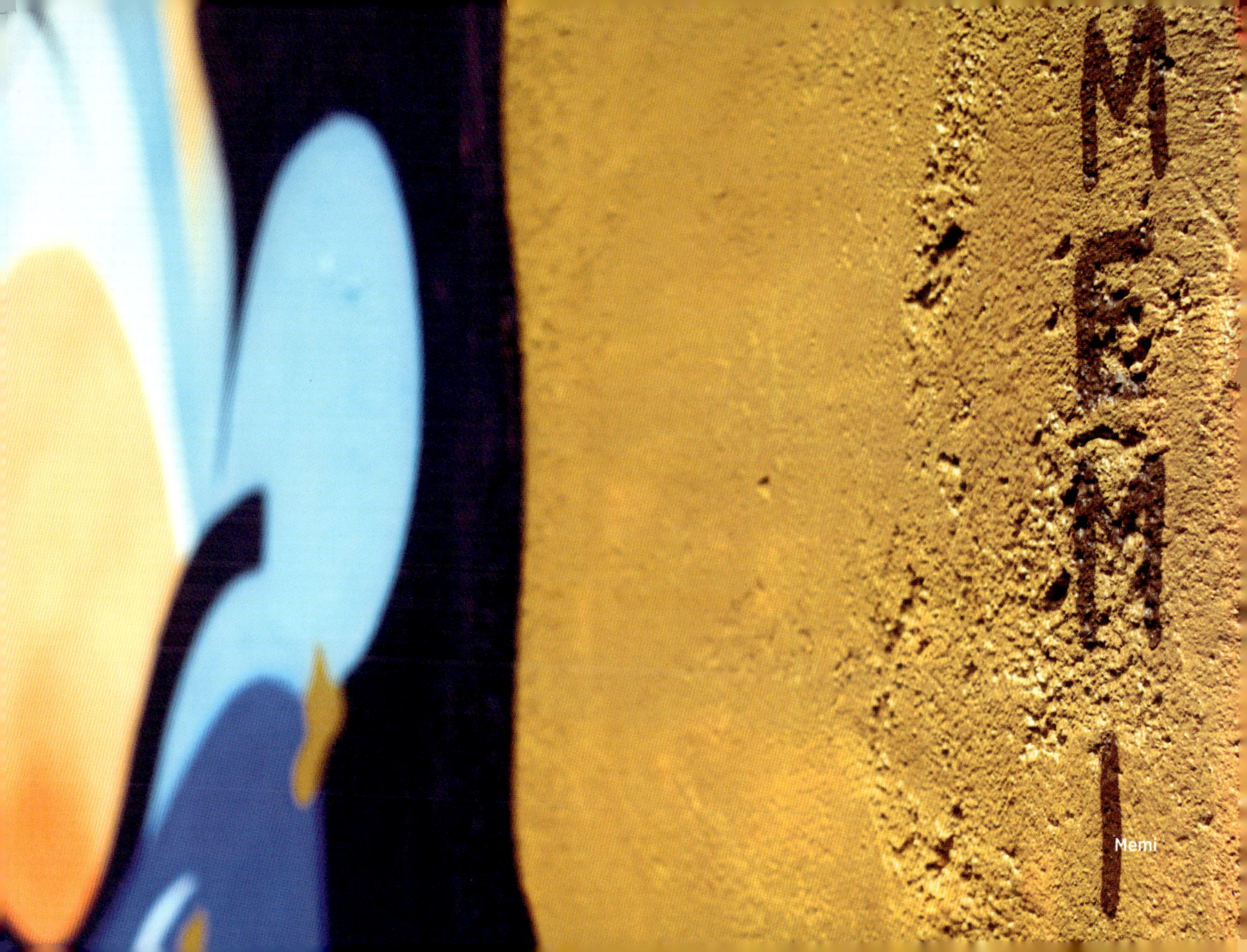

Memi

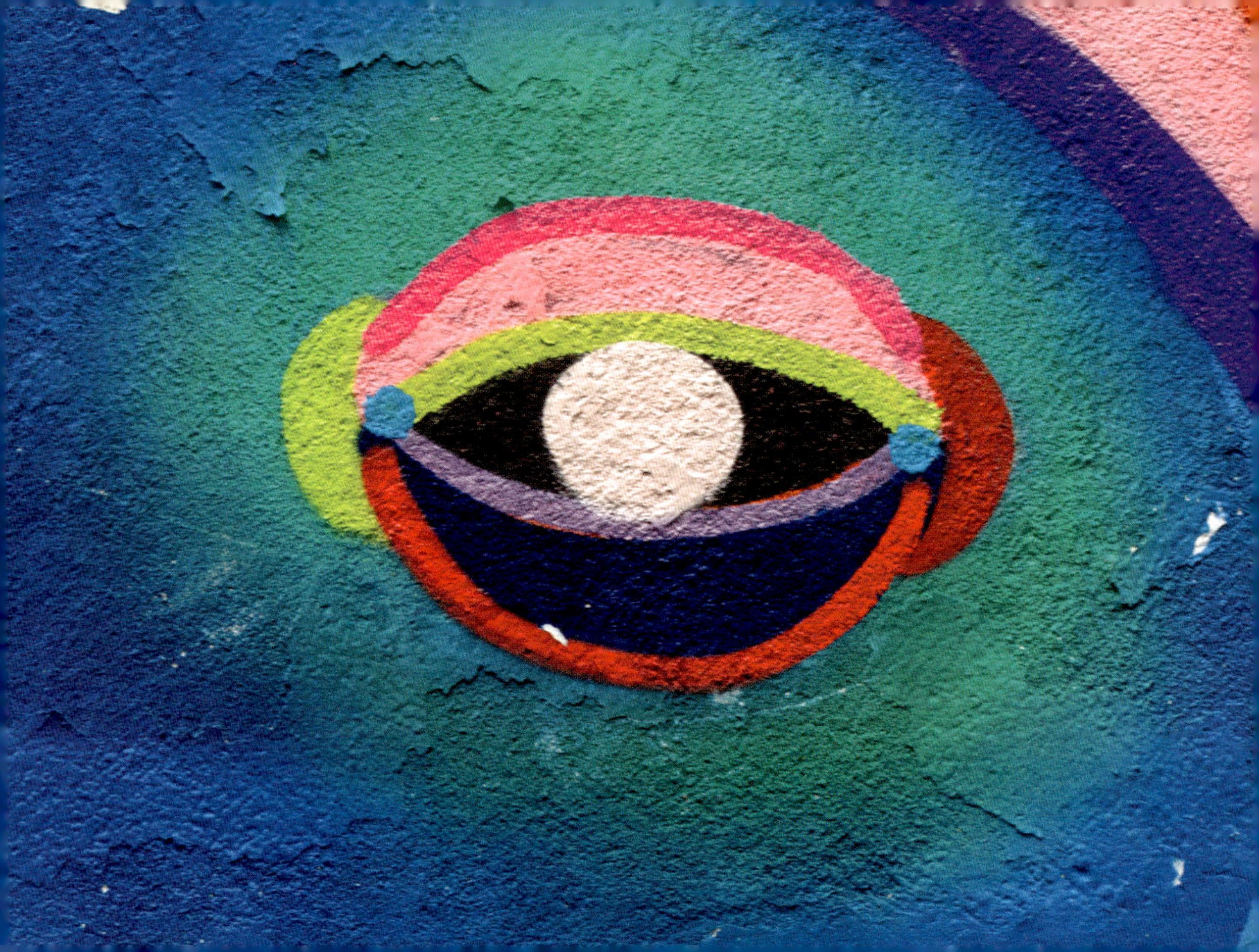

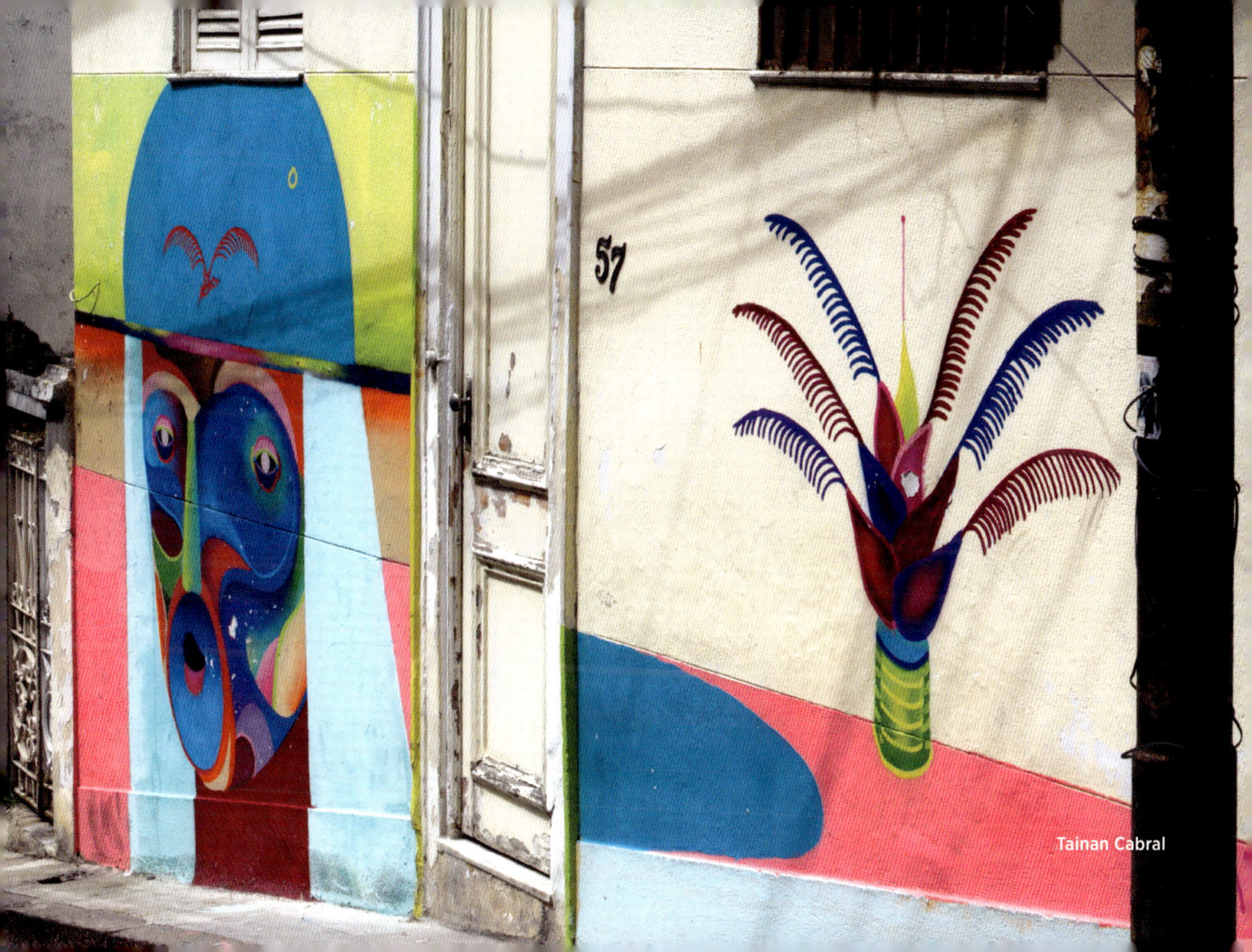

Tainan Cabral

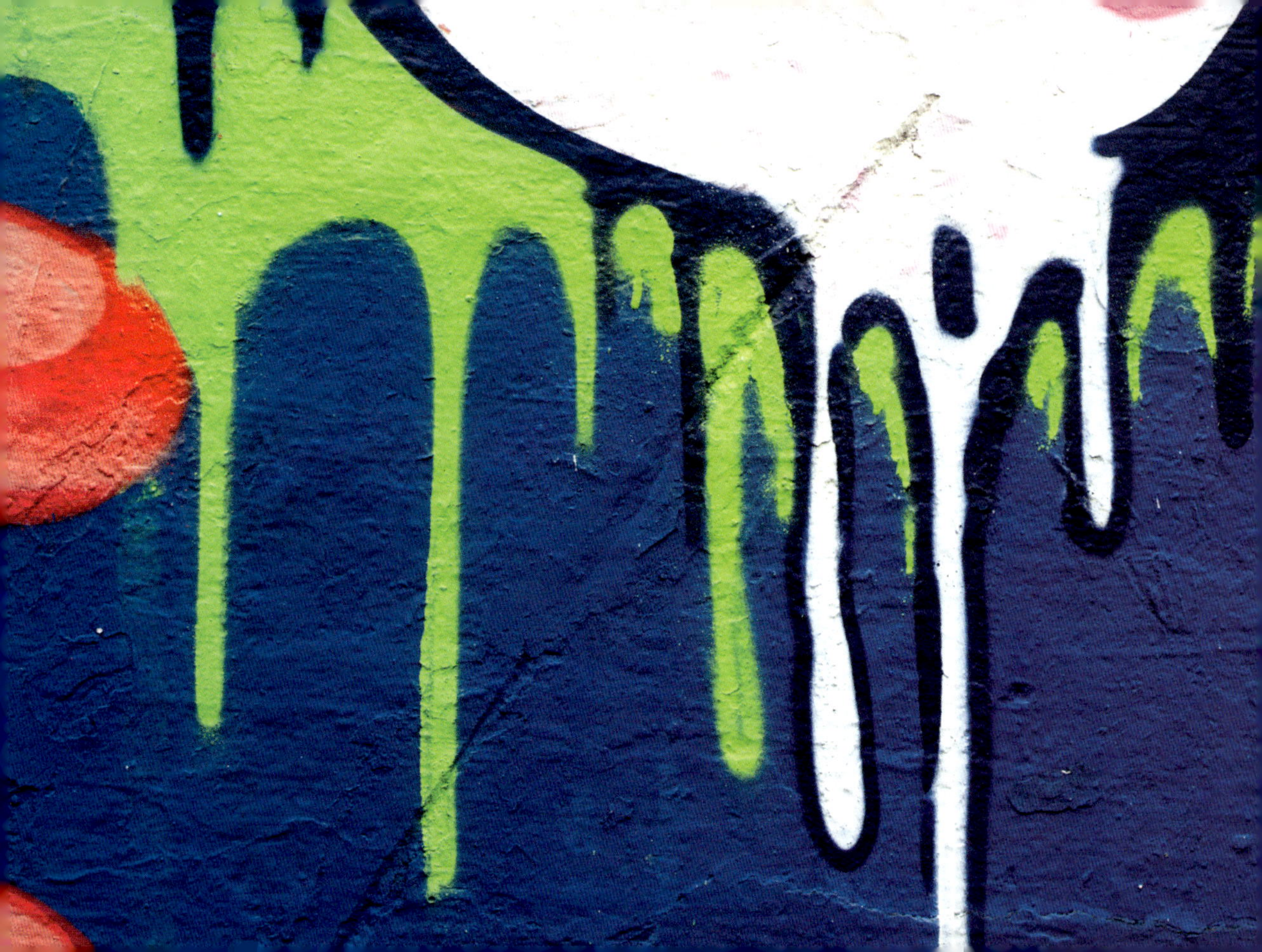

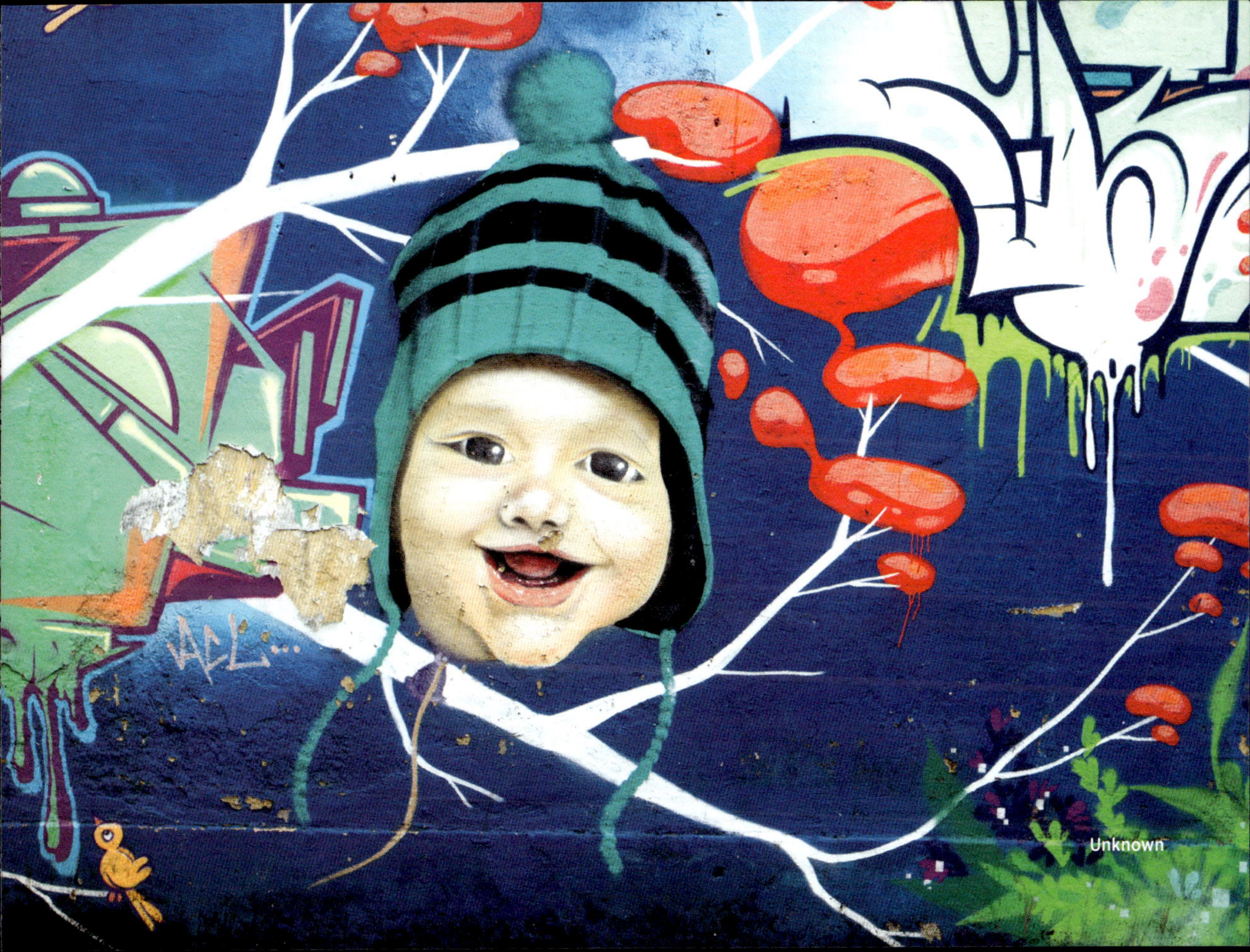

Unknown

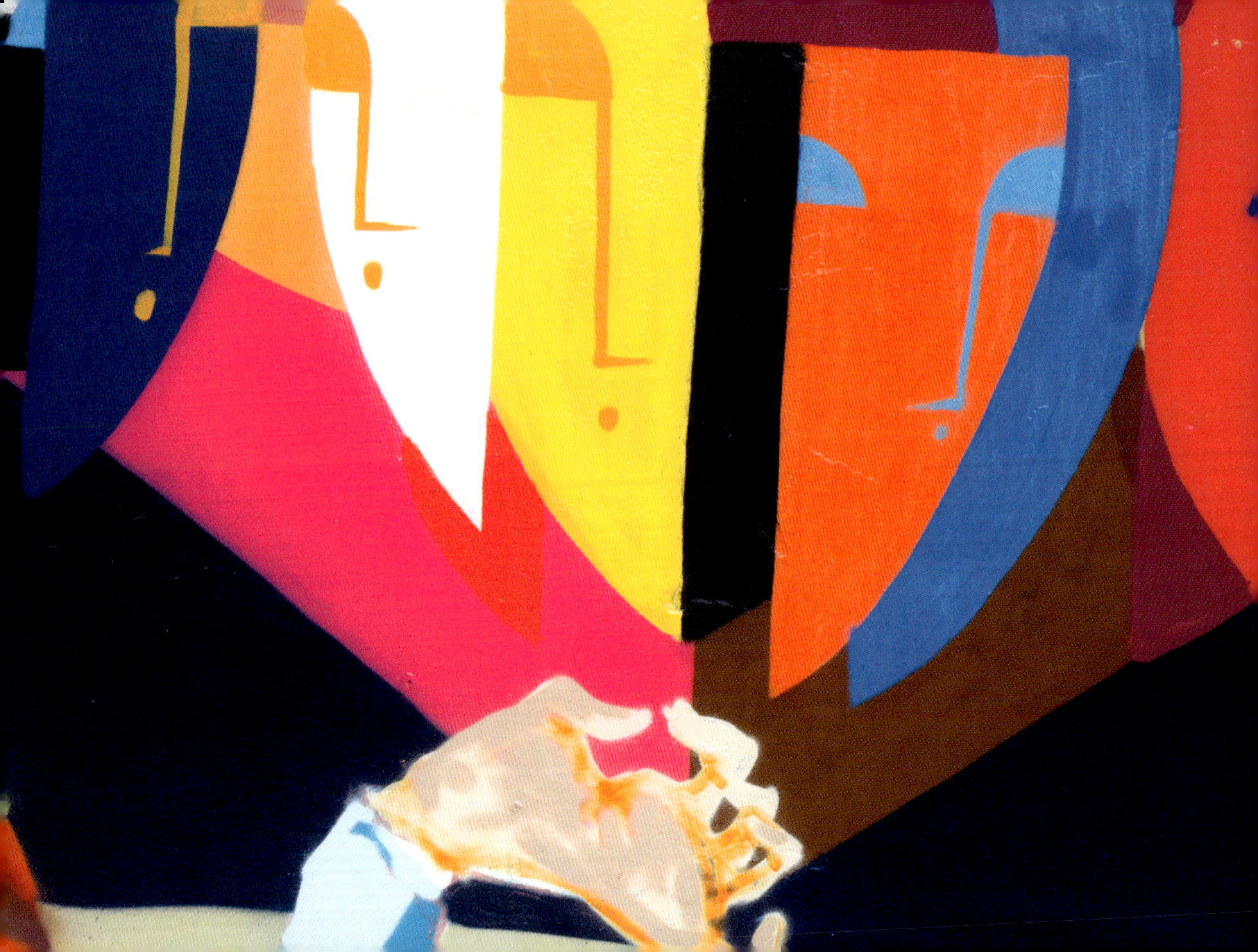

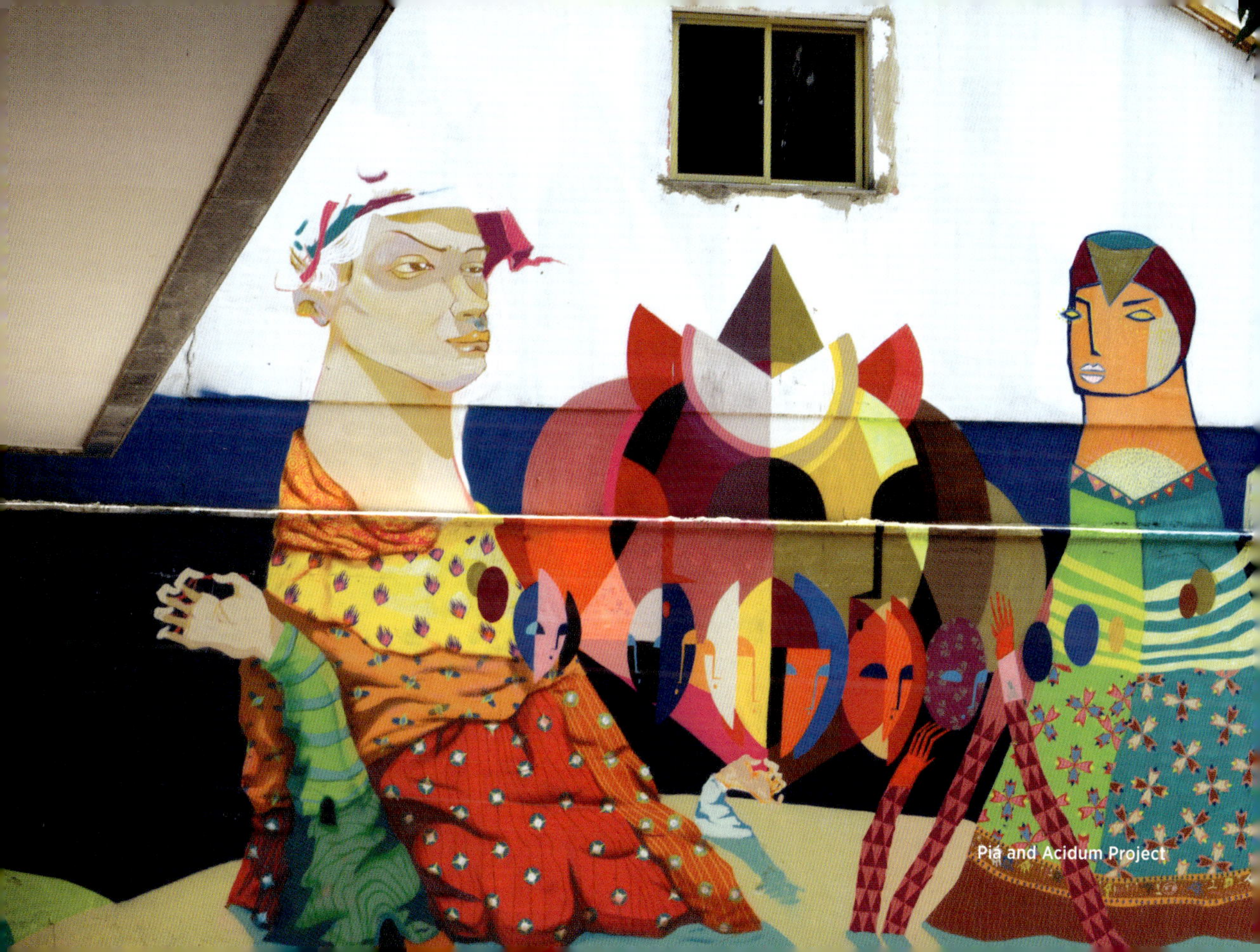

Piá and Acidum Project

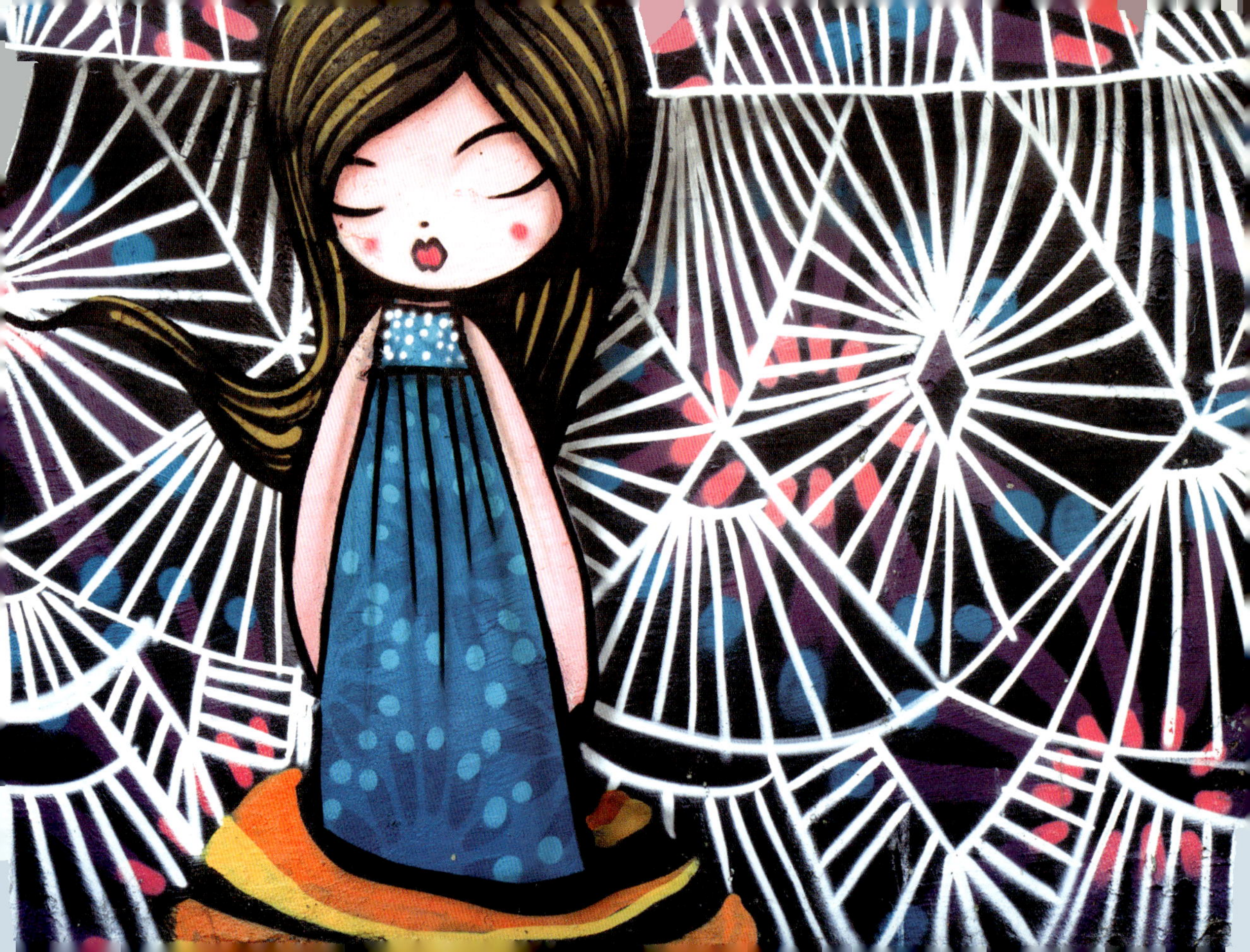

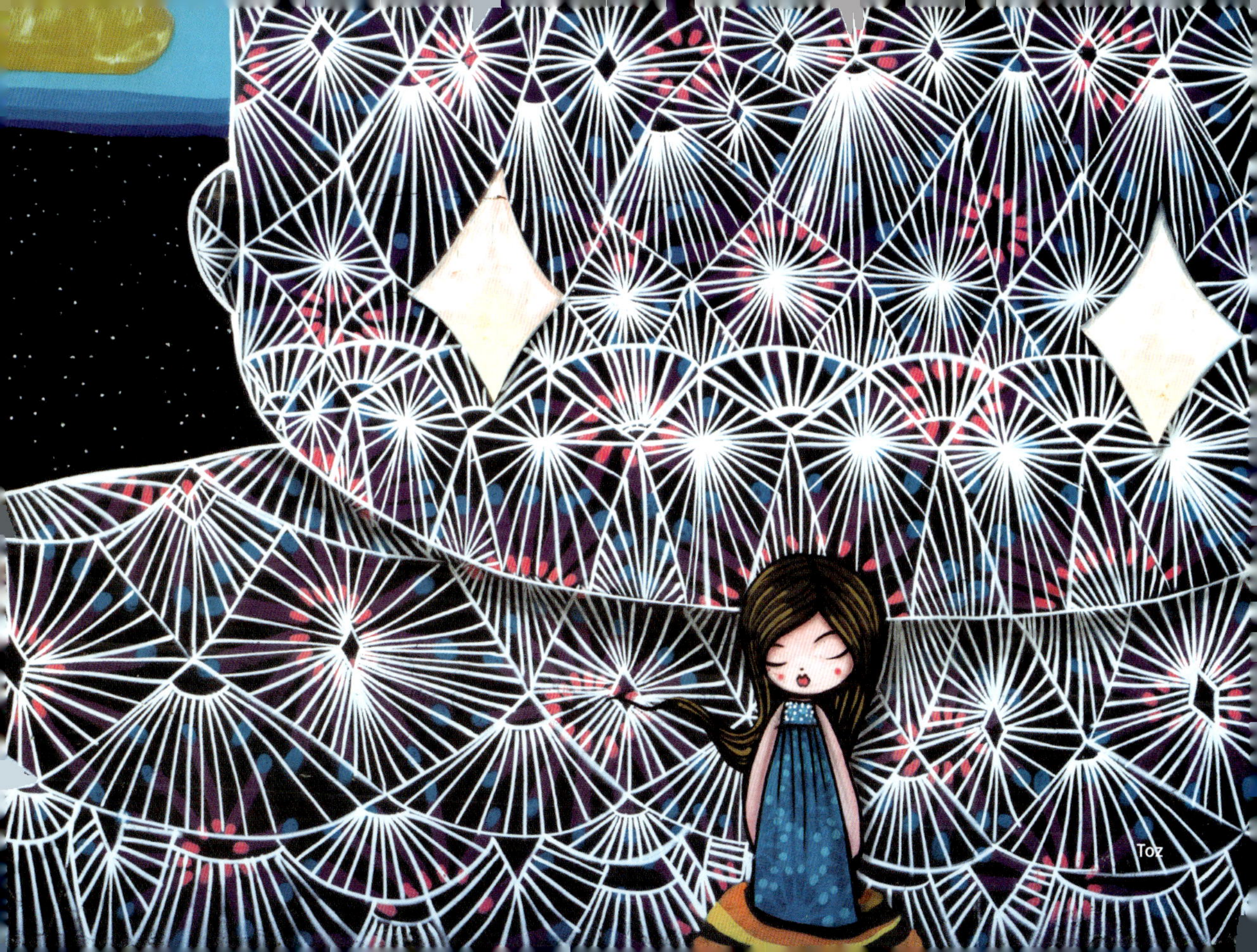
Toz

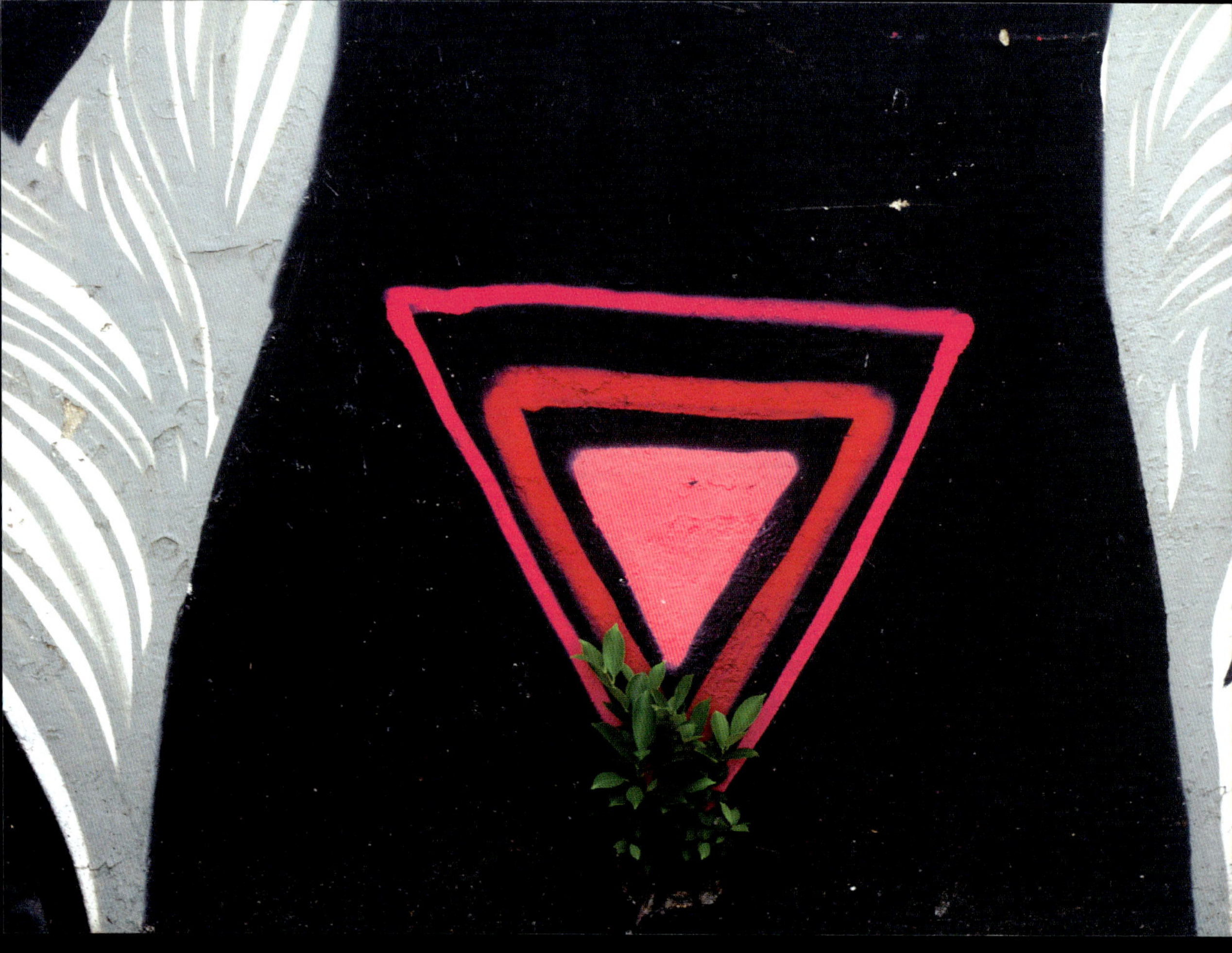

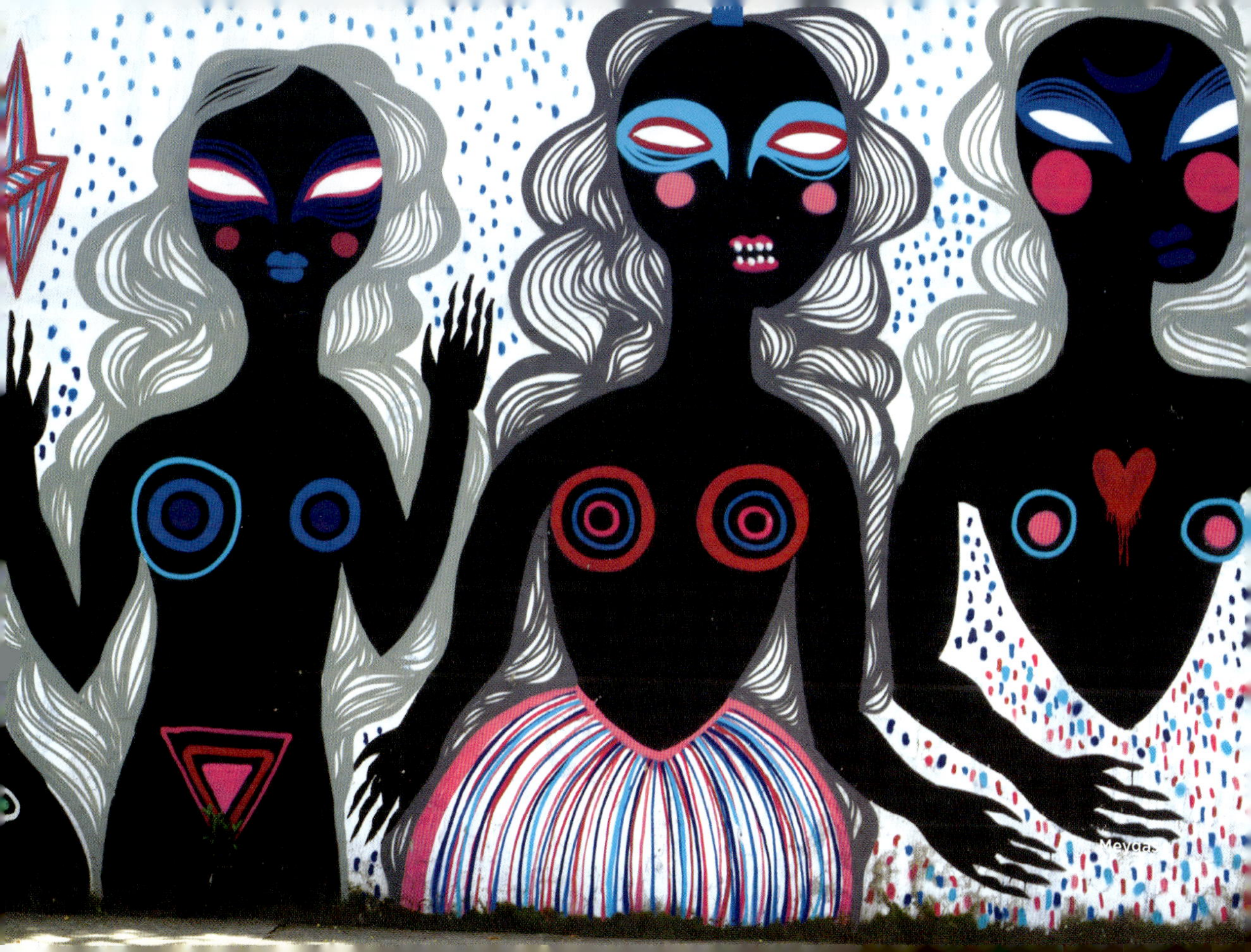

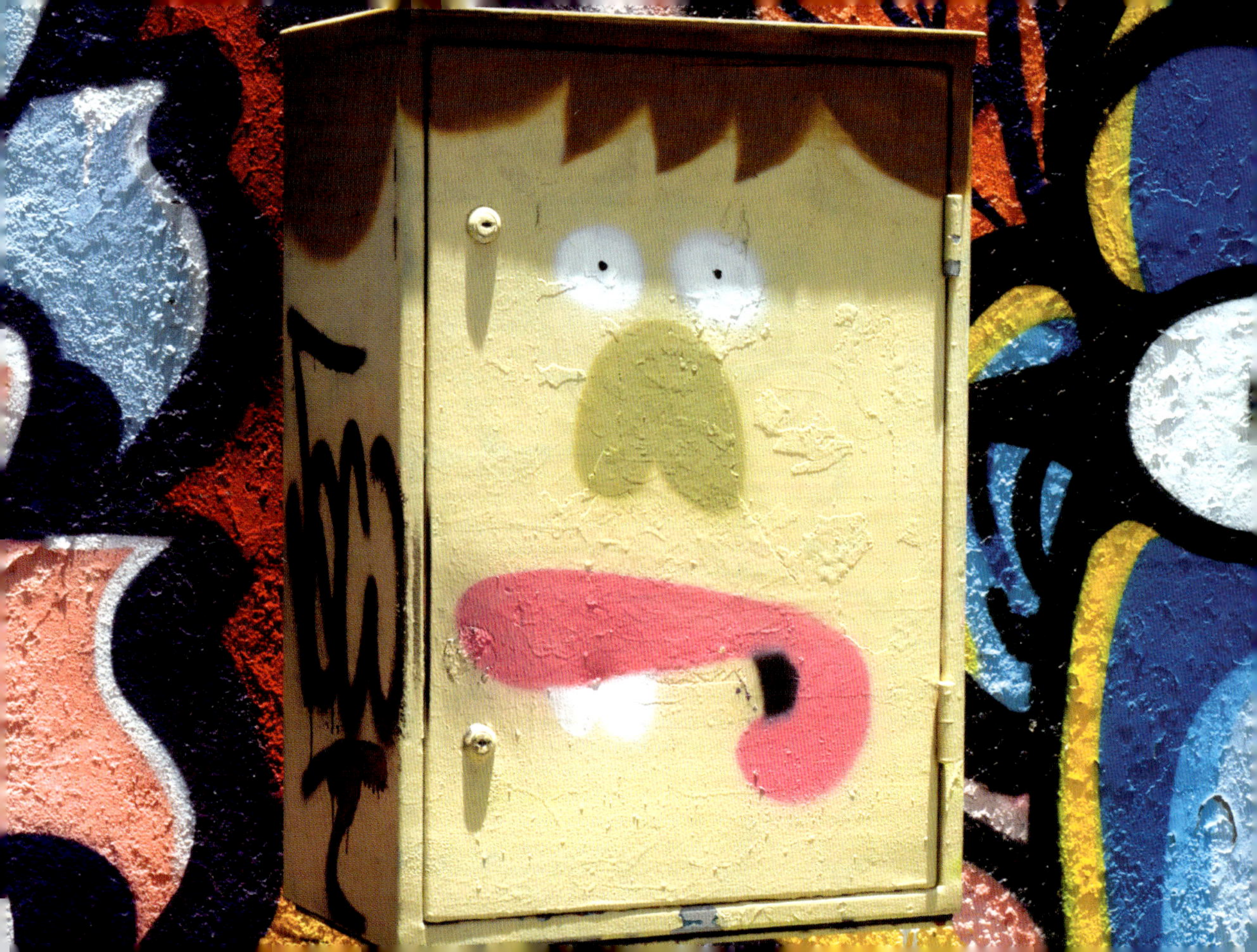

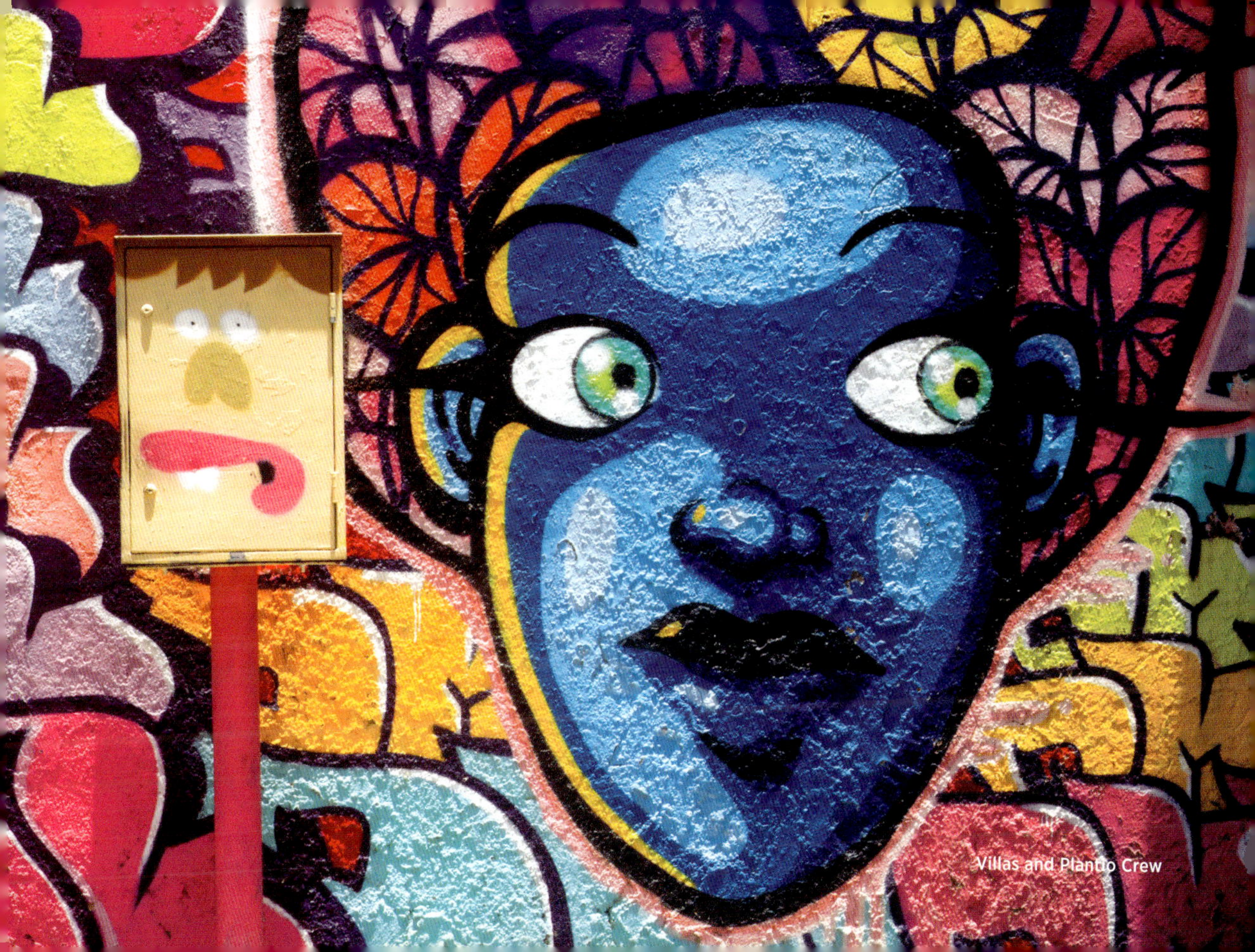
Villas and Plantio Crew

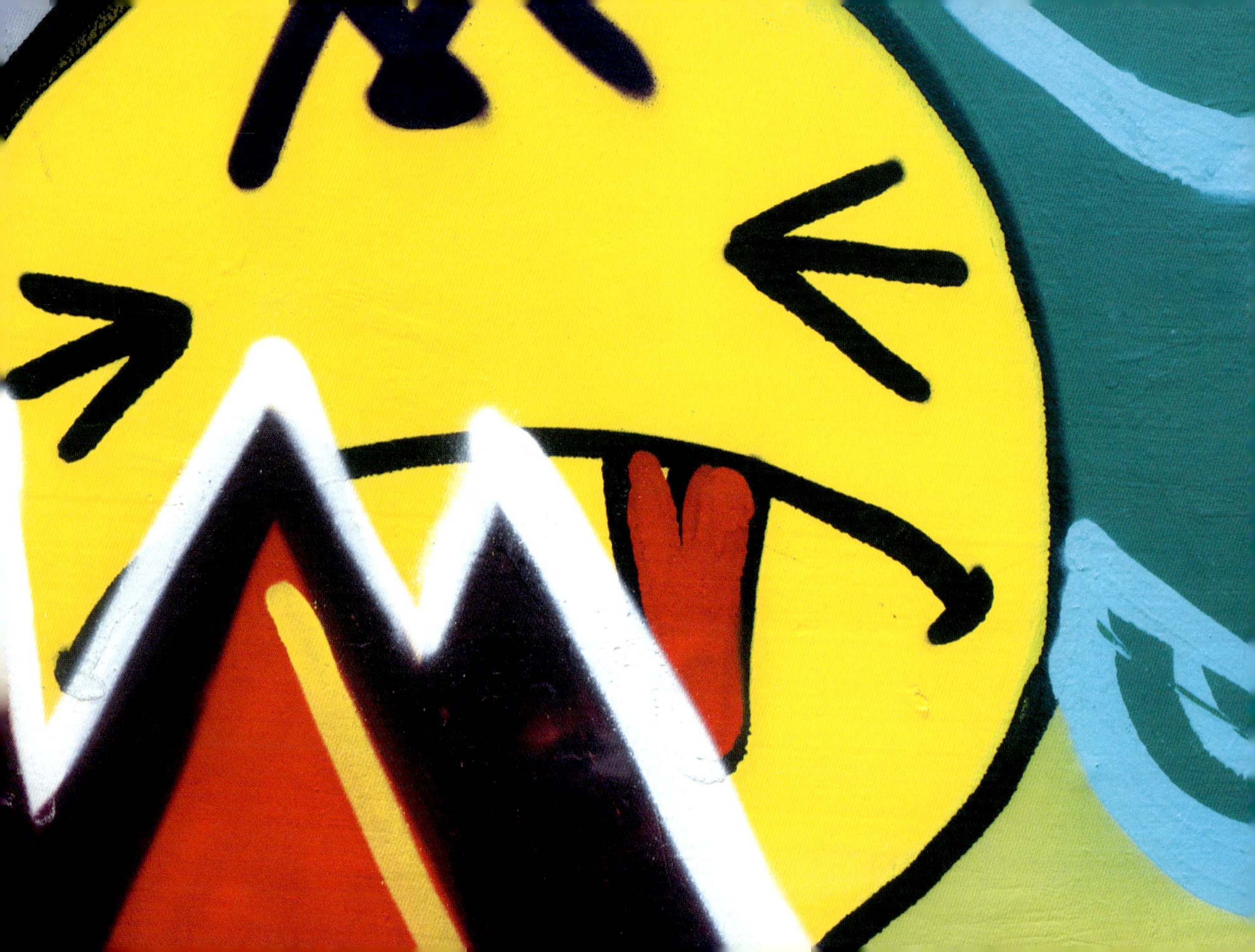

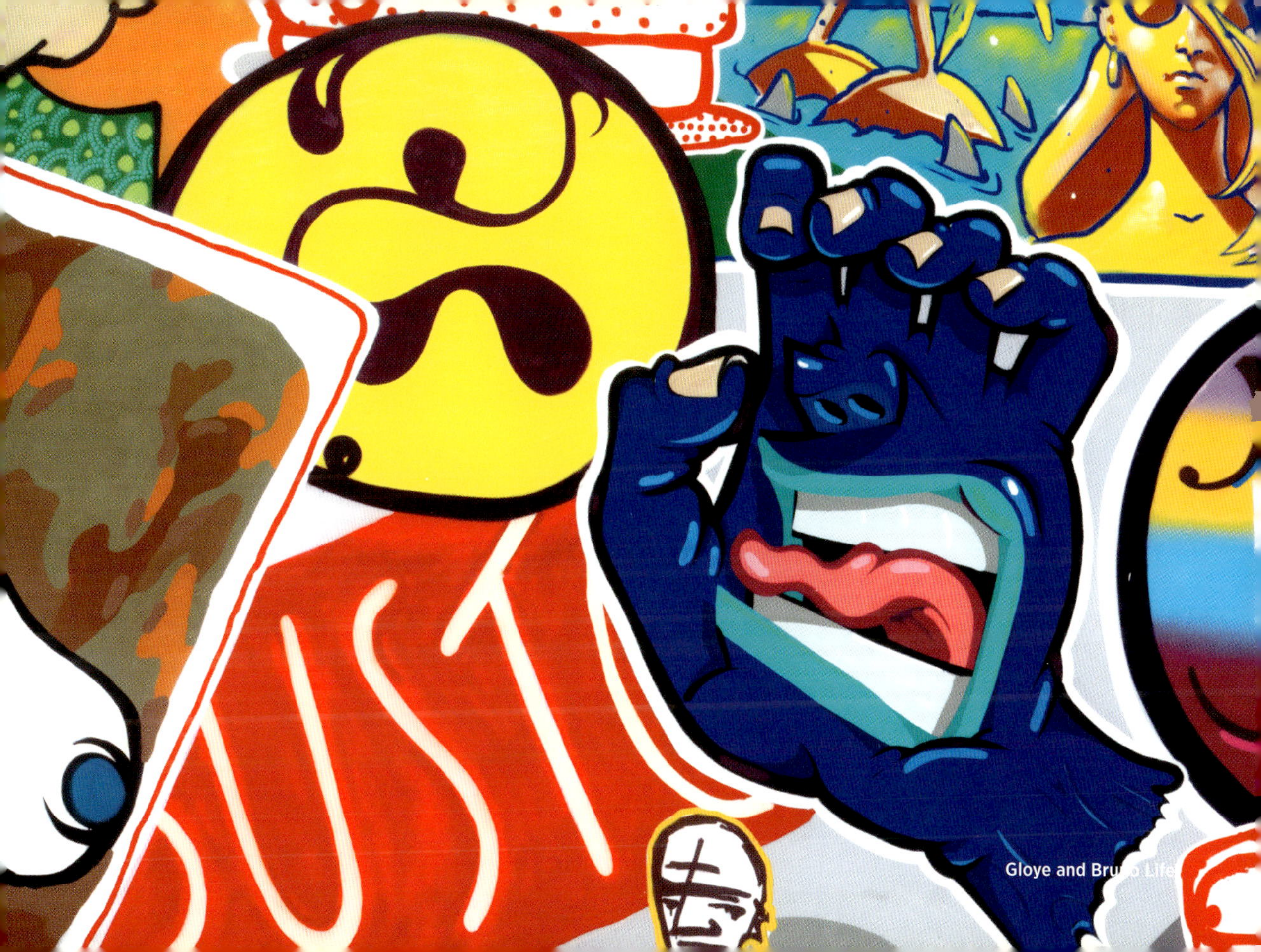

Gloye and Bruno Life

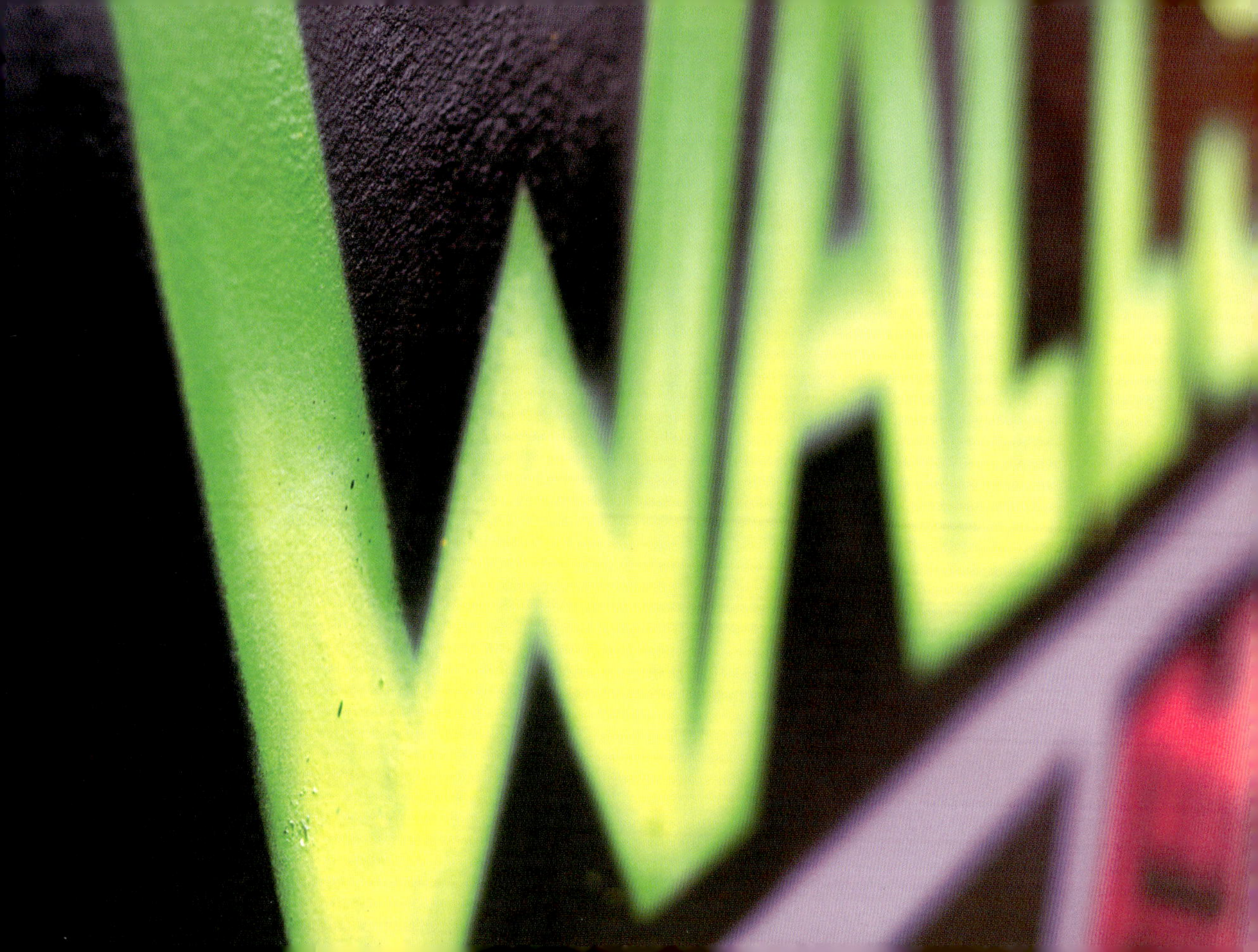
WAL

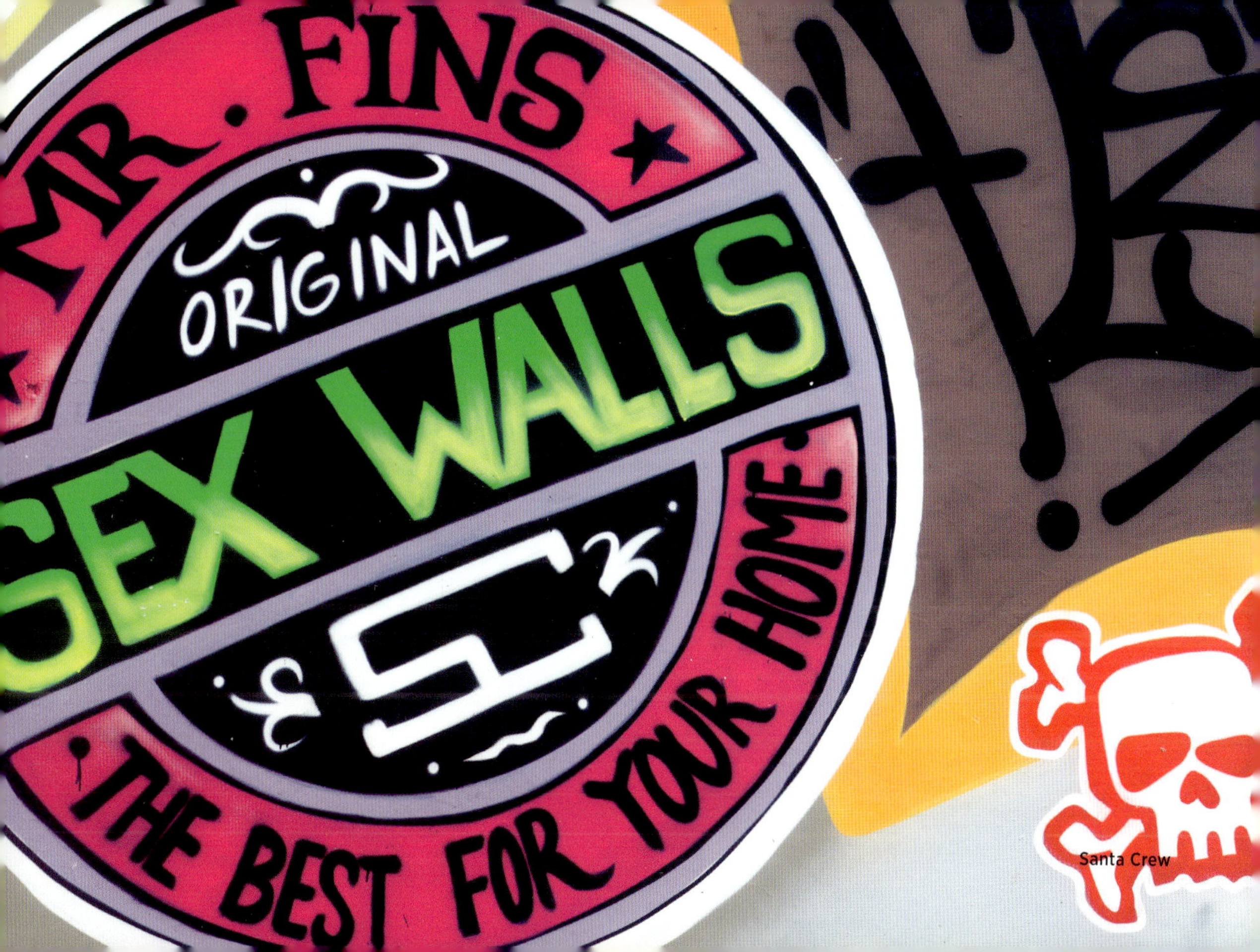

Santa Crew

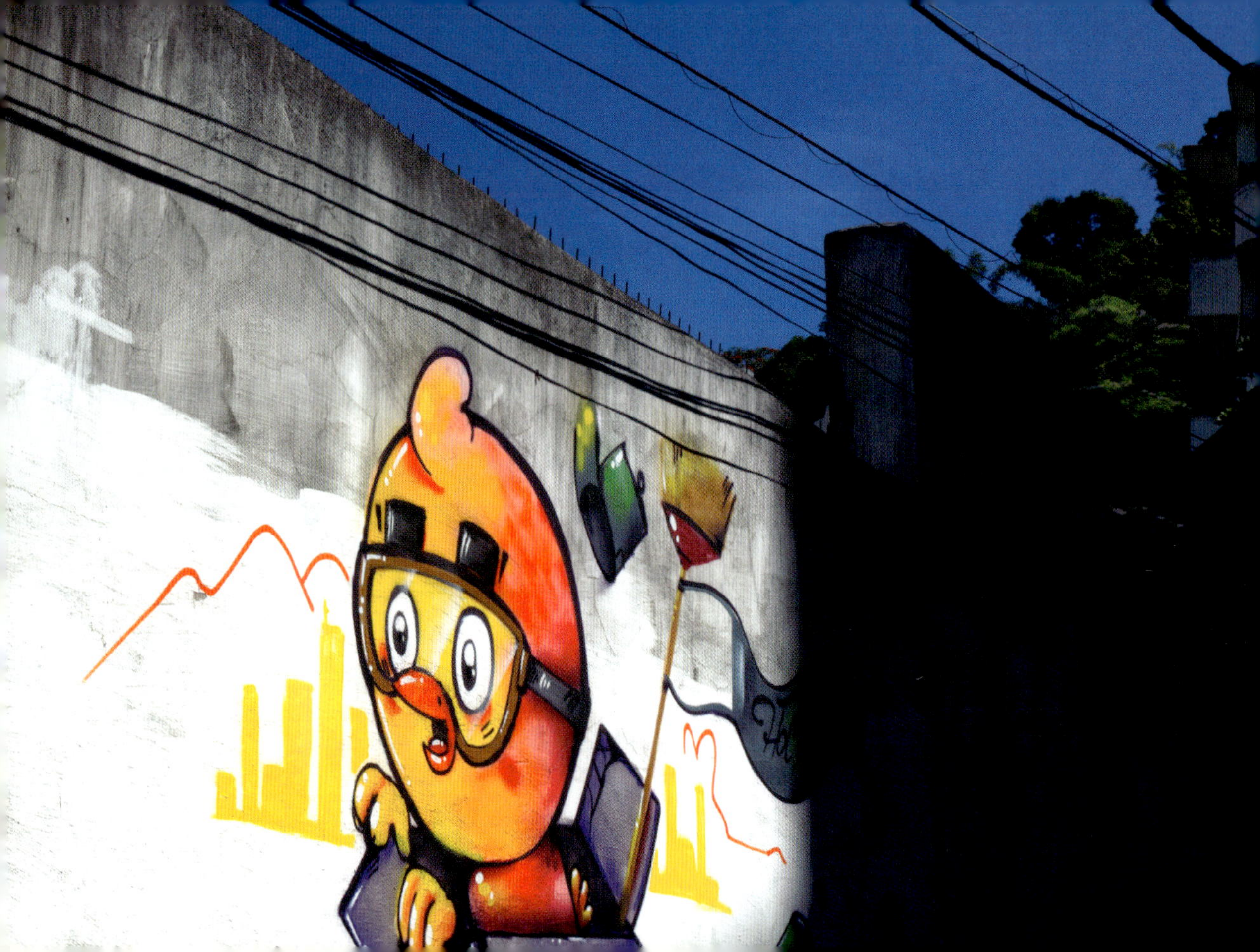

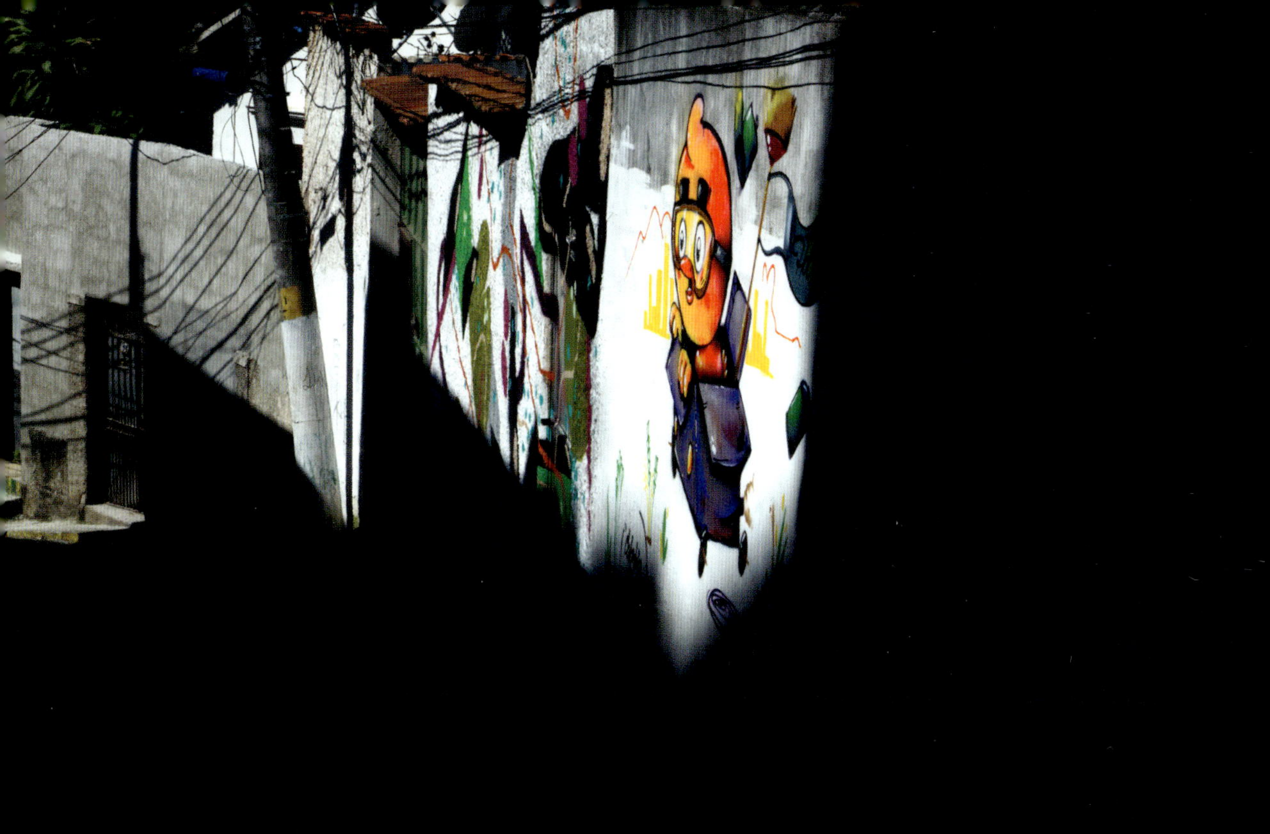

Hoc

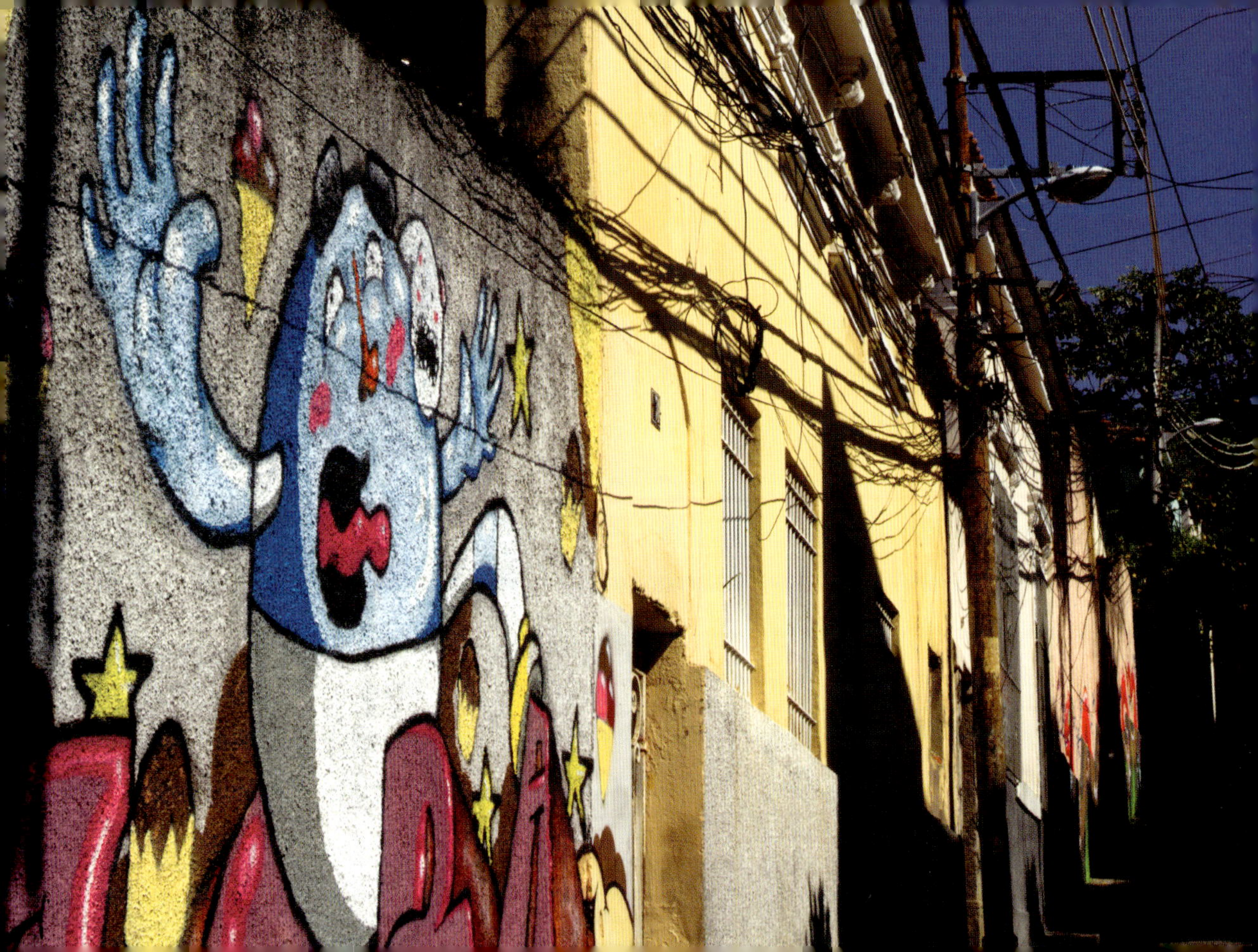

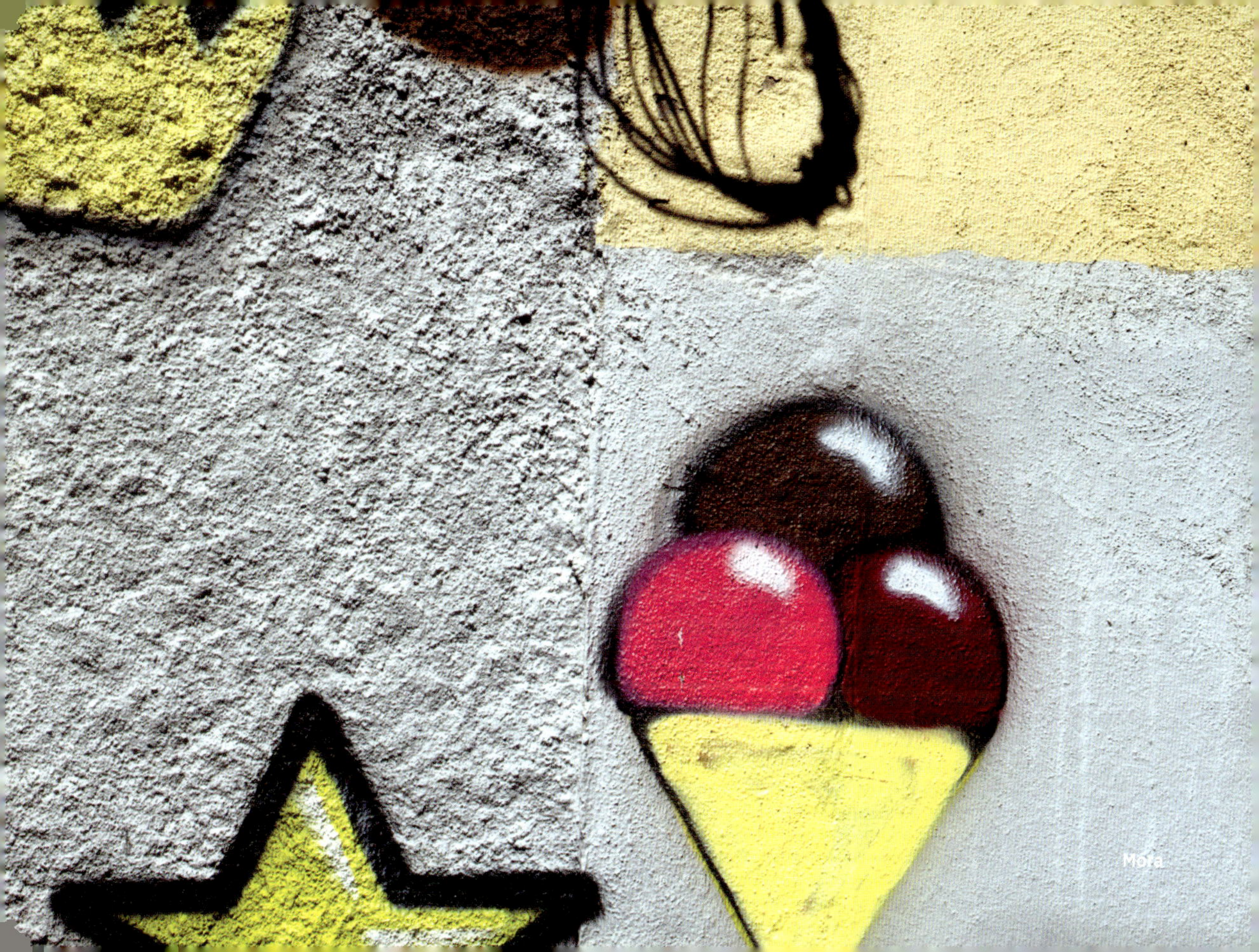
Mora

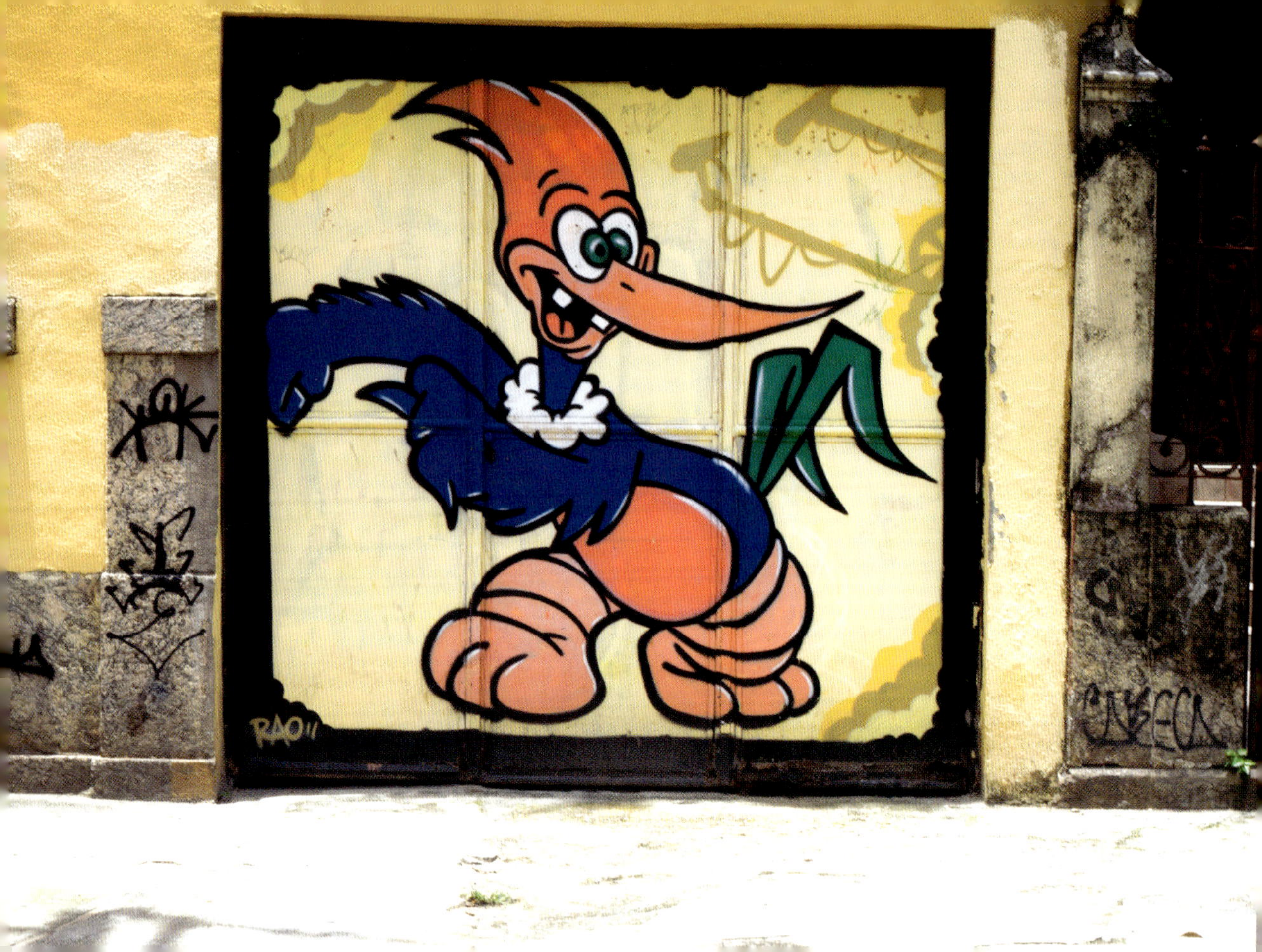
RAO

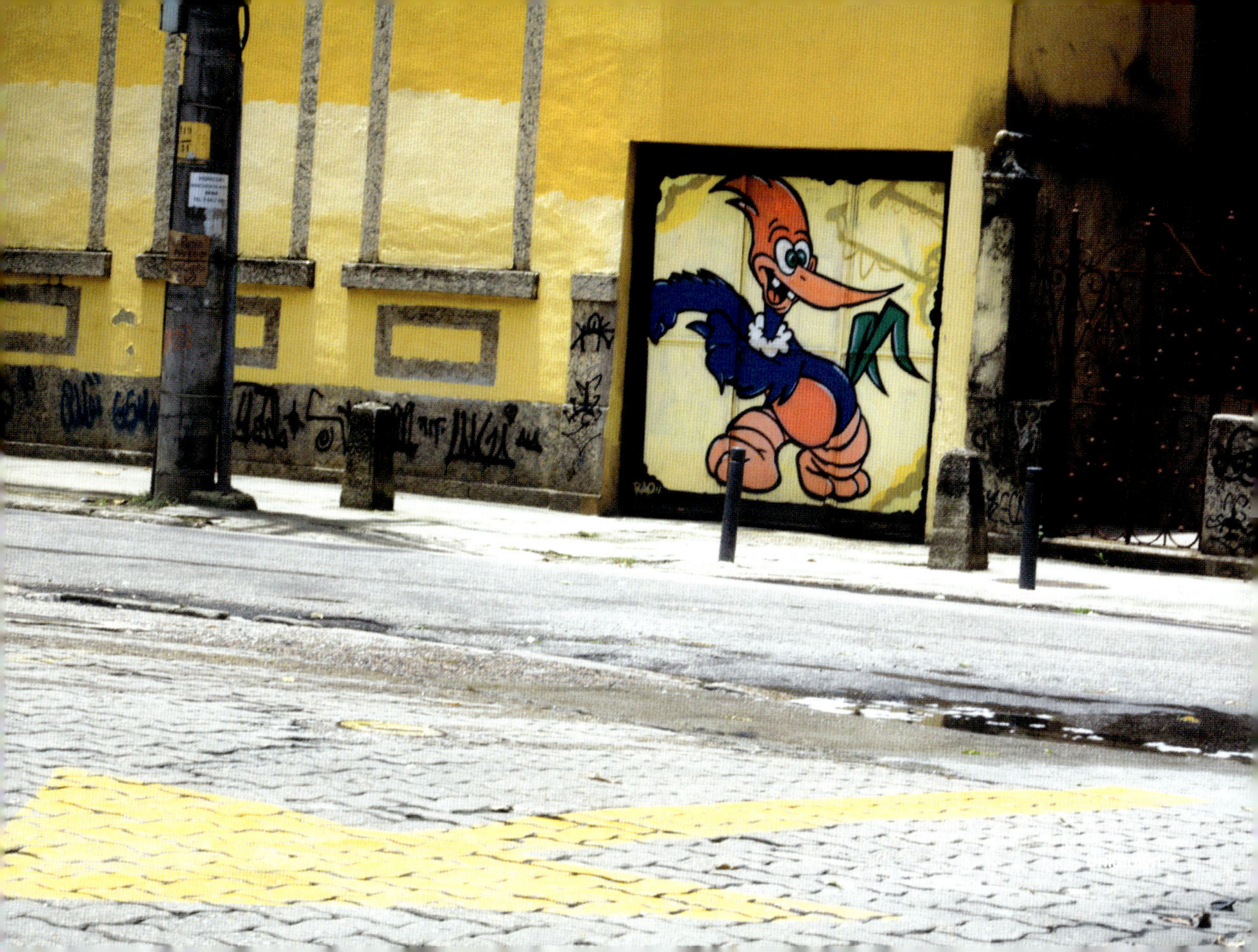

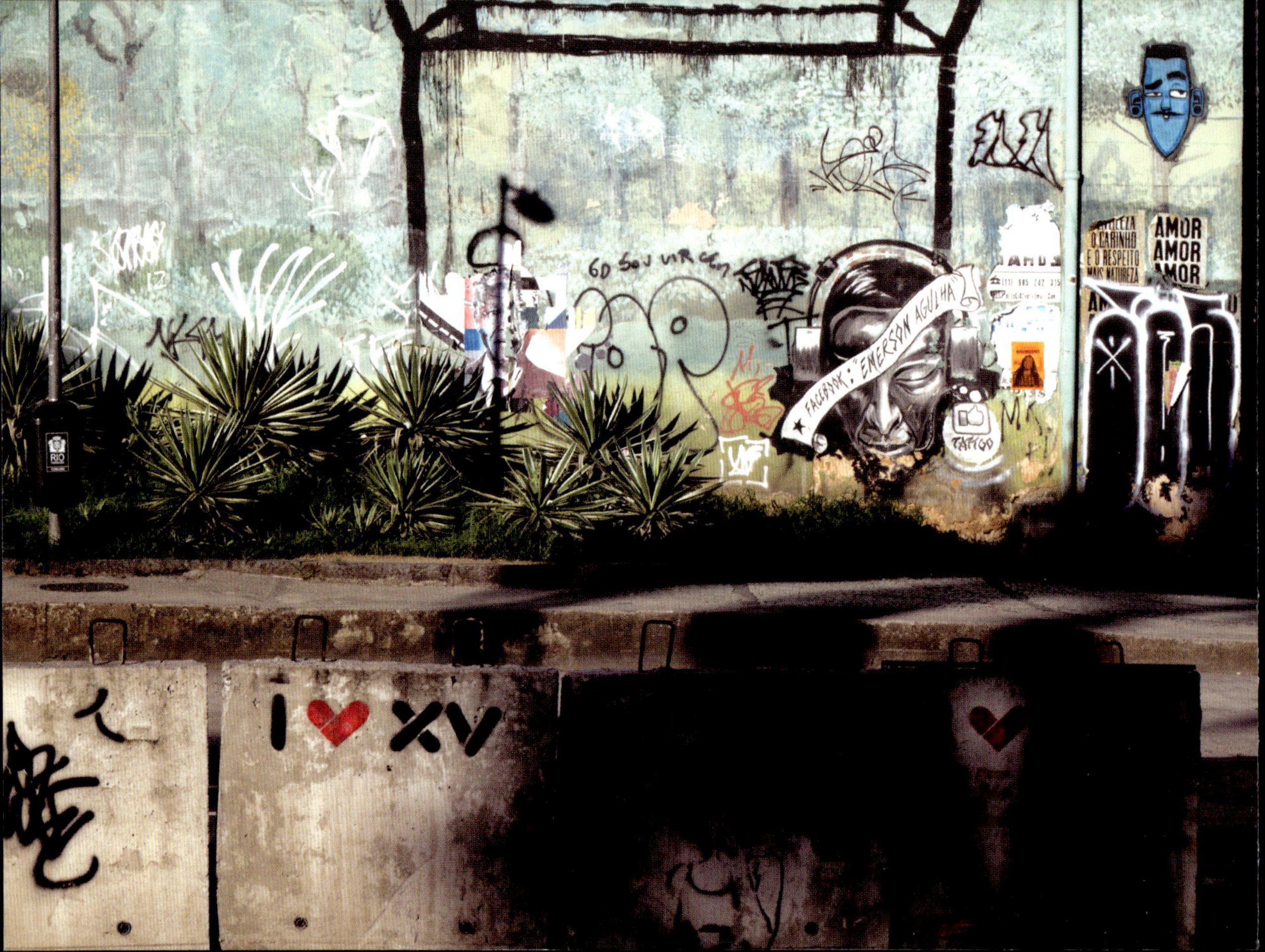
AMOR
AMOR
AMOR
FACEBOOK : EMERSON AGULHA
TATTOO
RIO
I XV

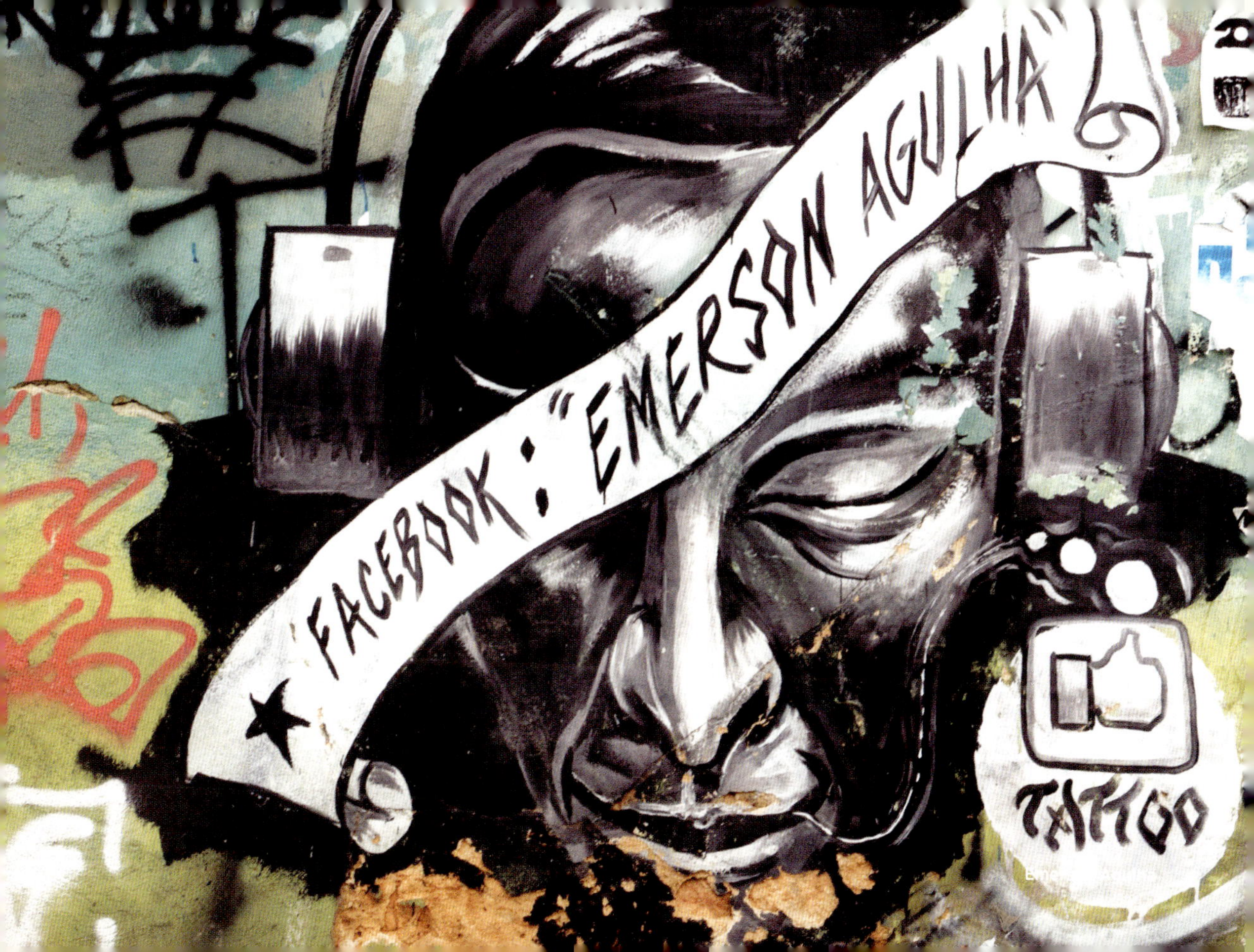
FACEBOOK: "EMERSON AGULHA"
TATTOO

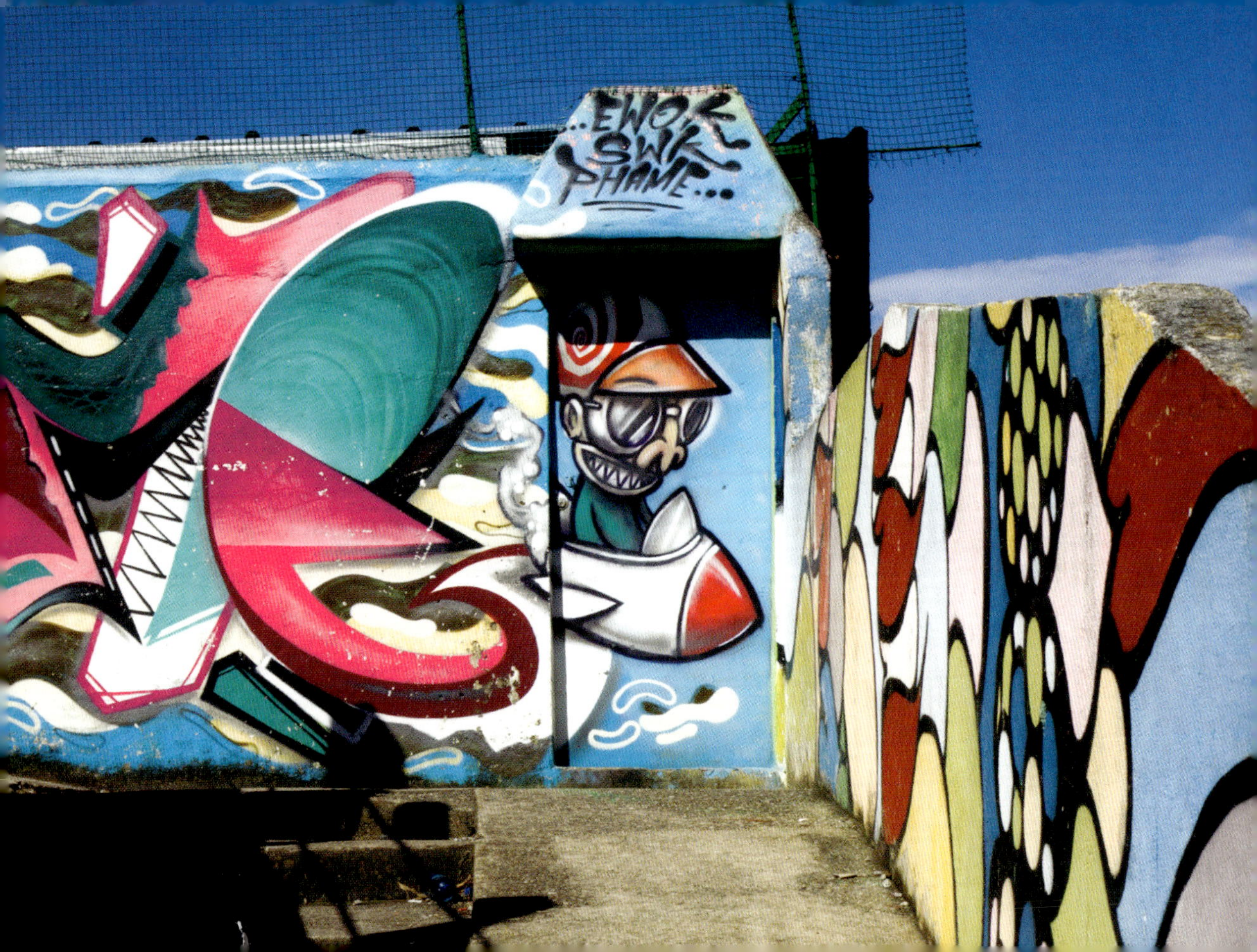
EWOK
SWK
PHAME

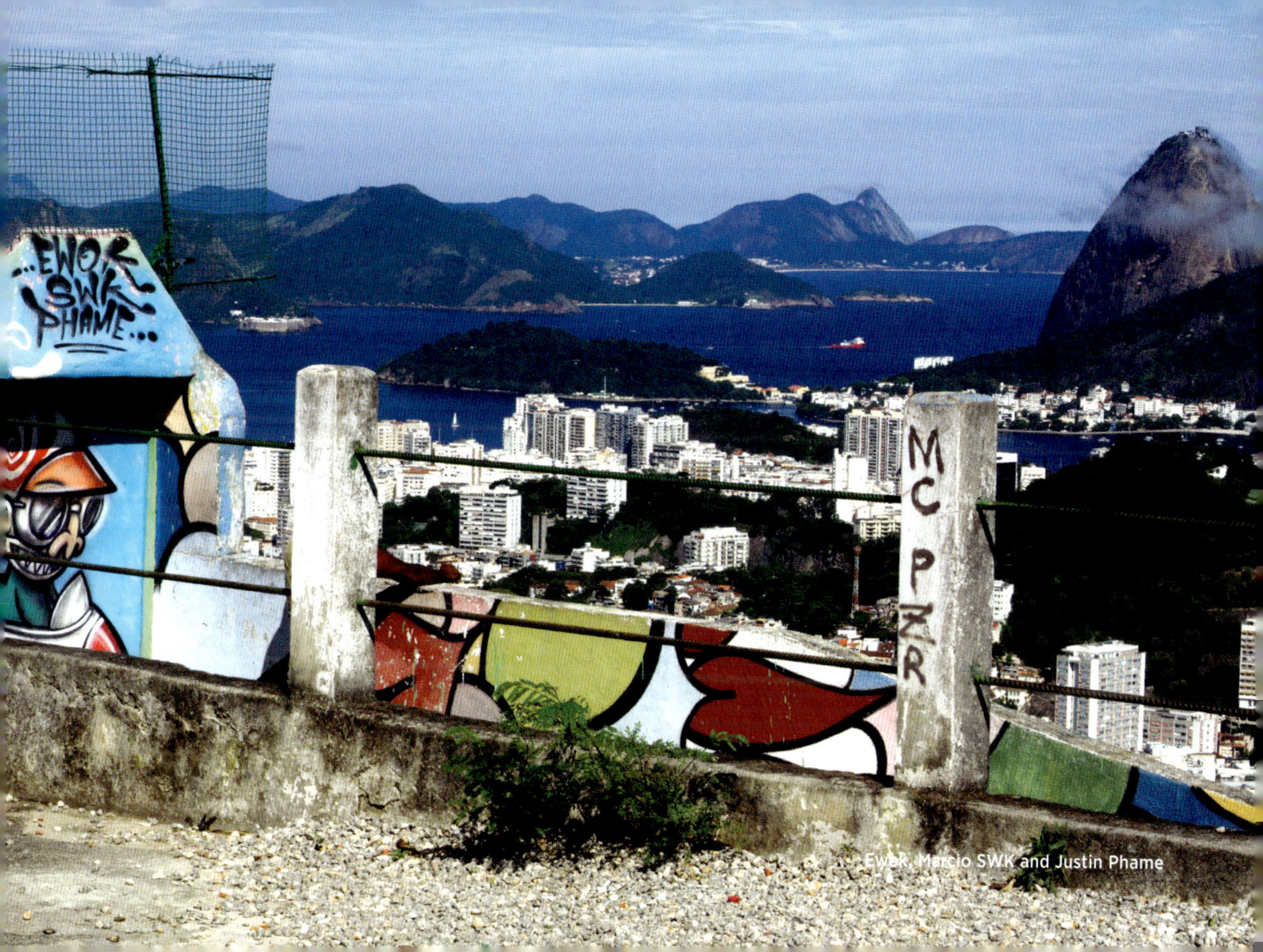

Ewok, Marcio SWK and Justin Phame

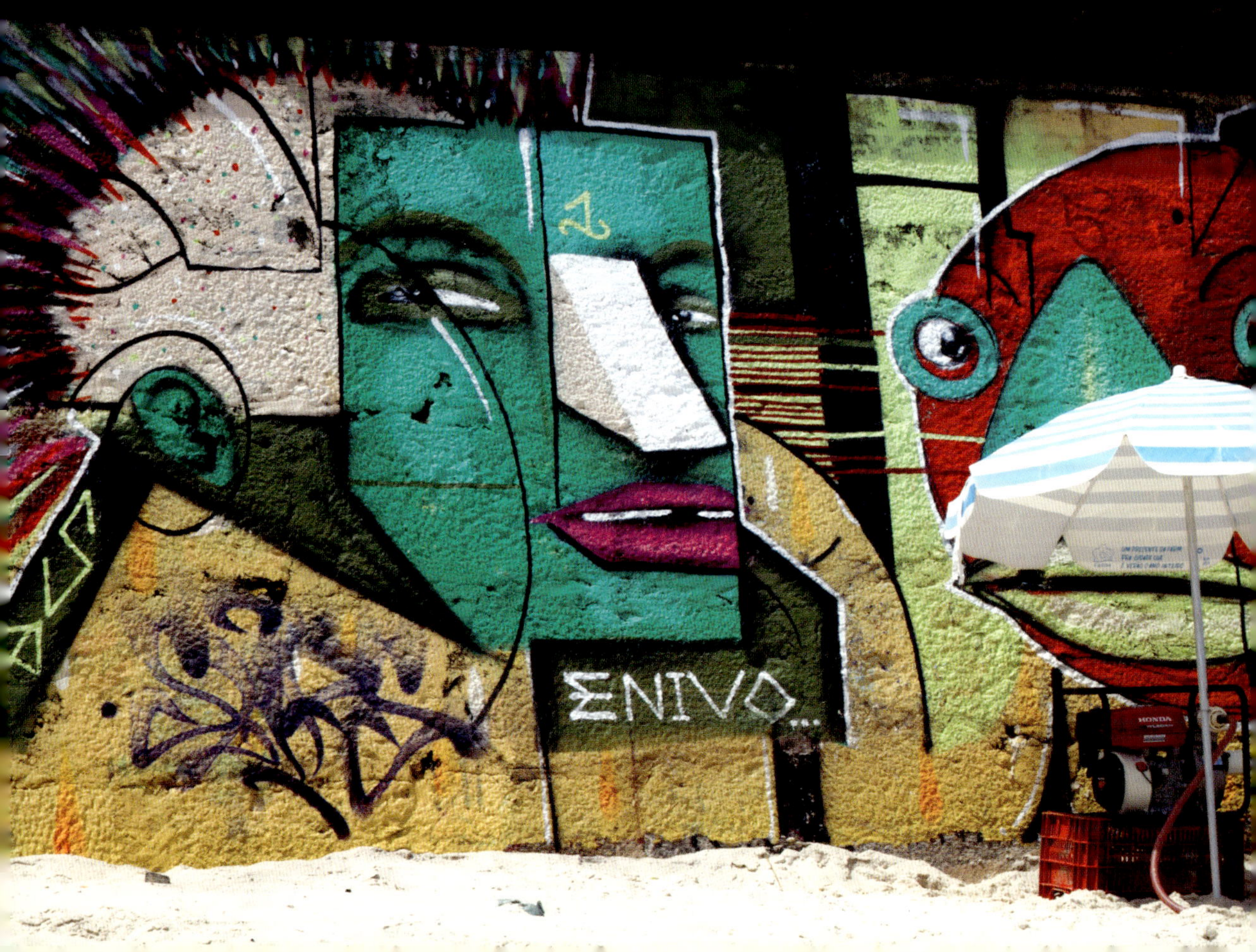
ENIVO...
HONDA

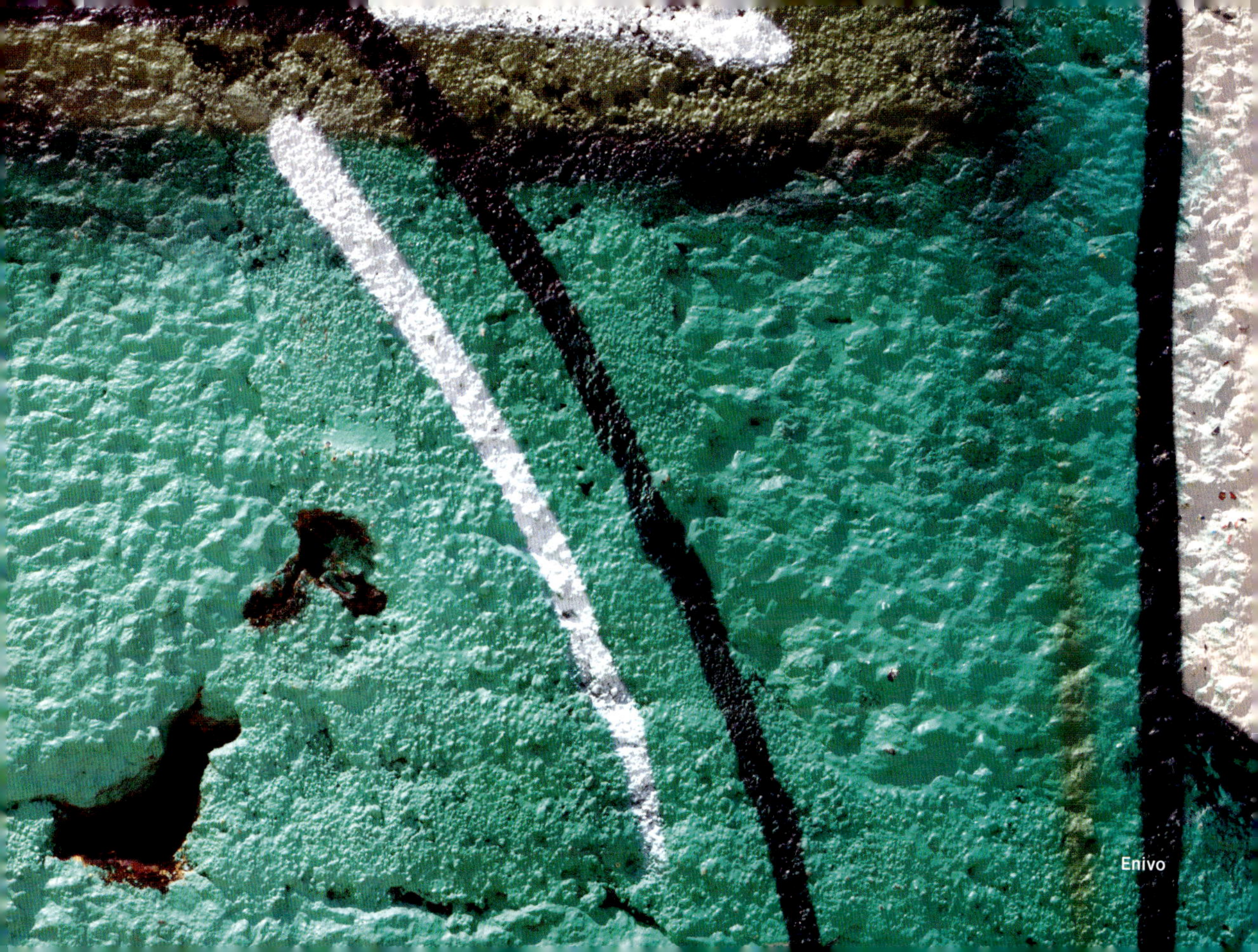
Enivo

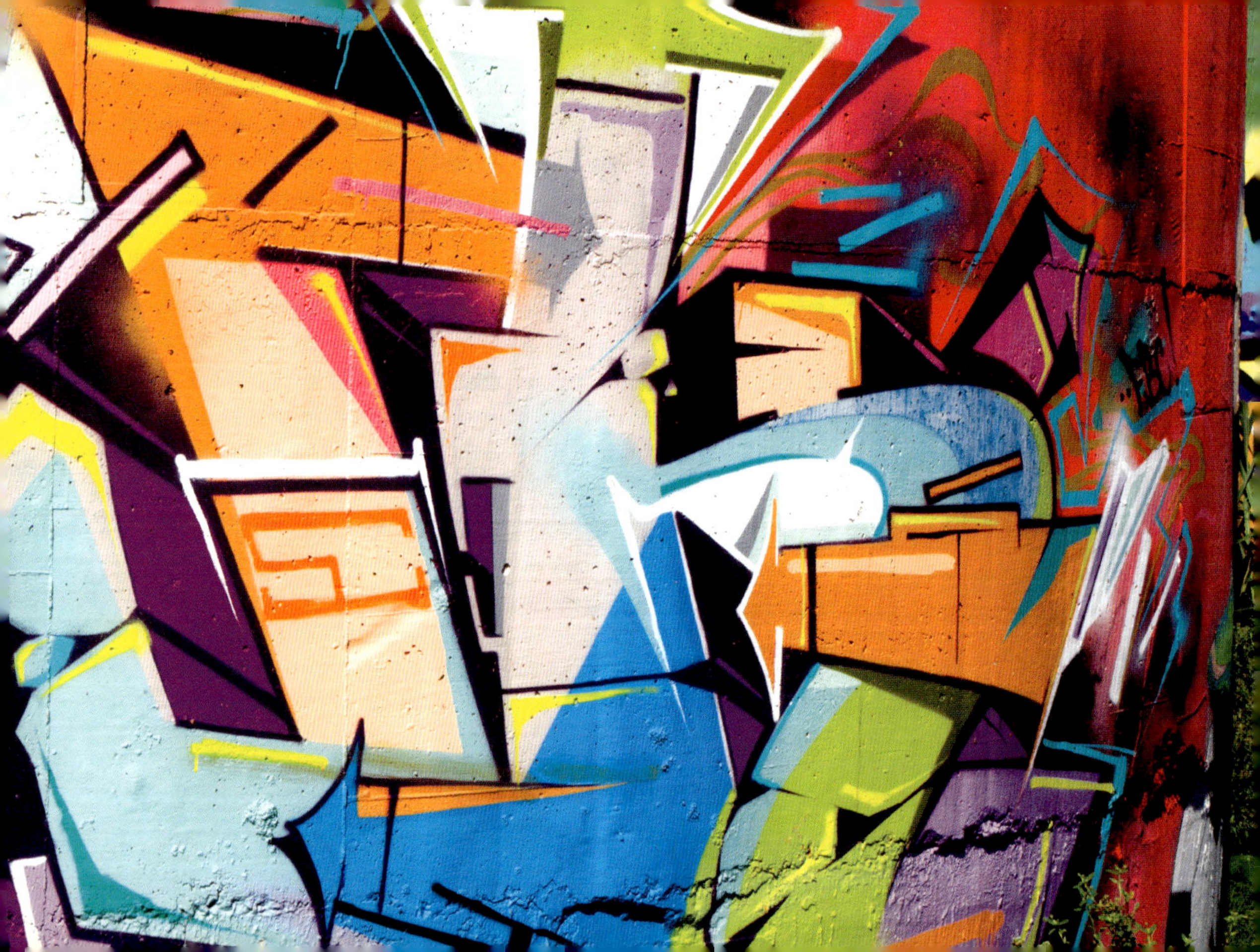

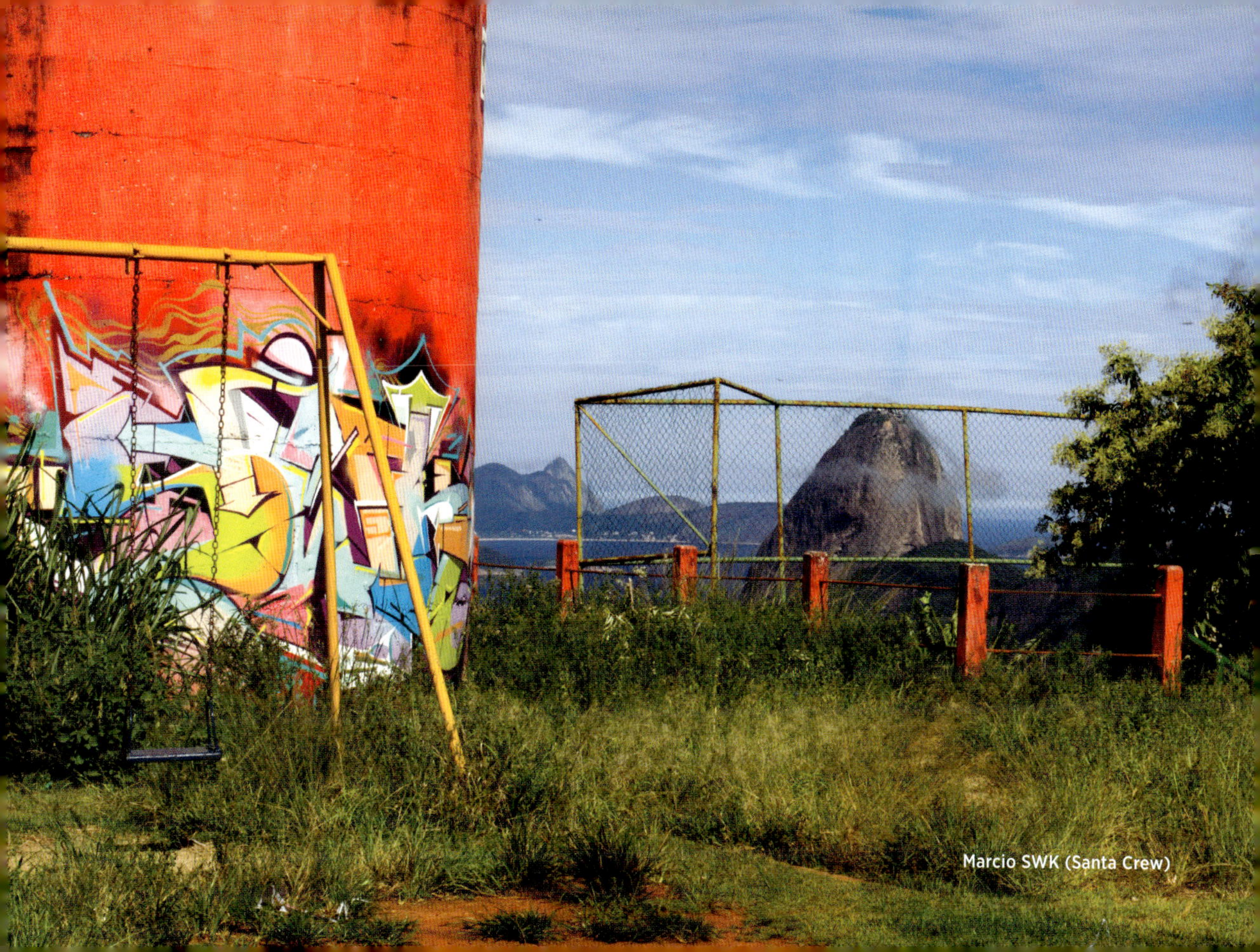

Marcio SWK (Santa Crew)

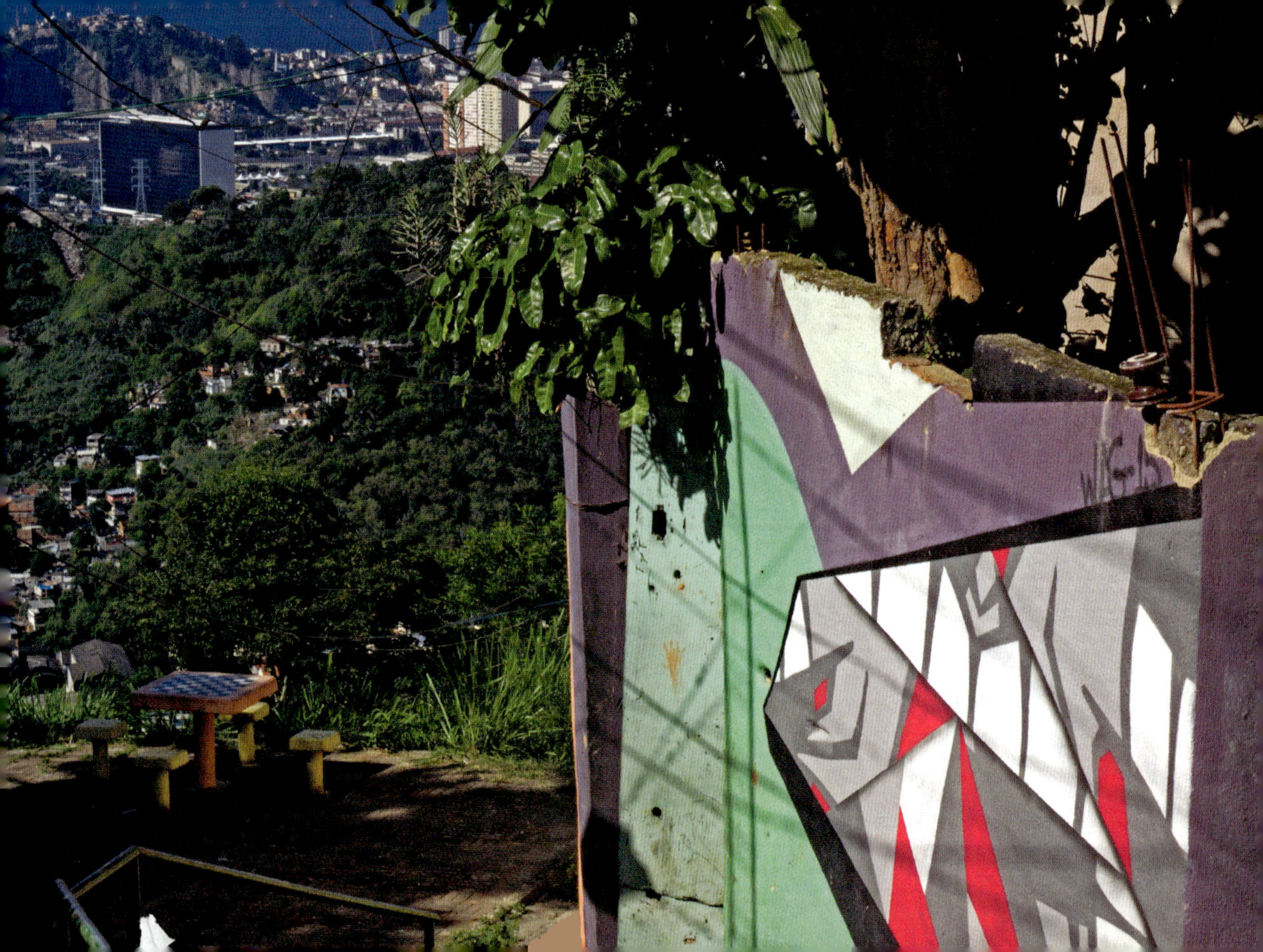

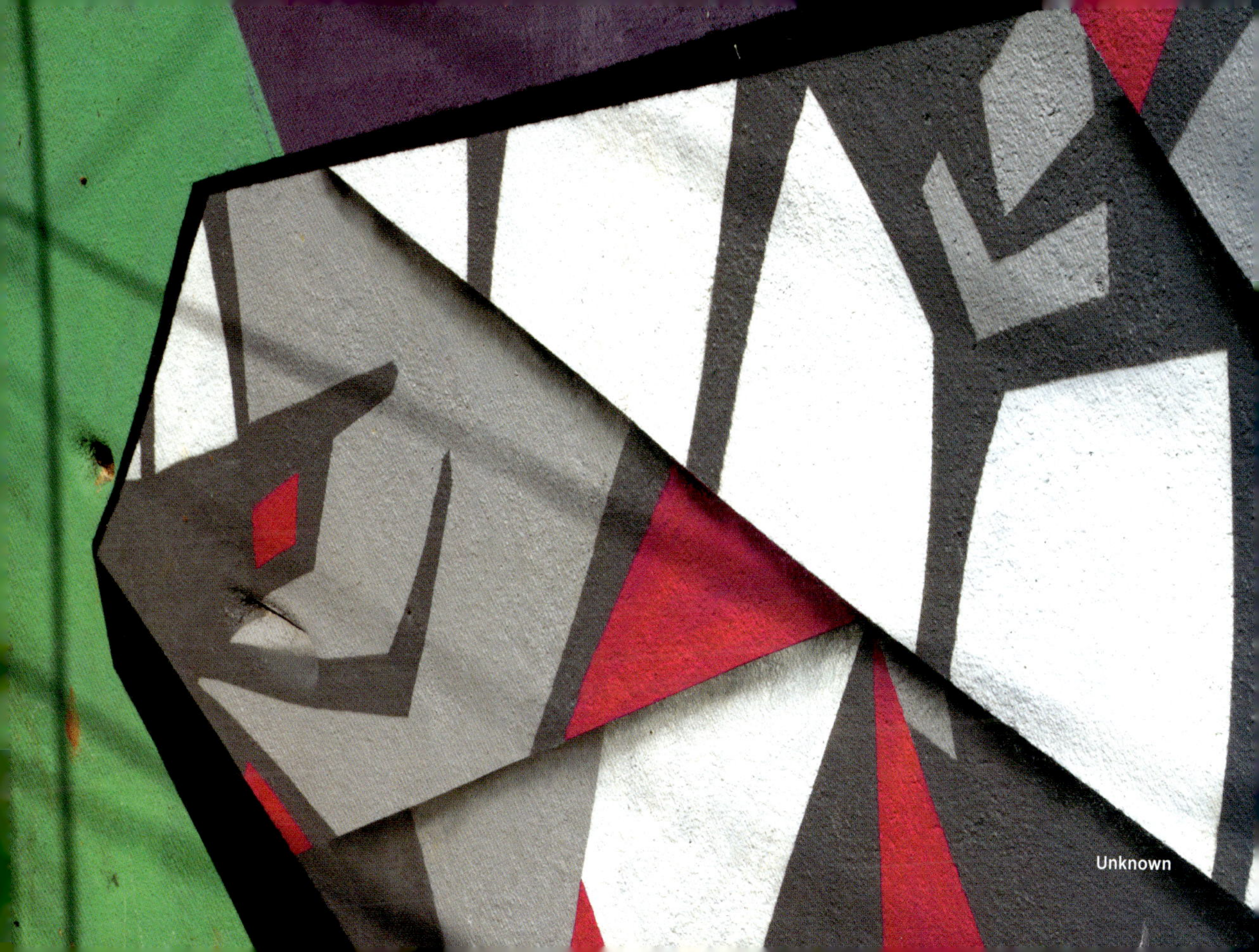

Unknown

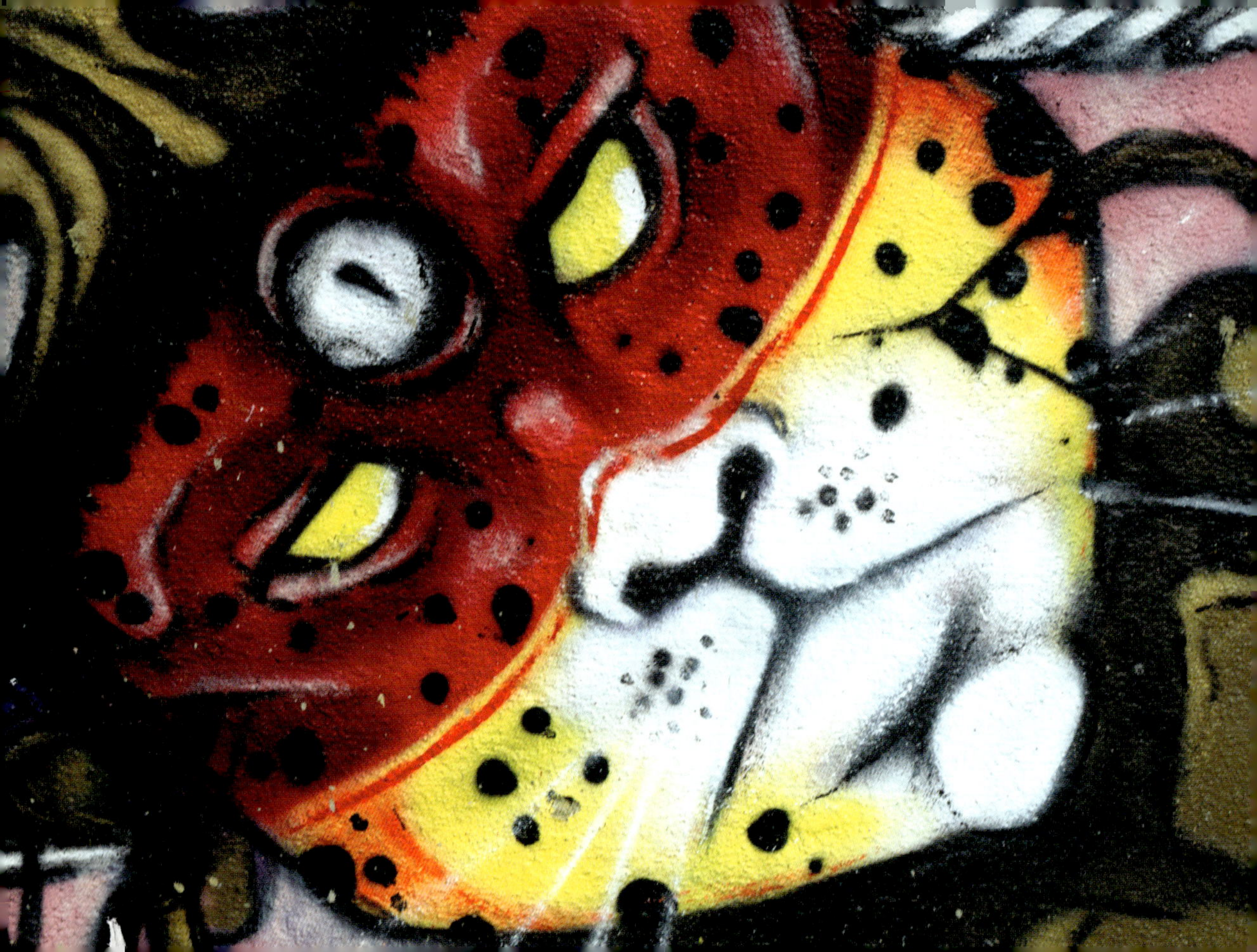

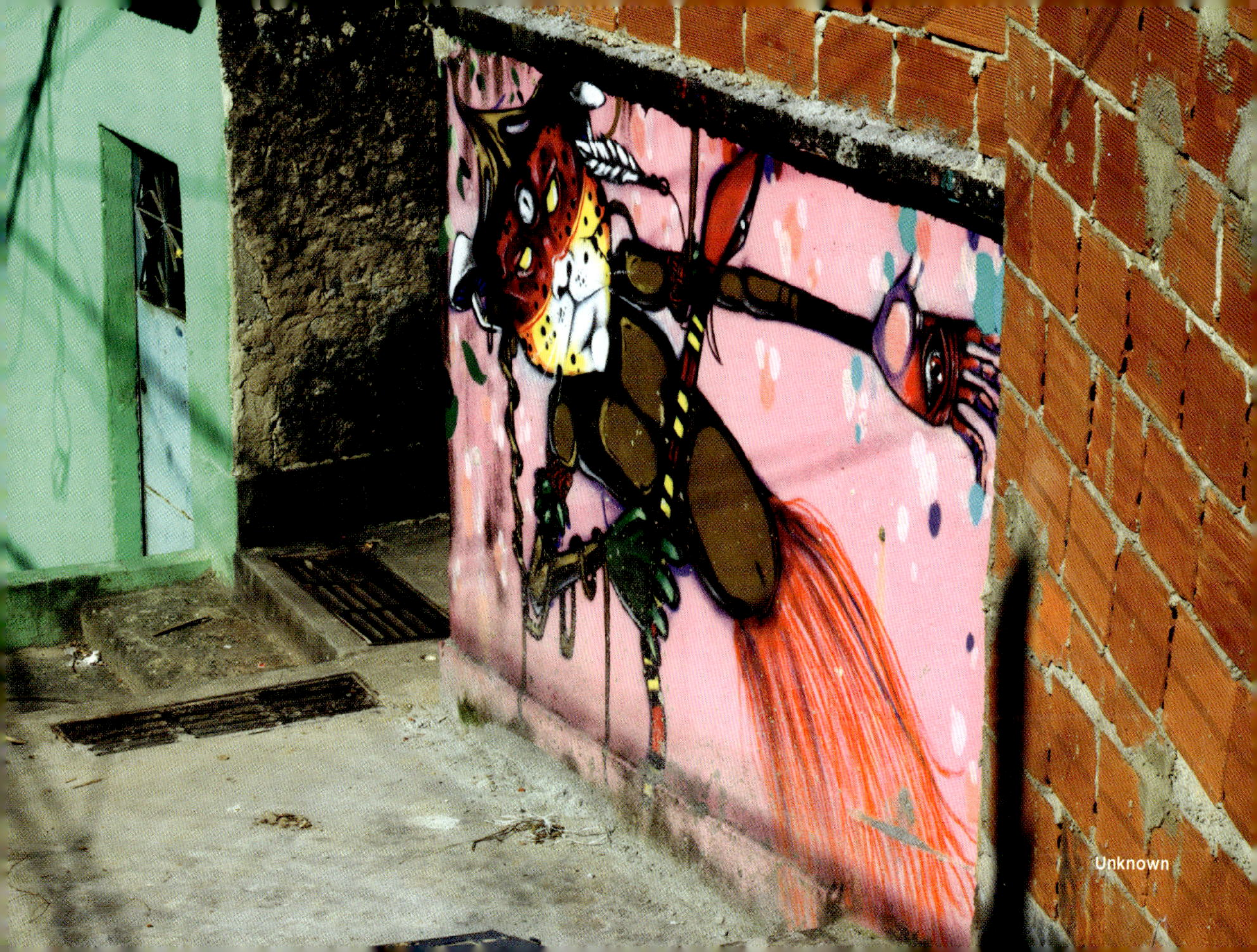

Unknown

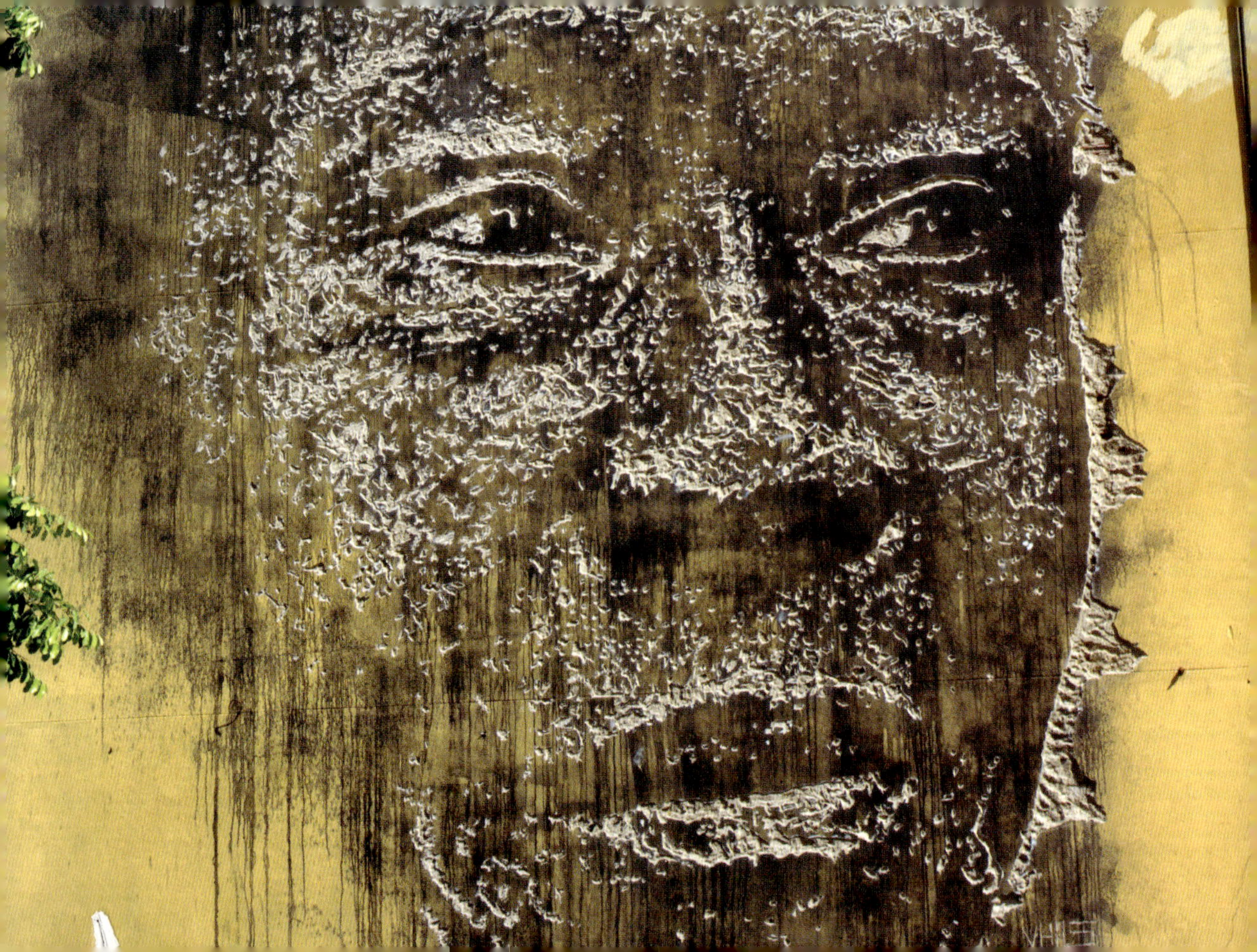

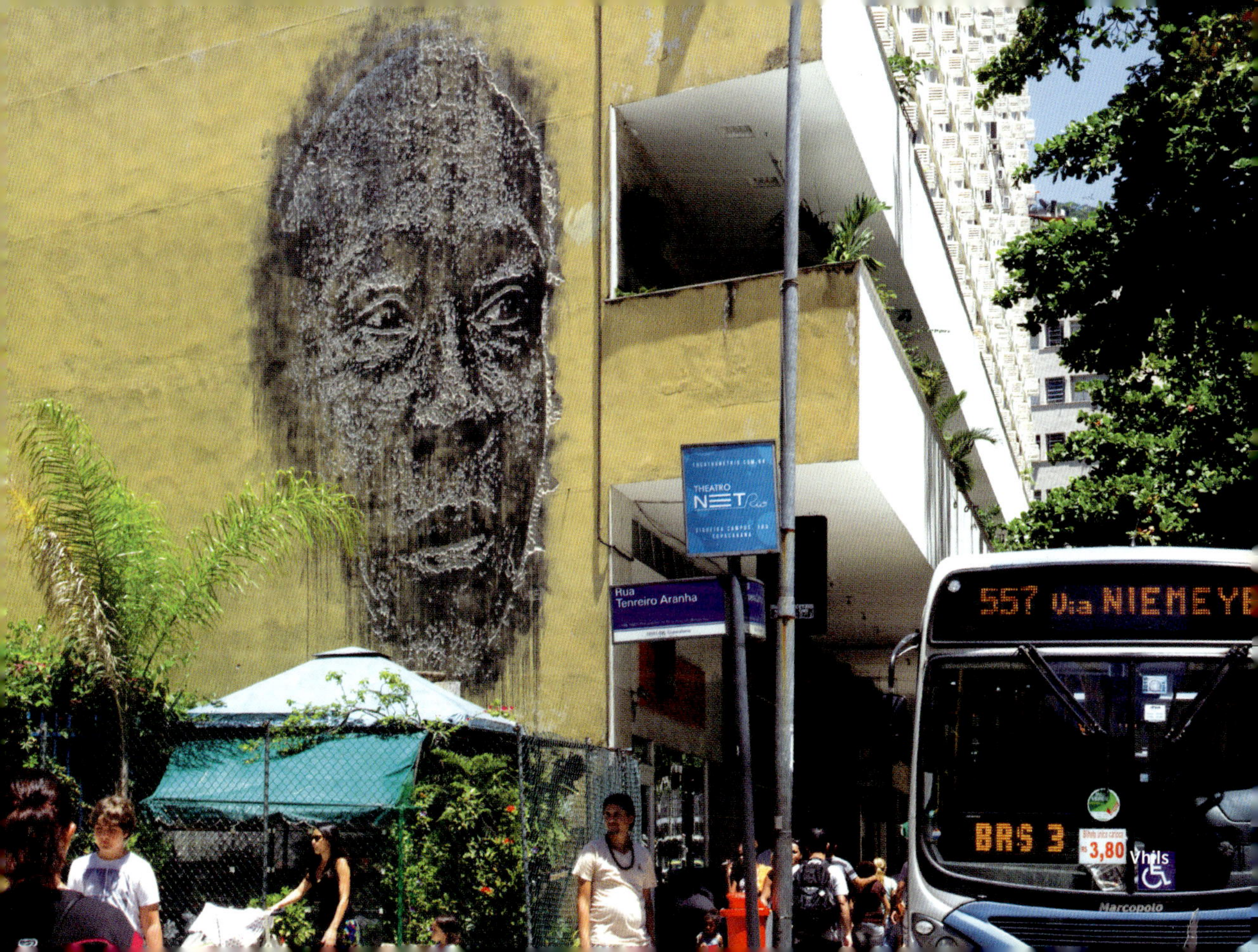
THEATRO
NET Rio
Rua
Tenreiro Aranha
557 Via NIEMEYE
BRS 3
3,80
Marcopolo

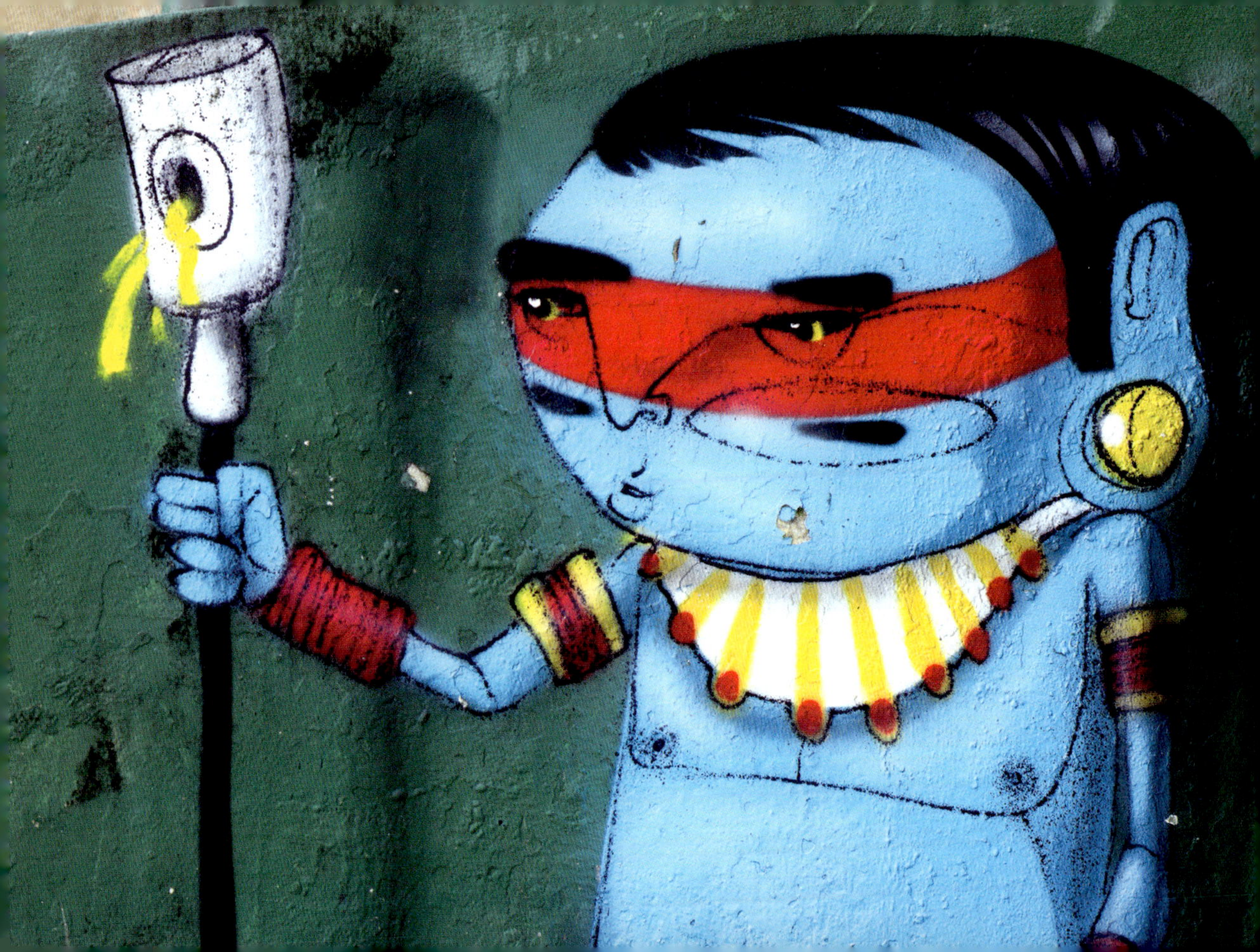

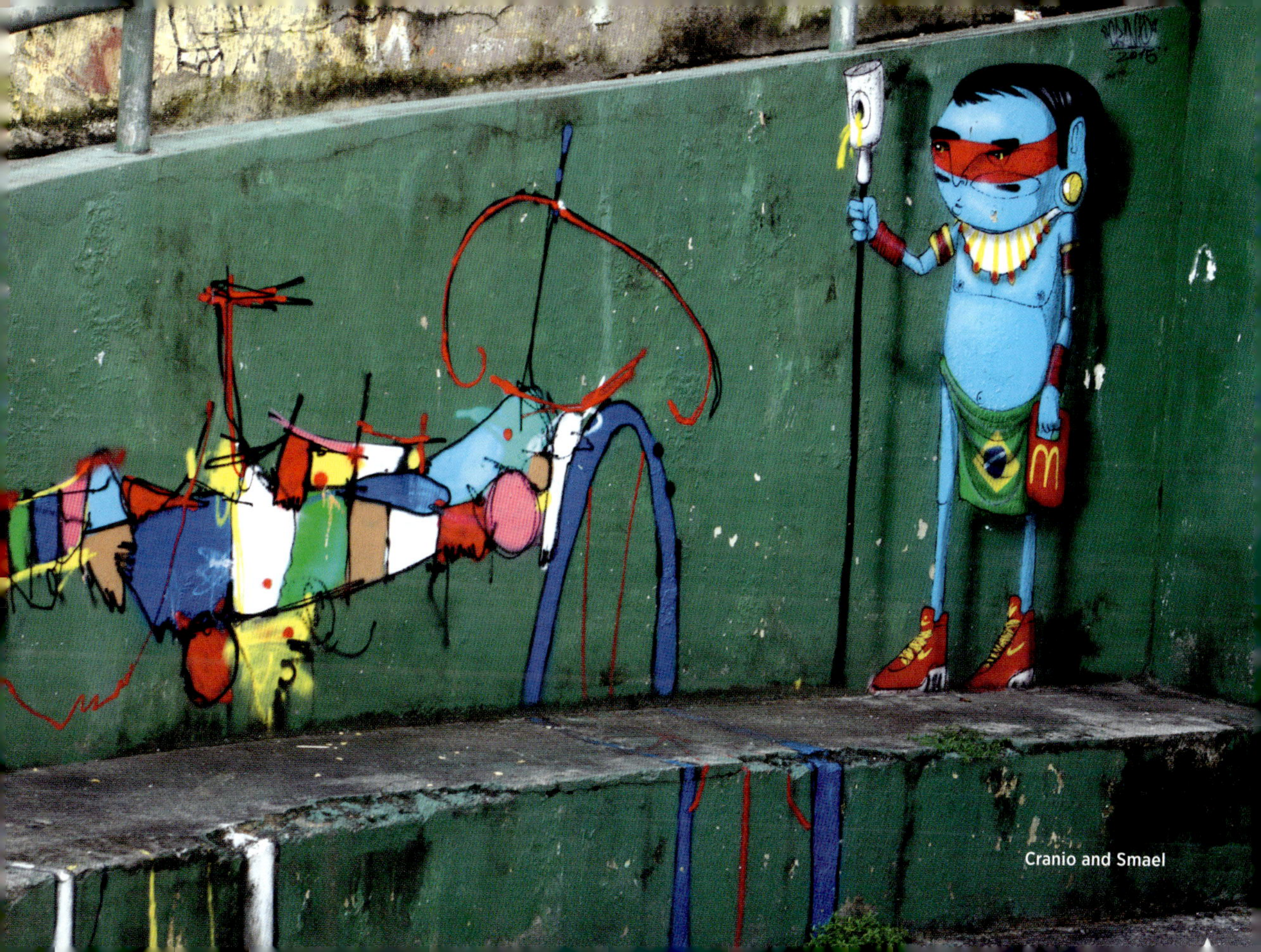

Cranio and Smael

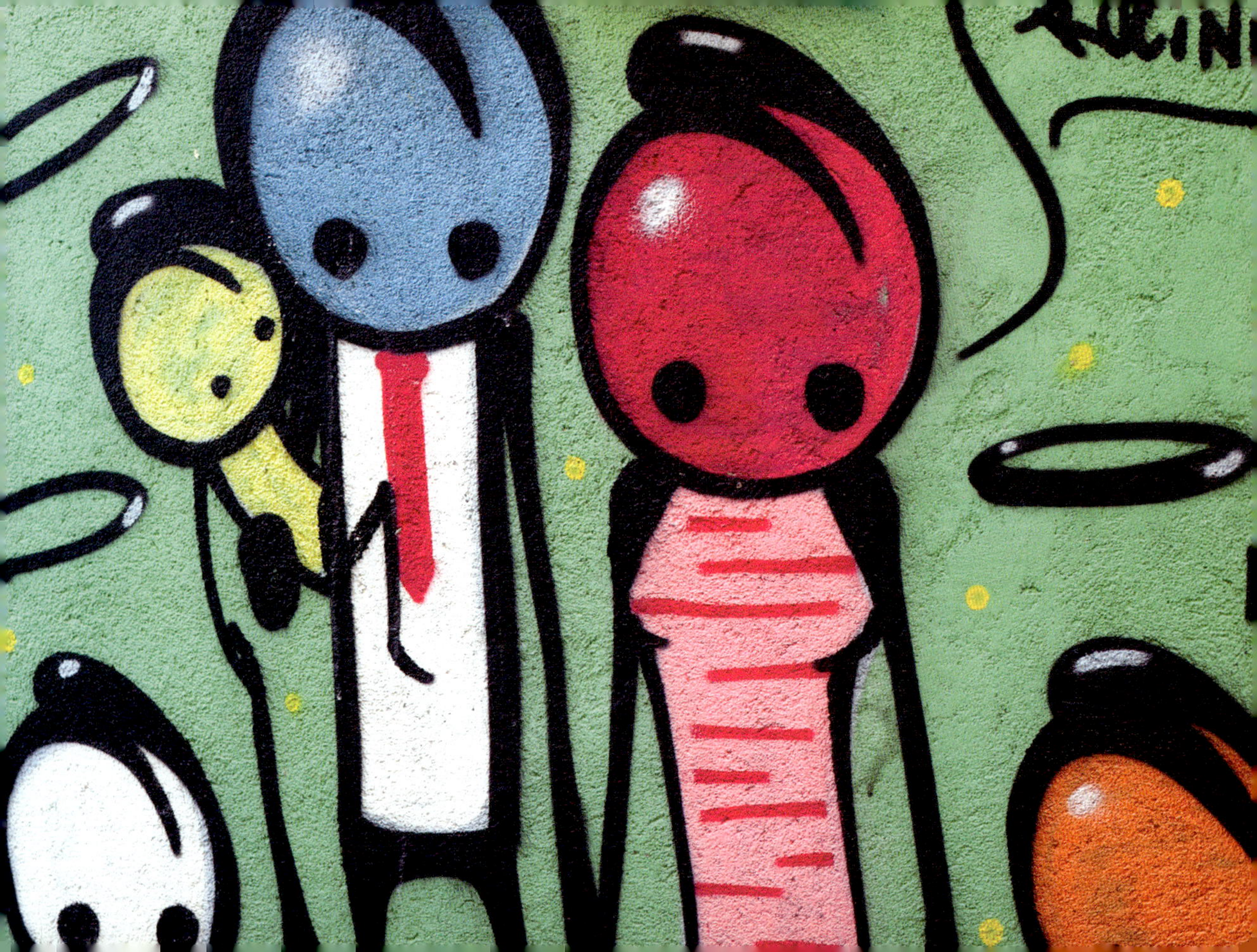

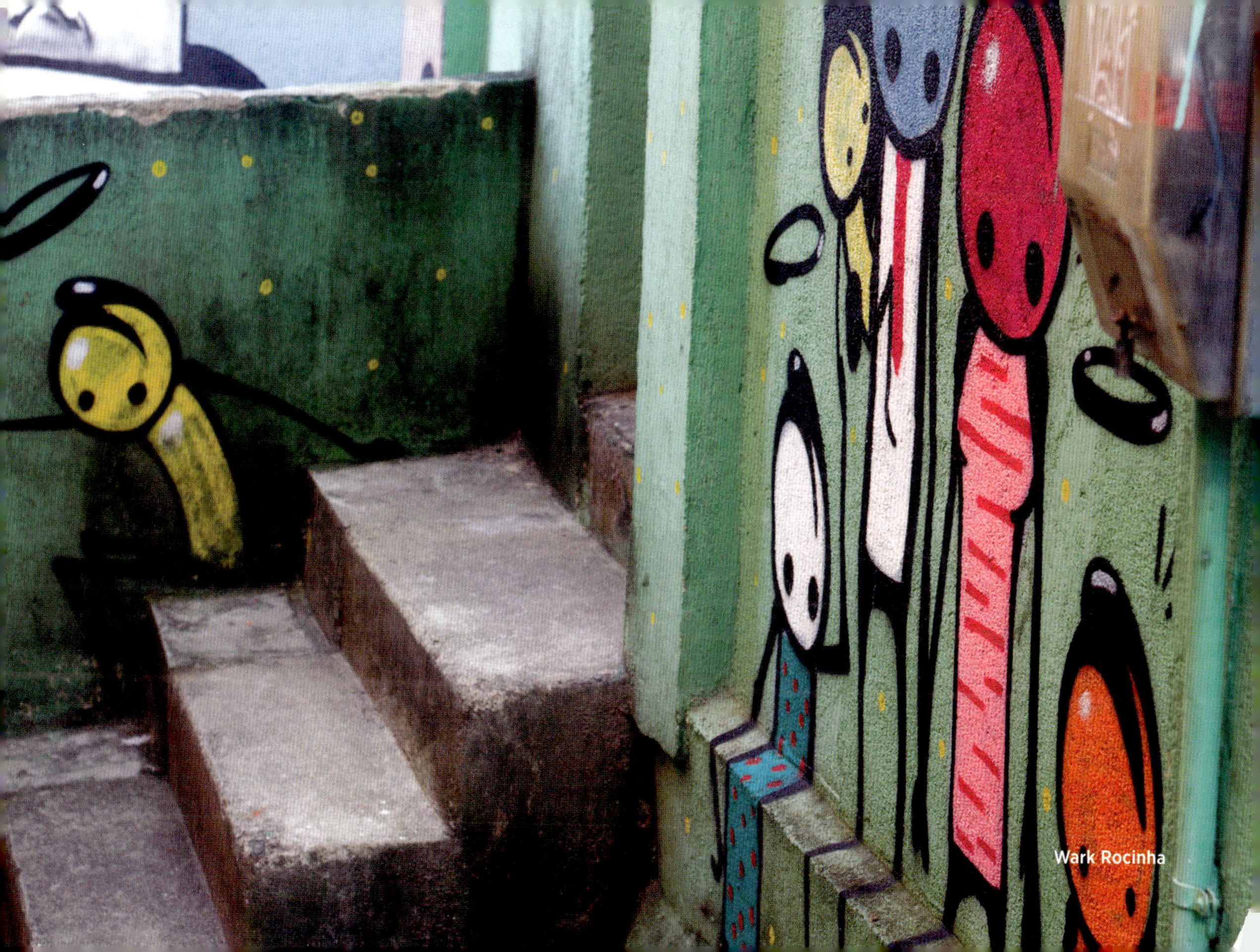

Wark Rocinha

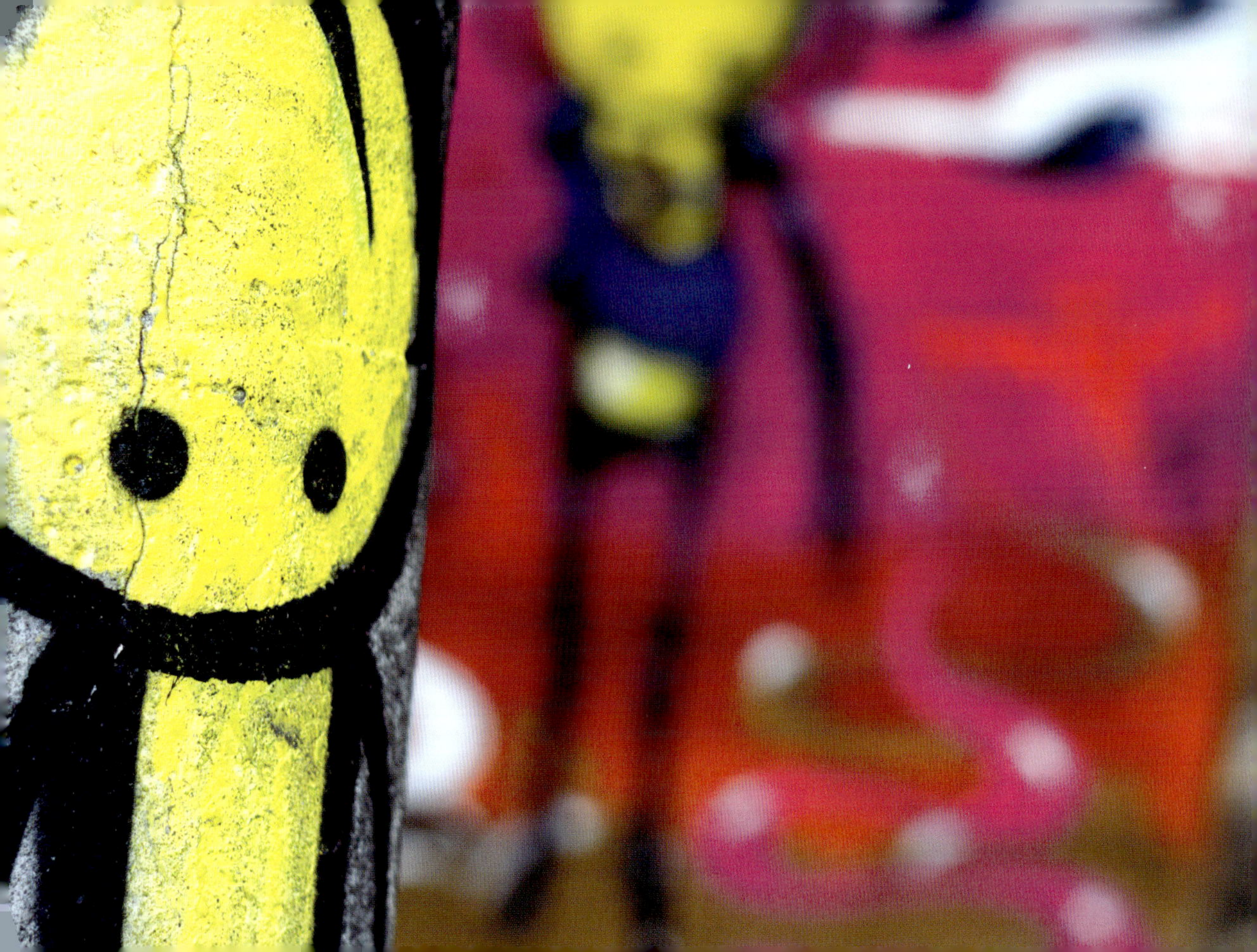

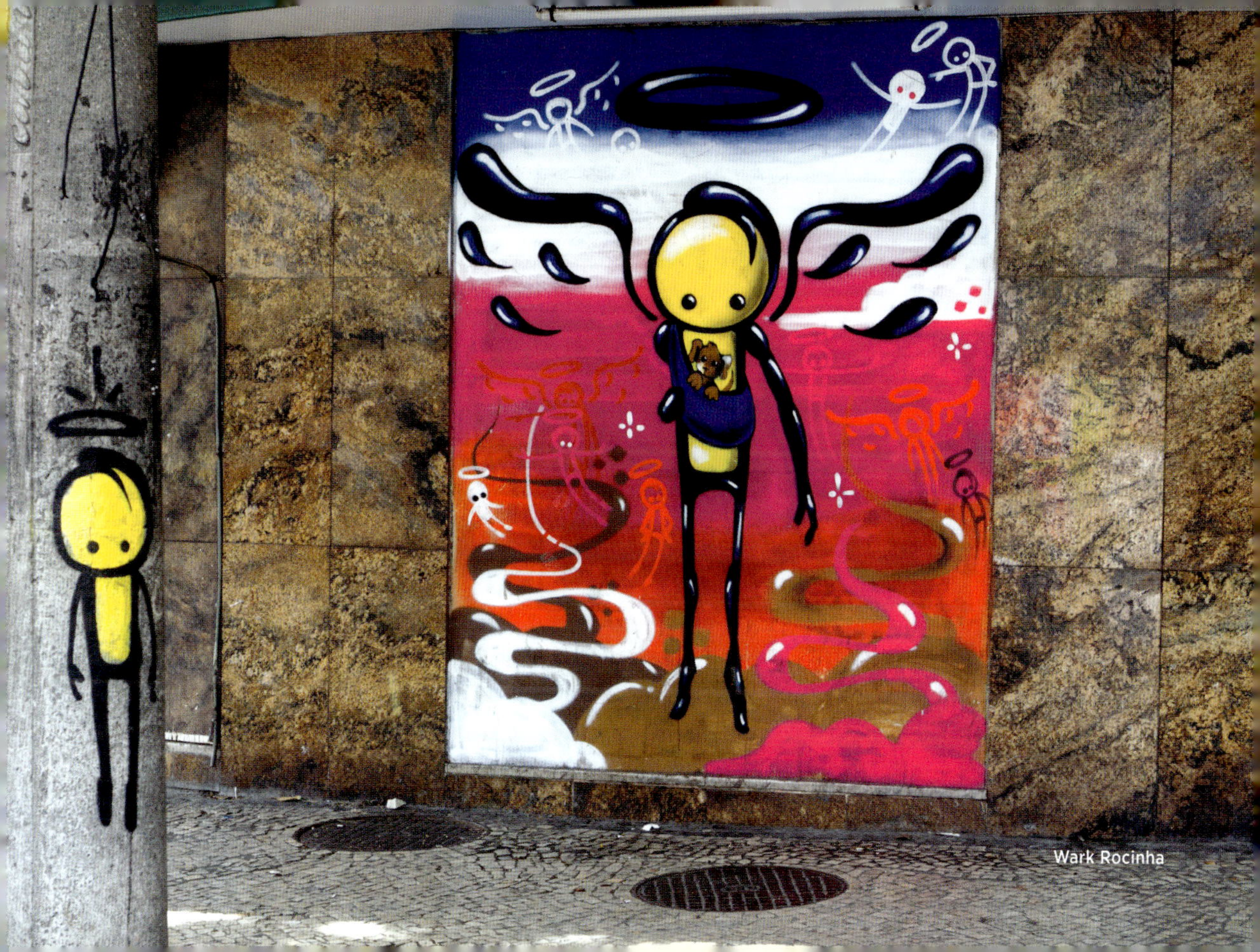

Wark Rocinha

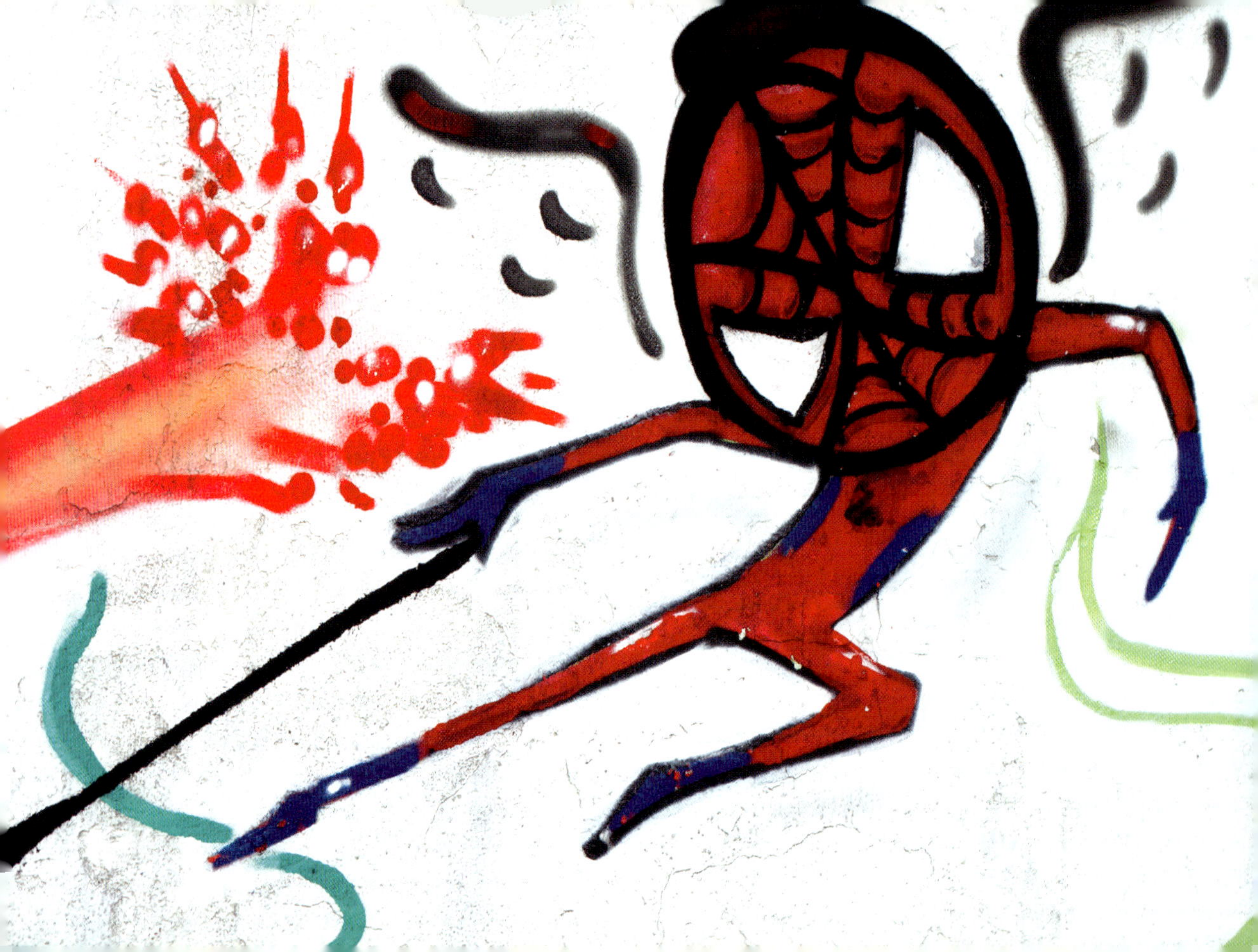

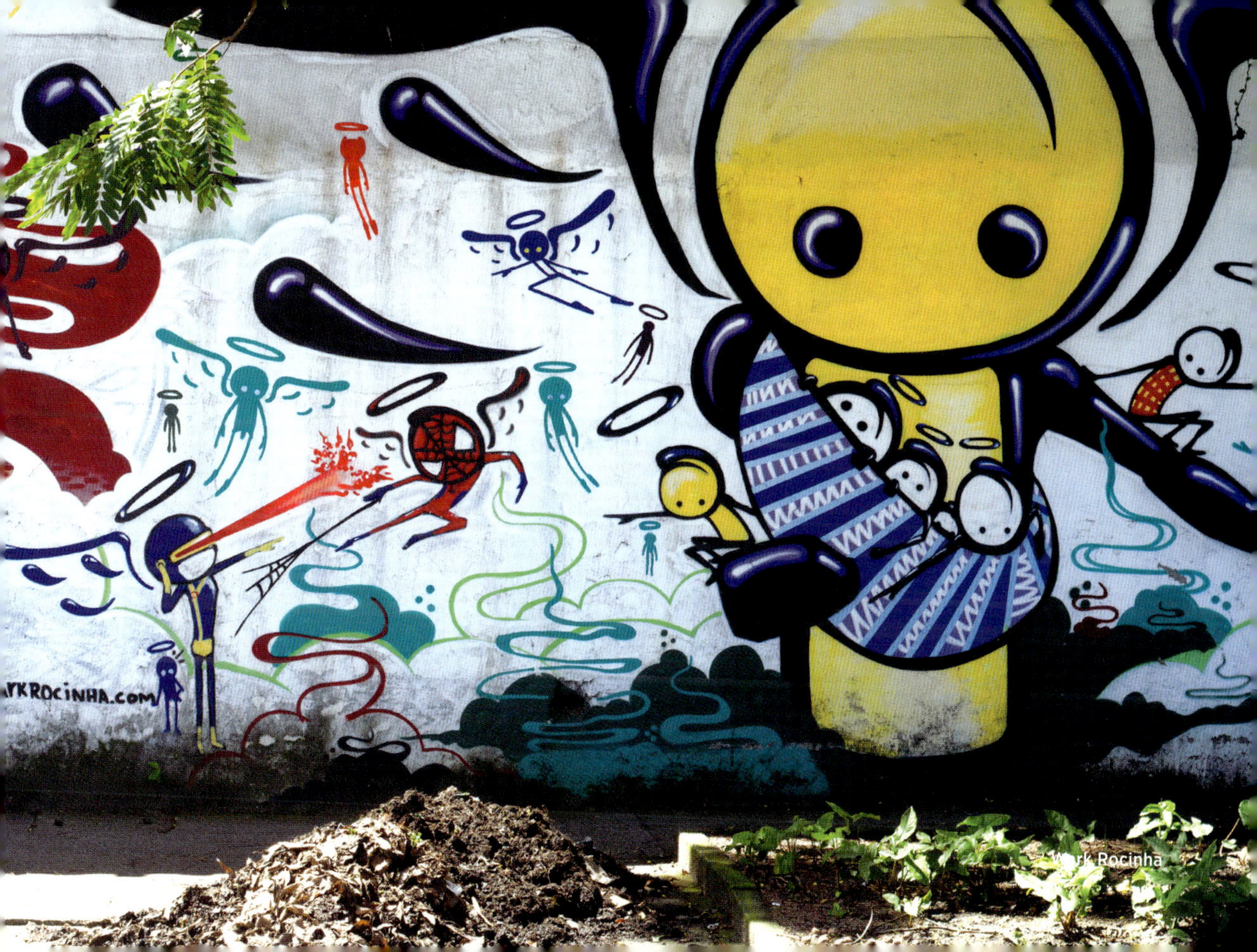

Work Rocinha

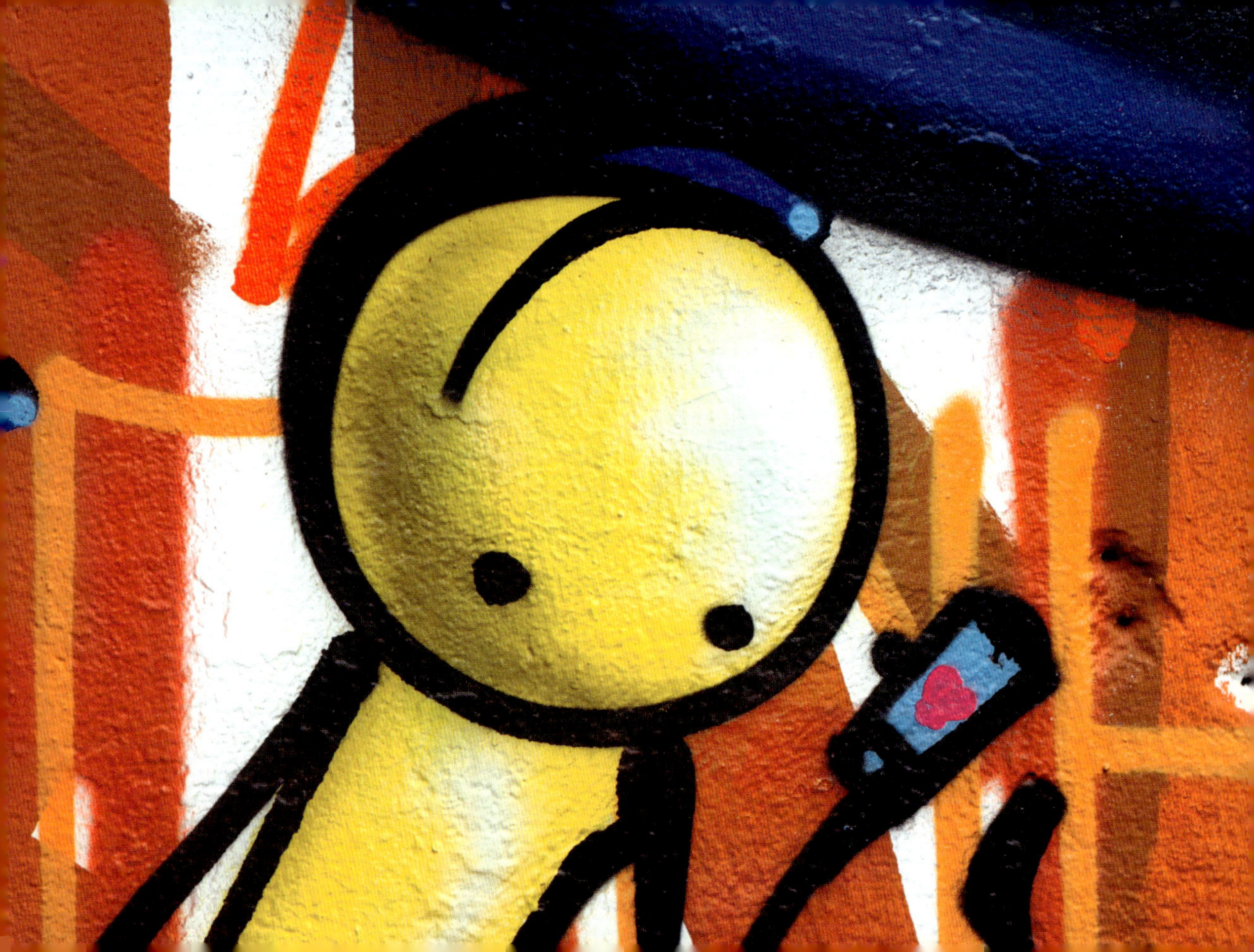

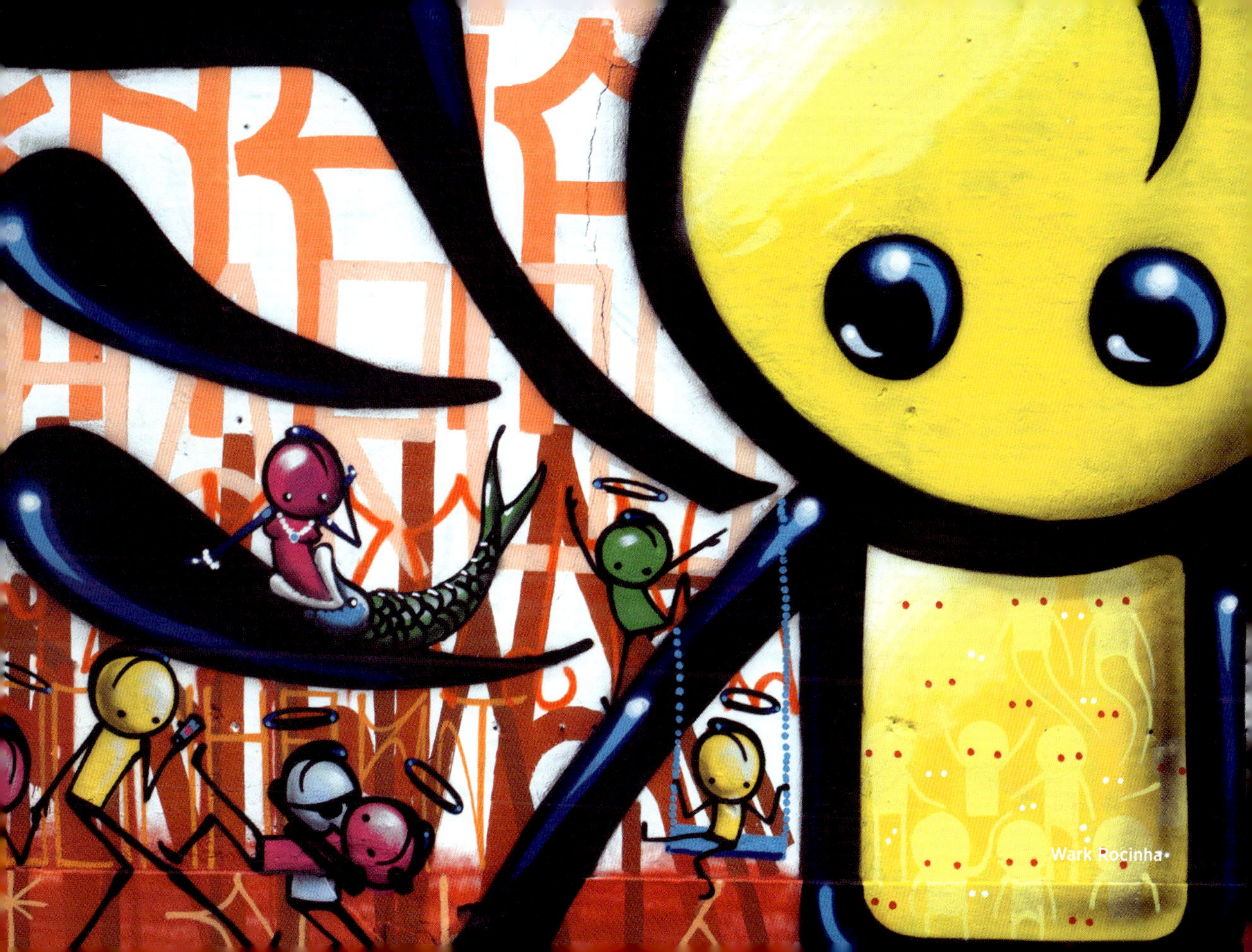

Wark Rocinha

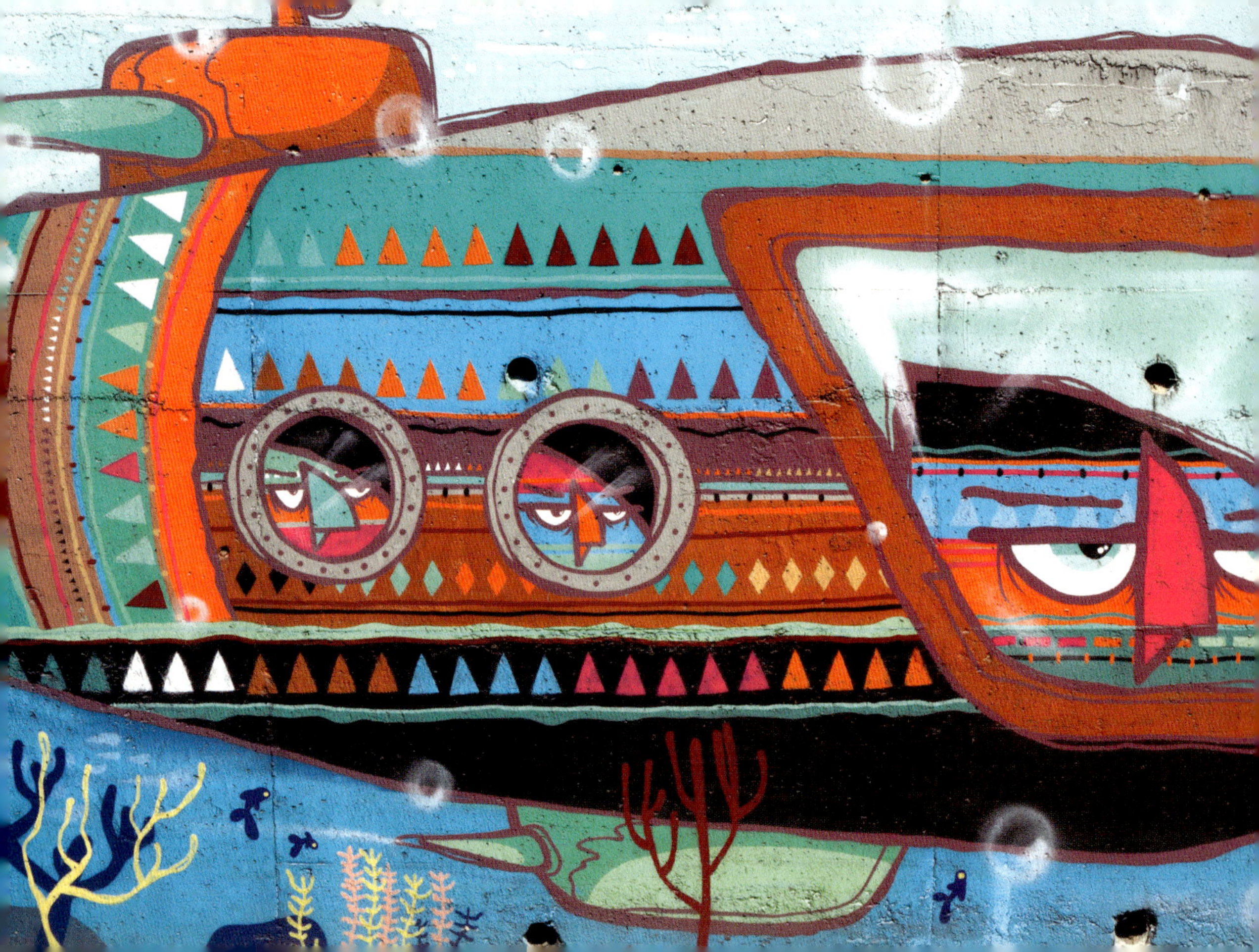

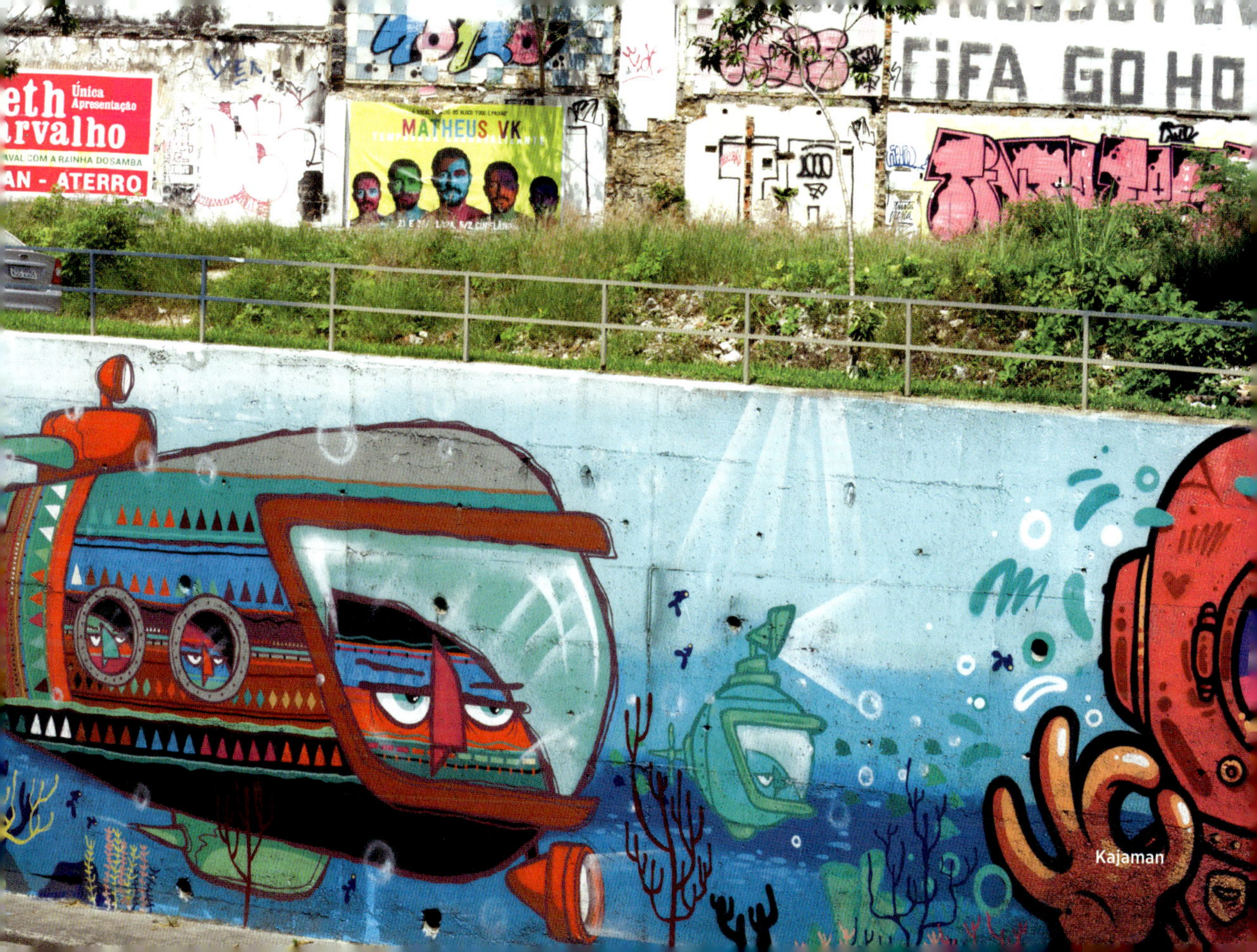
eth
Única Apresentação
rvalho
AVAL COM A RAINHA DO SAMBA
AN - ATERRO
MATHEUS VK
FIFA GO HO
Kajaman

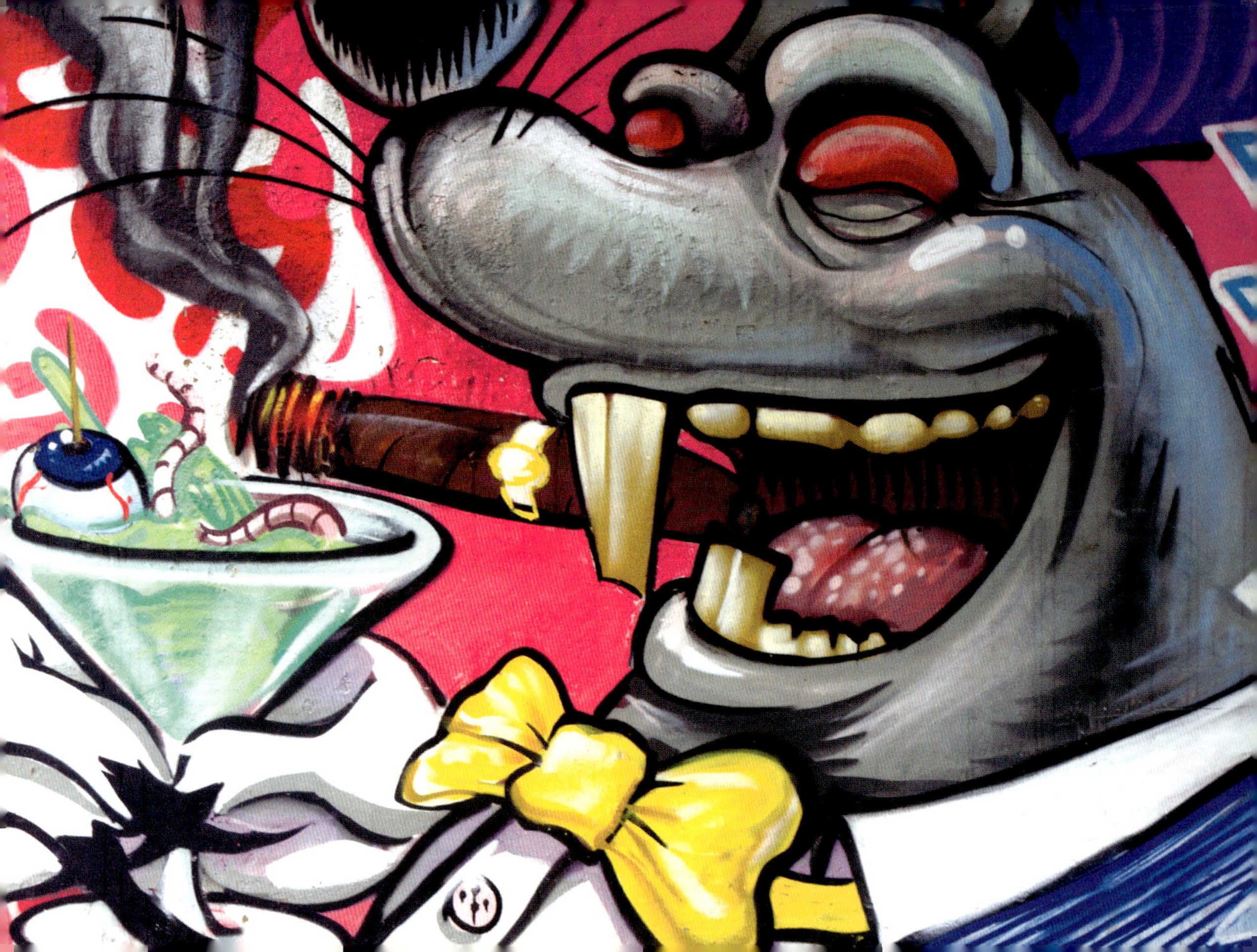

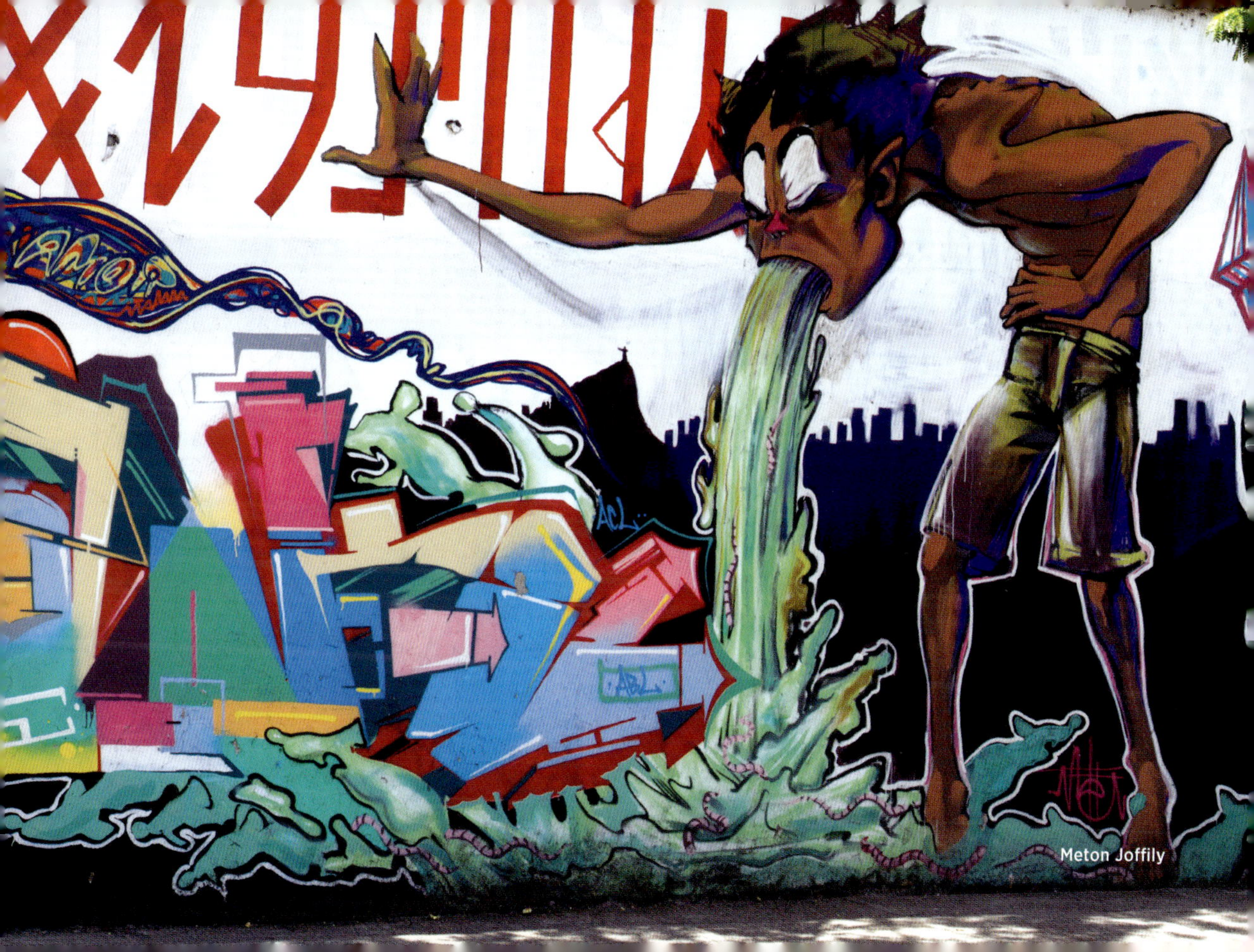

Meton Joffily

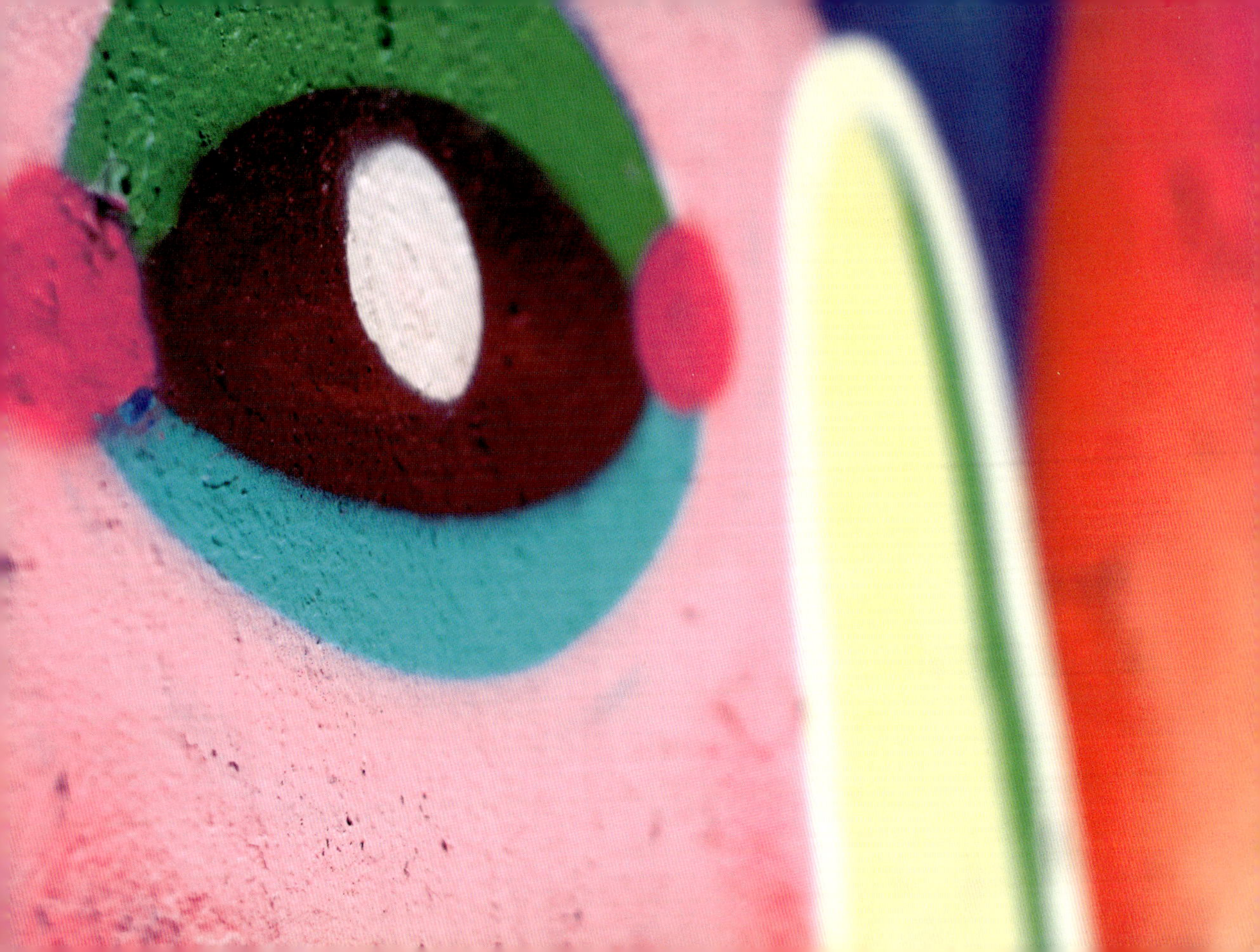

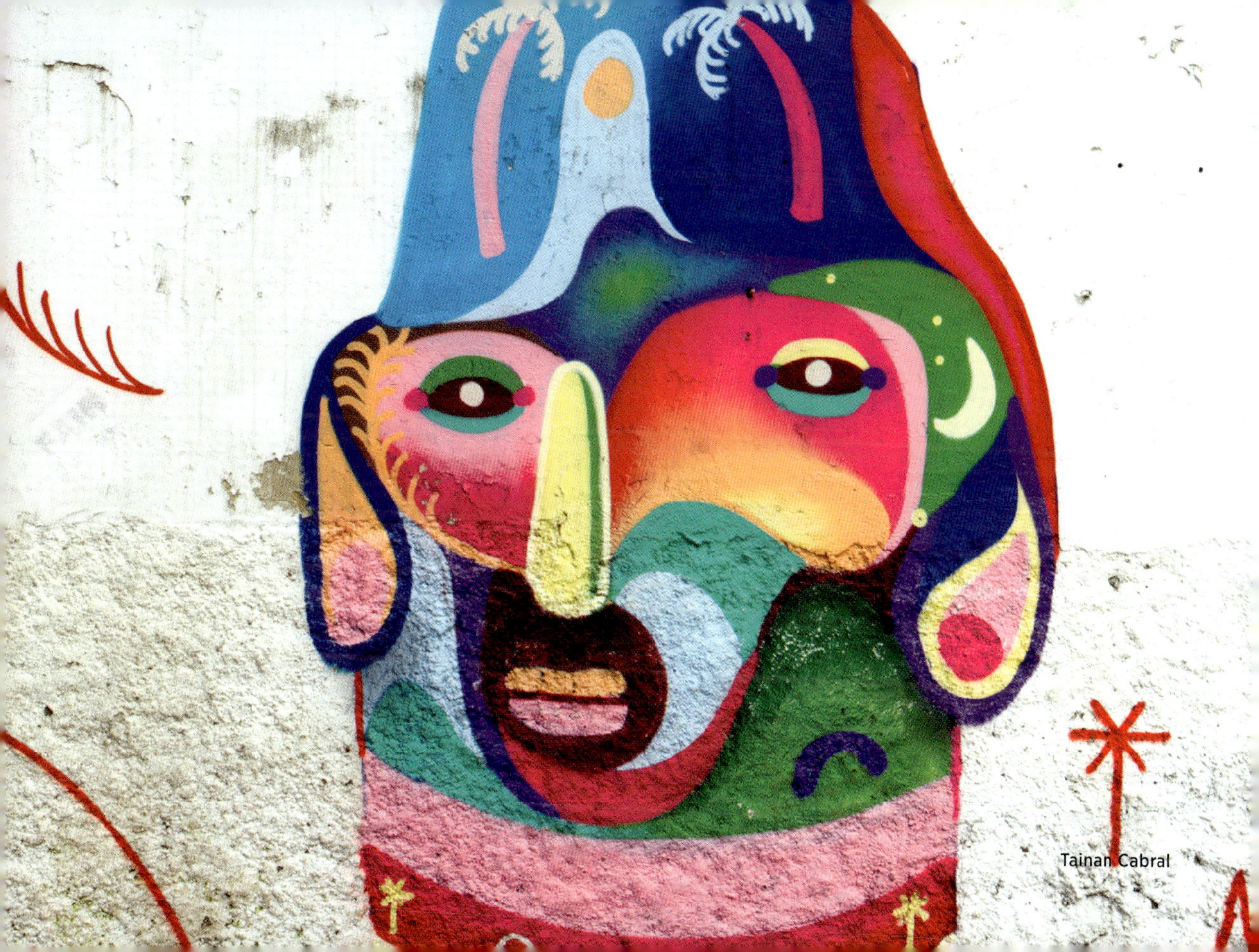

Tainan Cabral

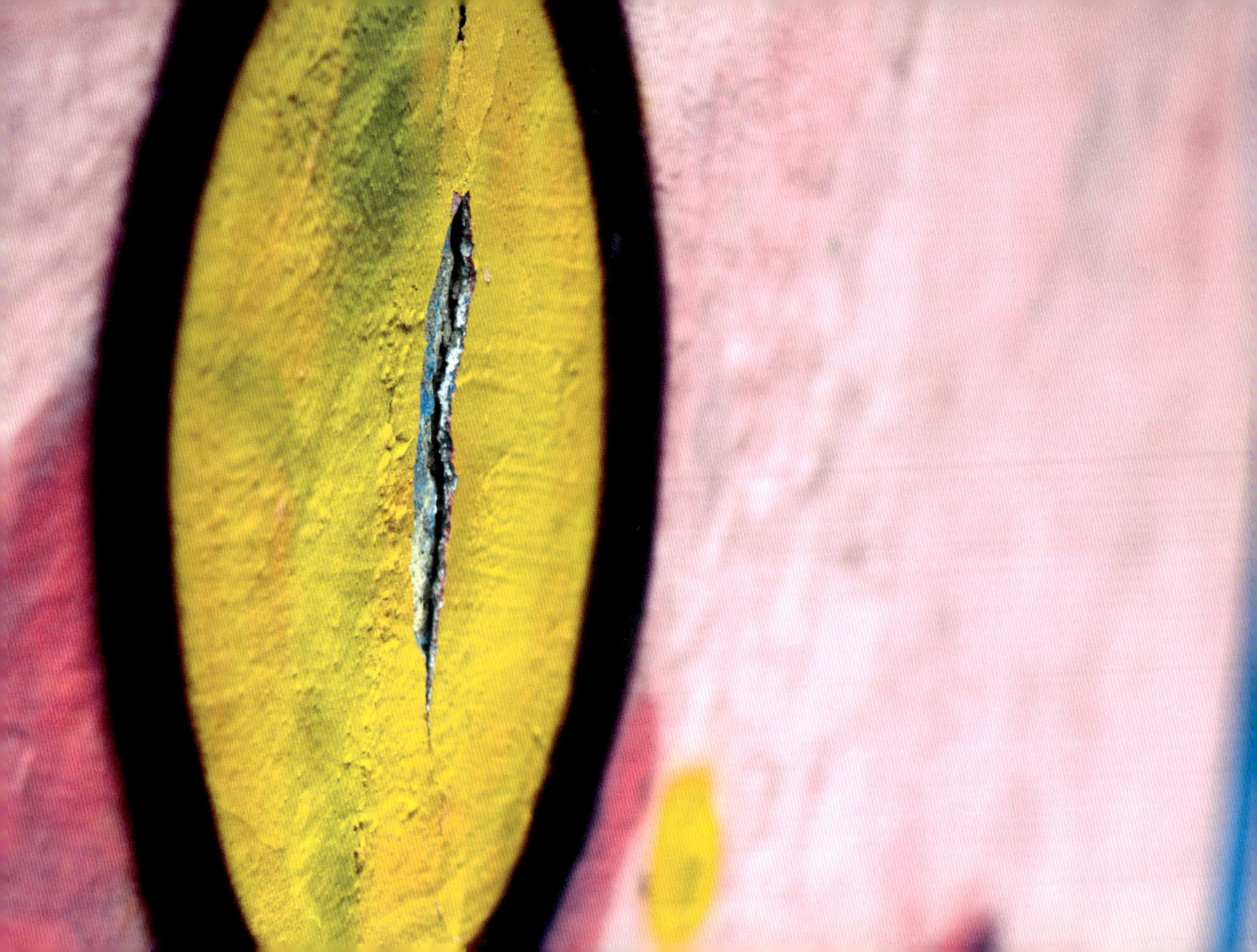

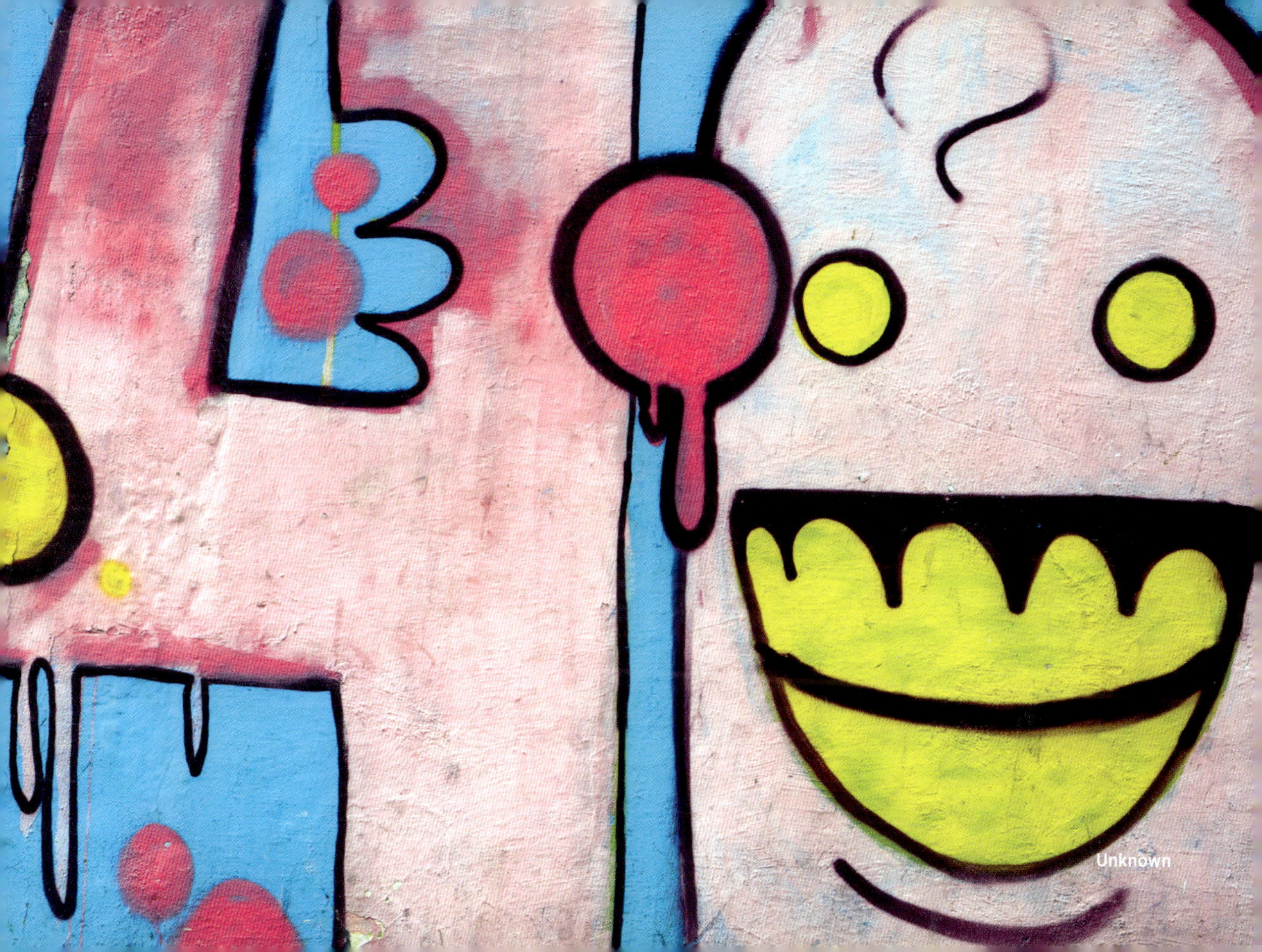

Unknown

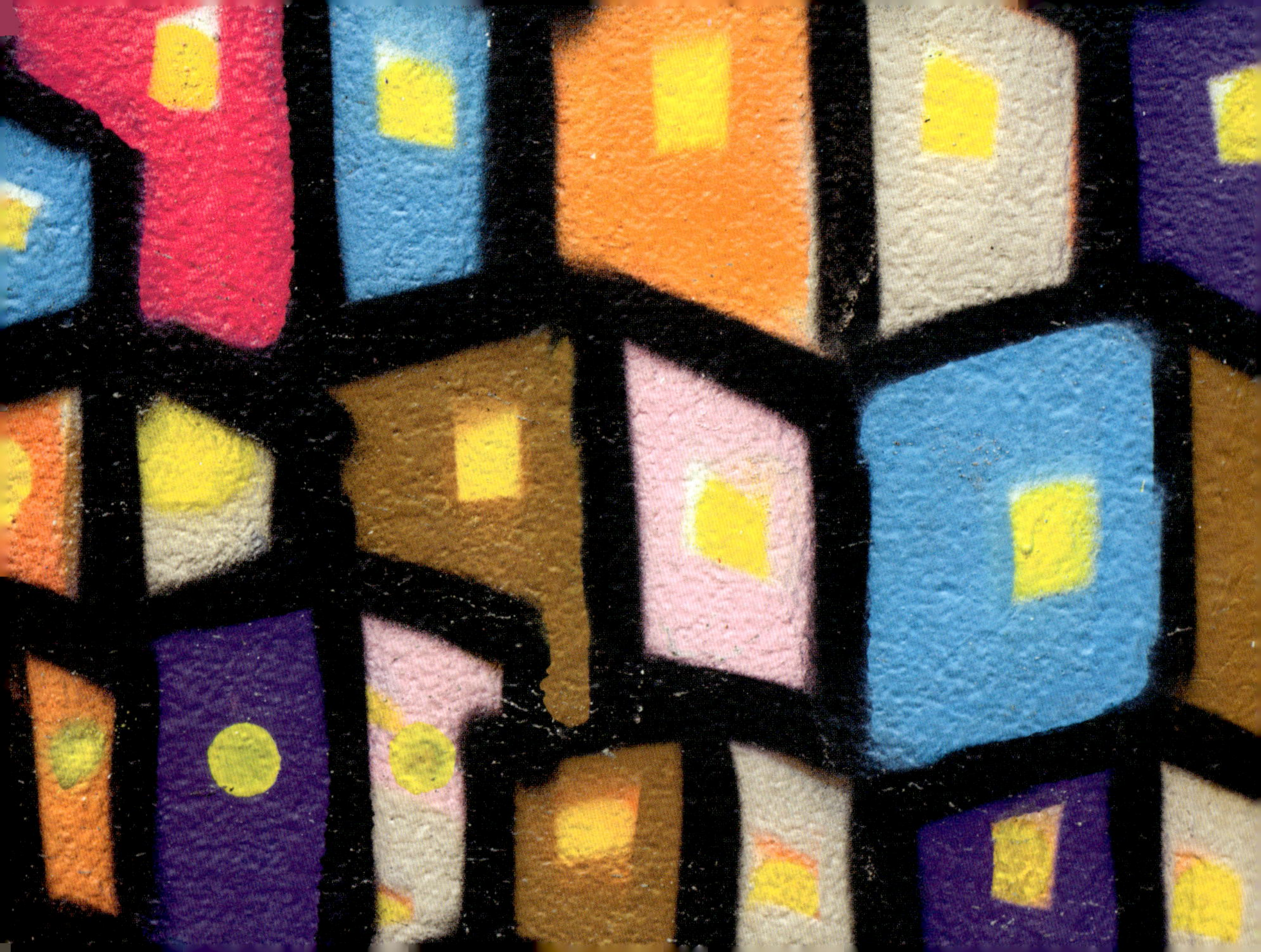

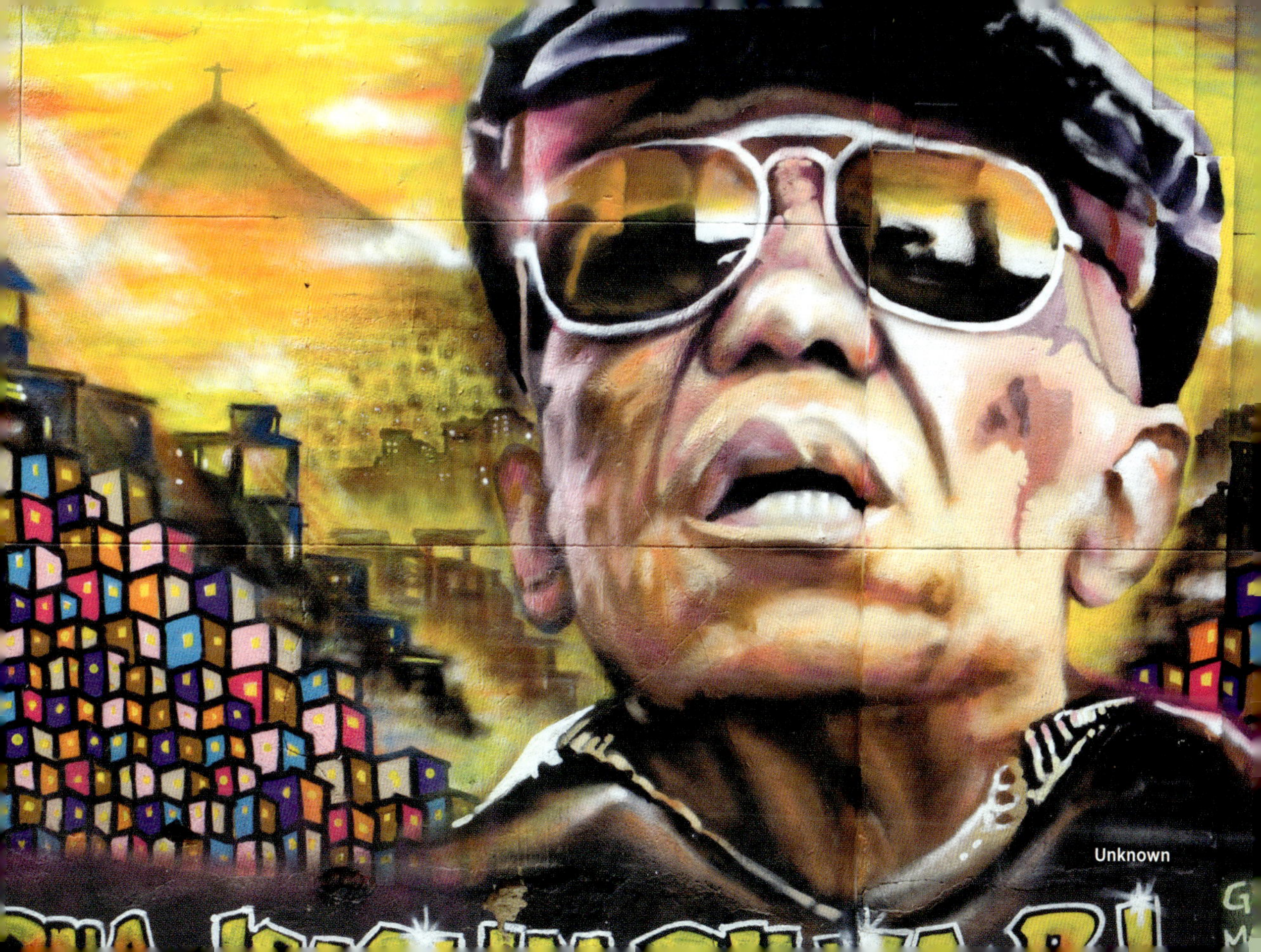

Unknown

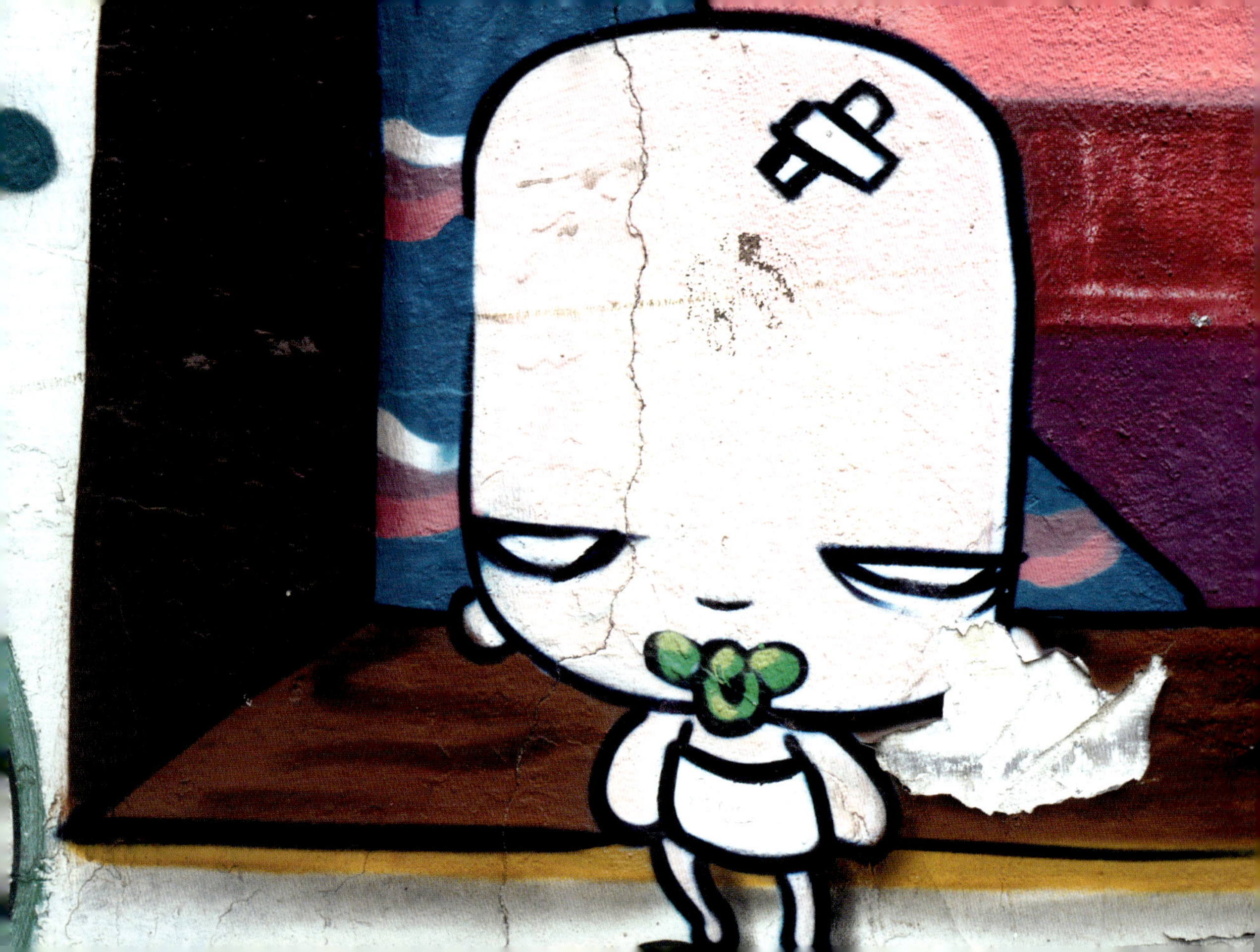

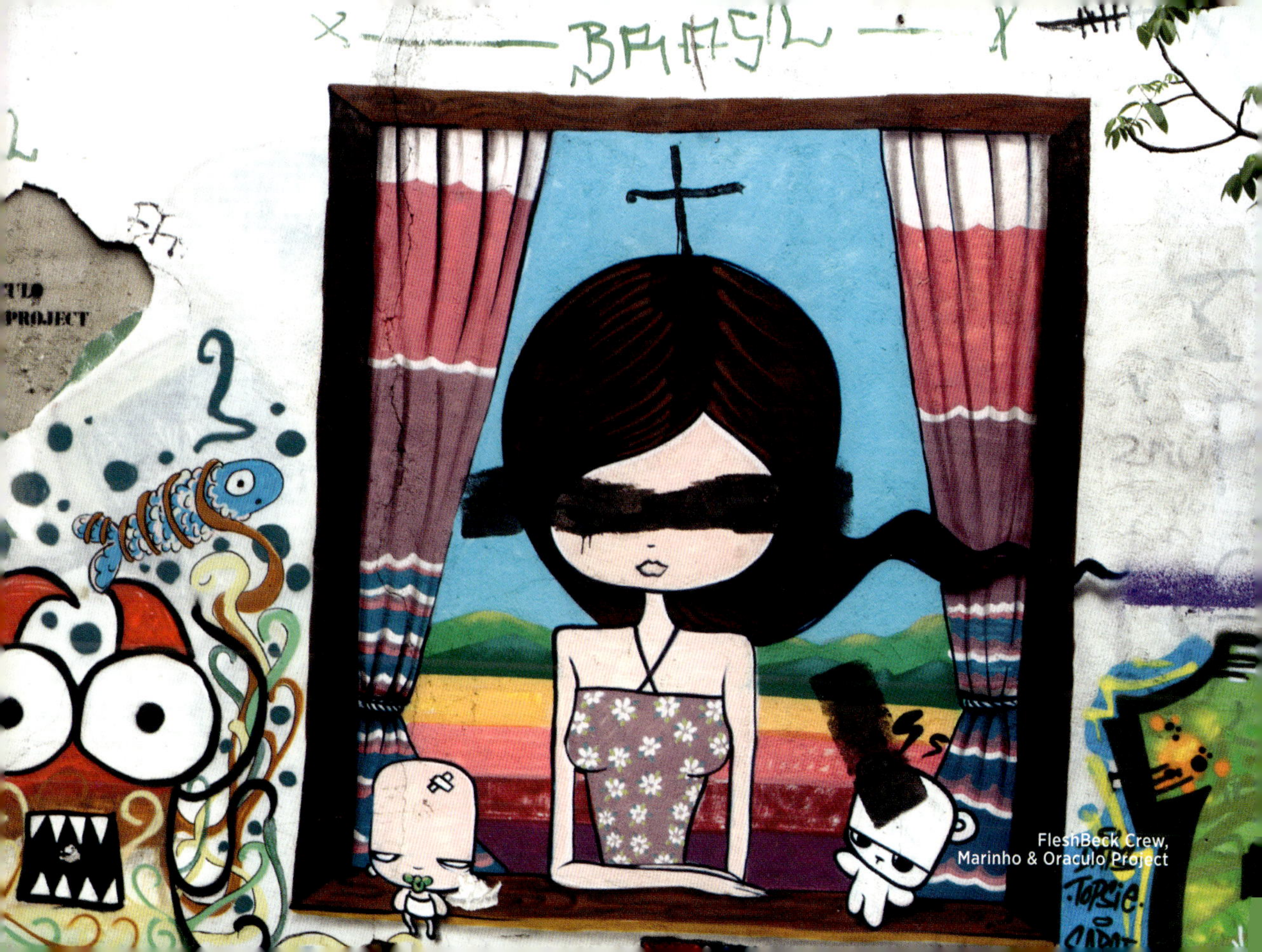

FleshBeck Crew,
Marinho & Oraculo Project

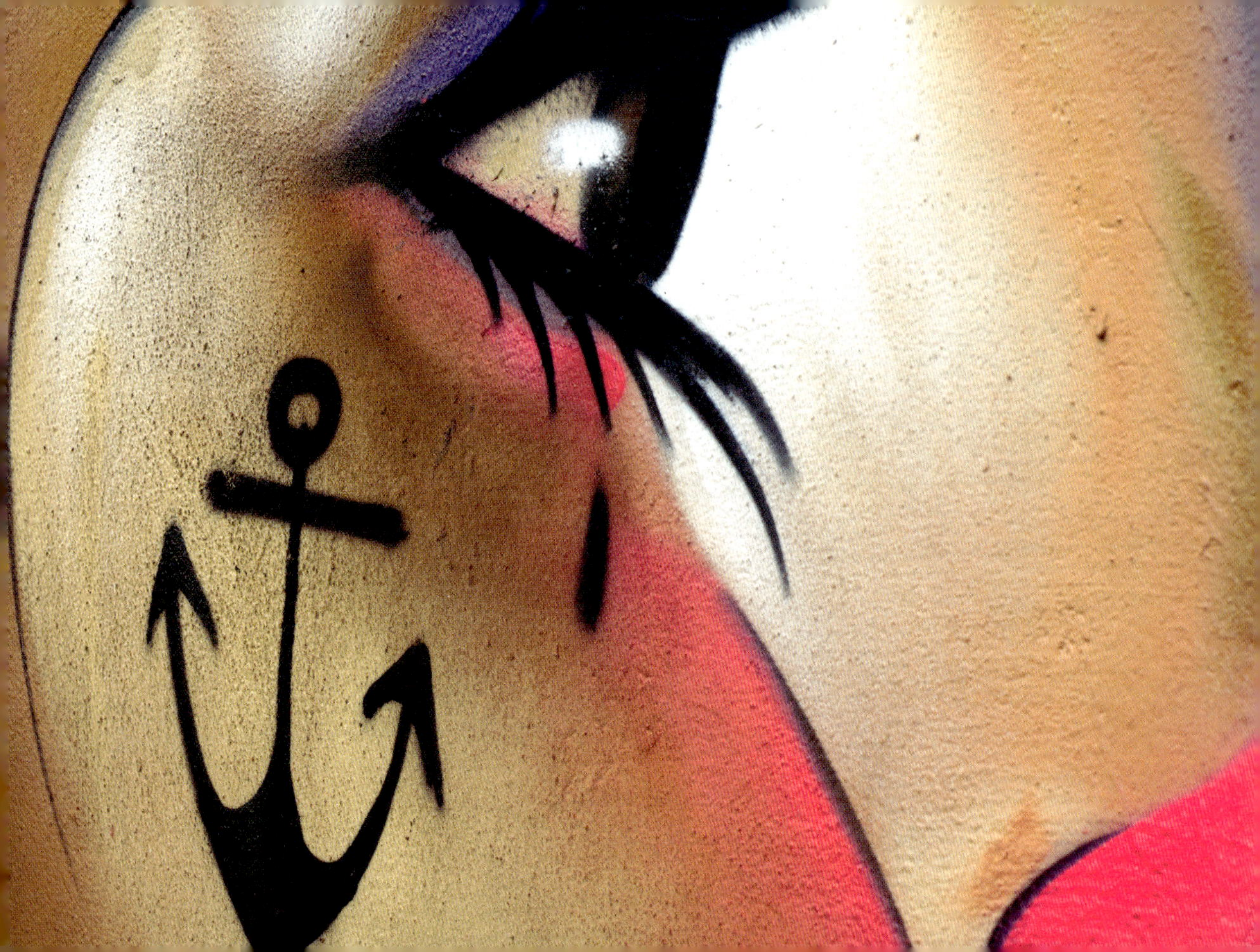

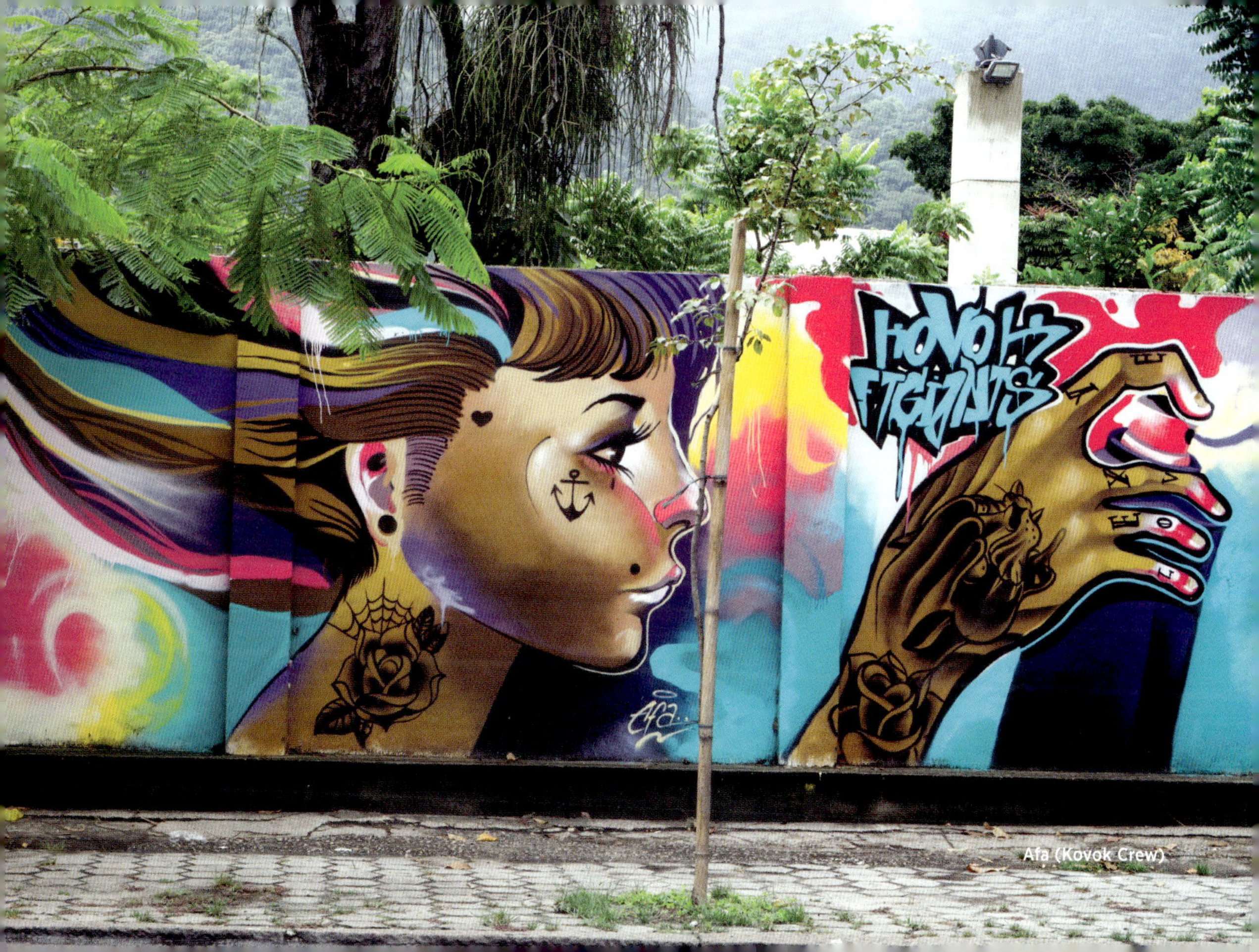

Afa (Kovok Crew)

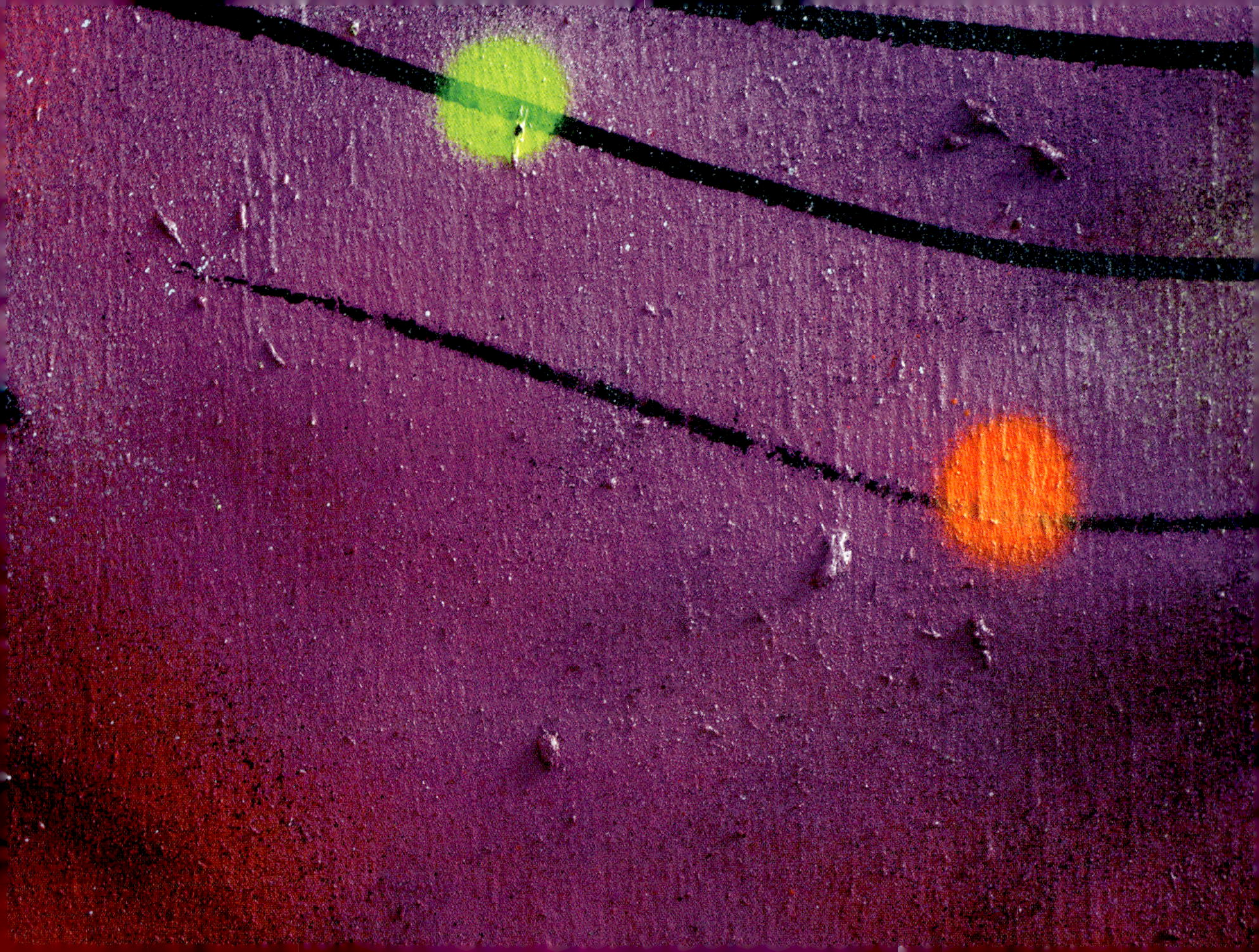

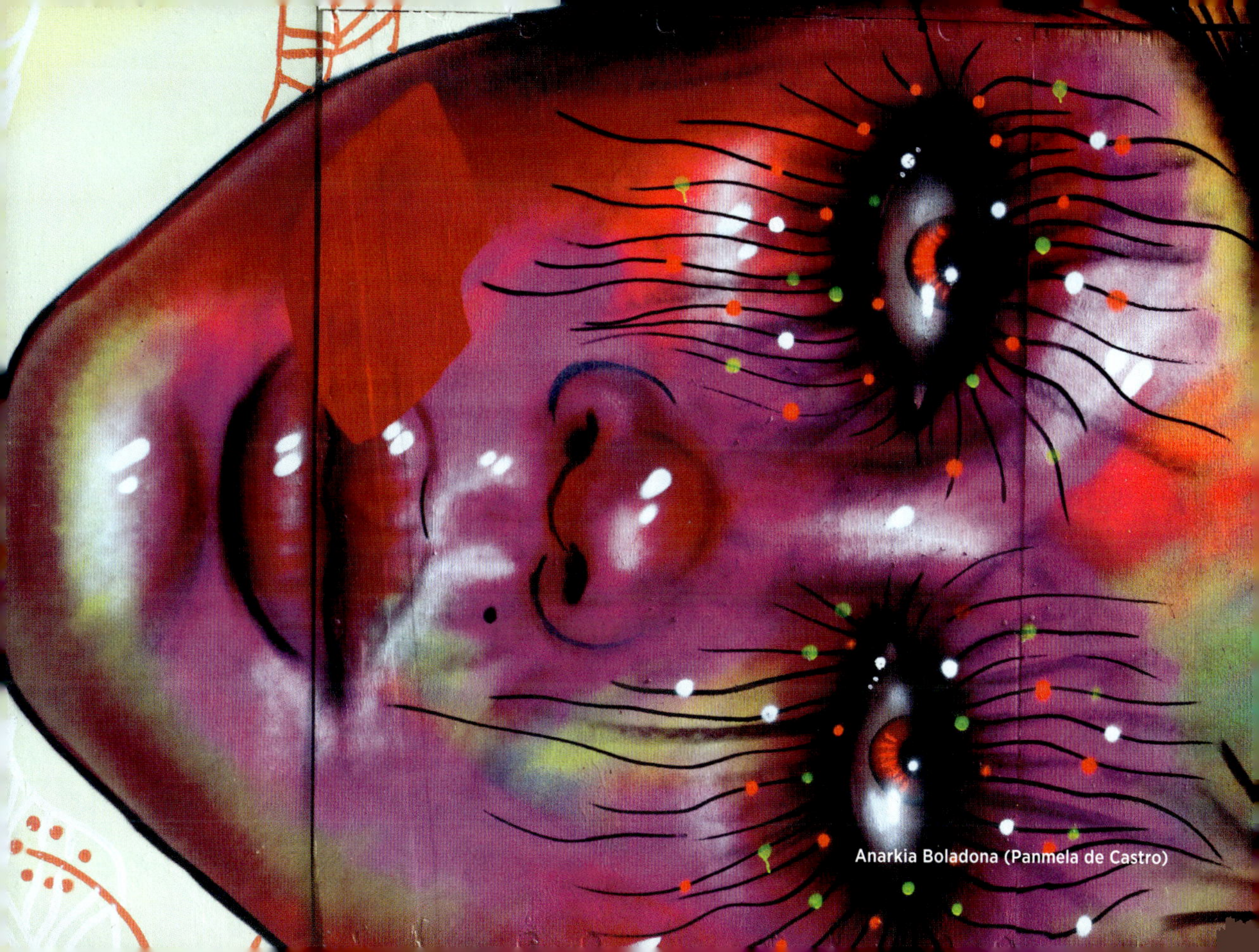

Anarkia Boladona (Panmela de Castro)

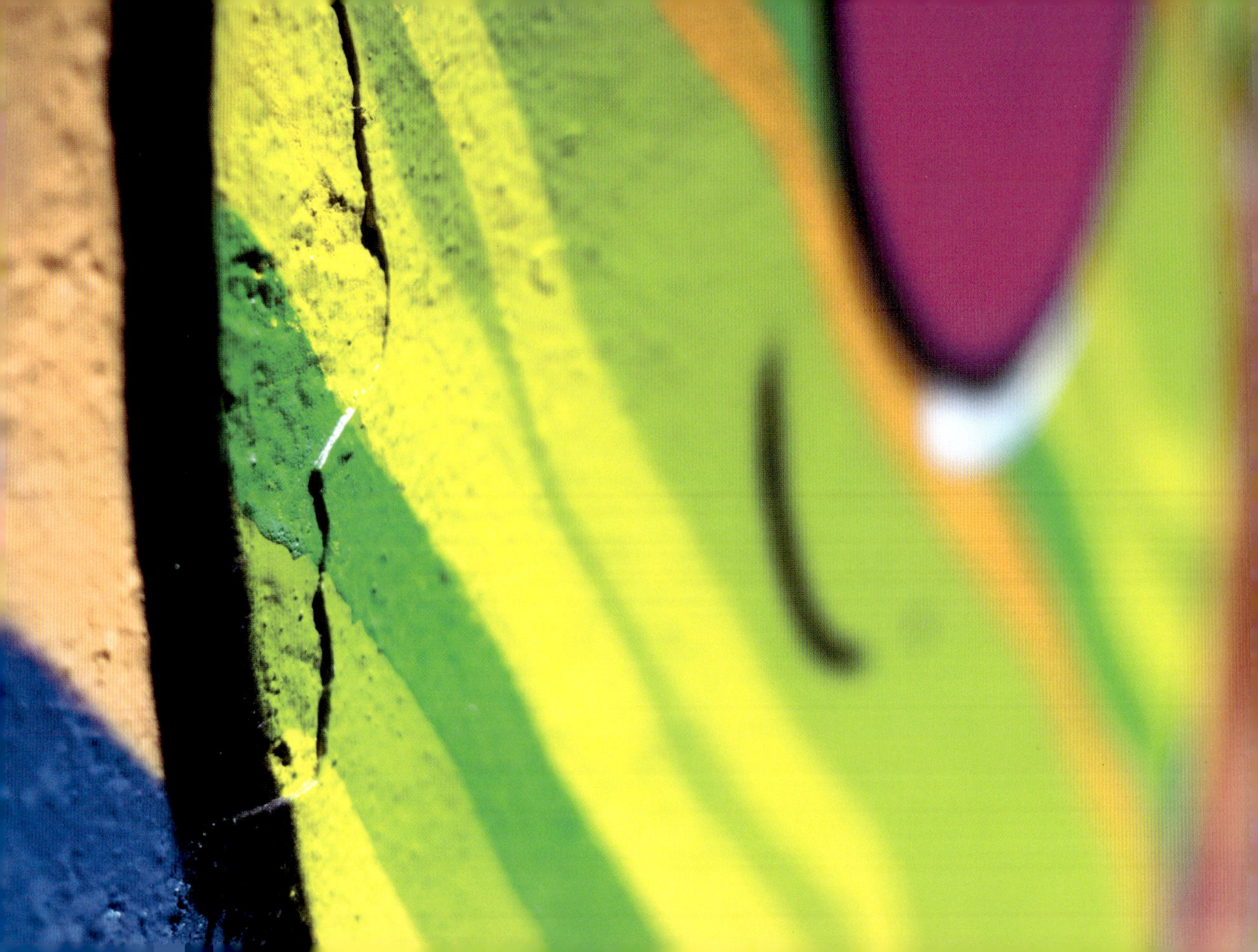

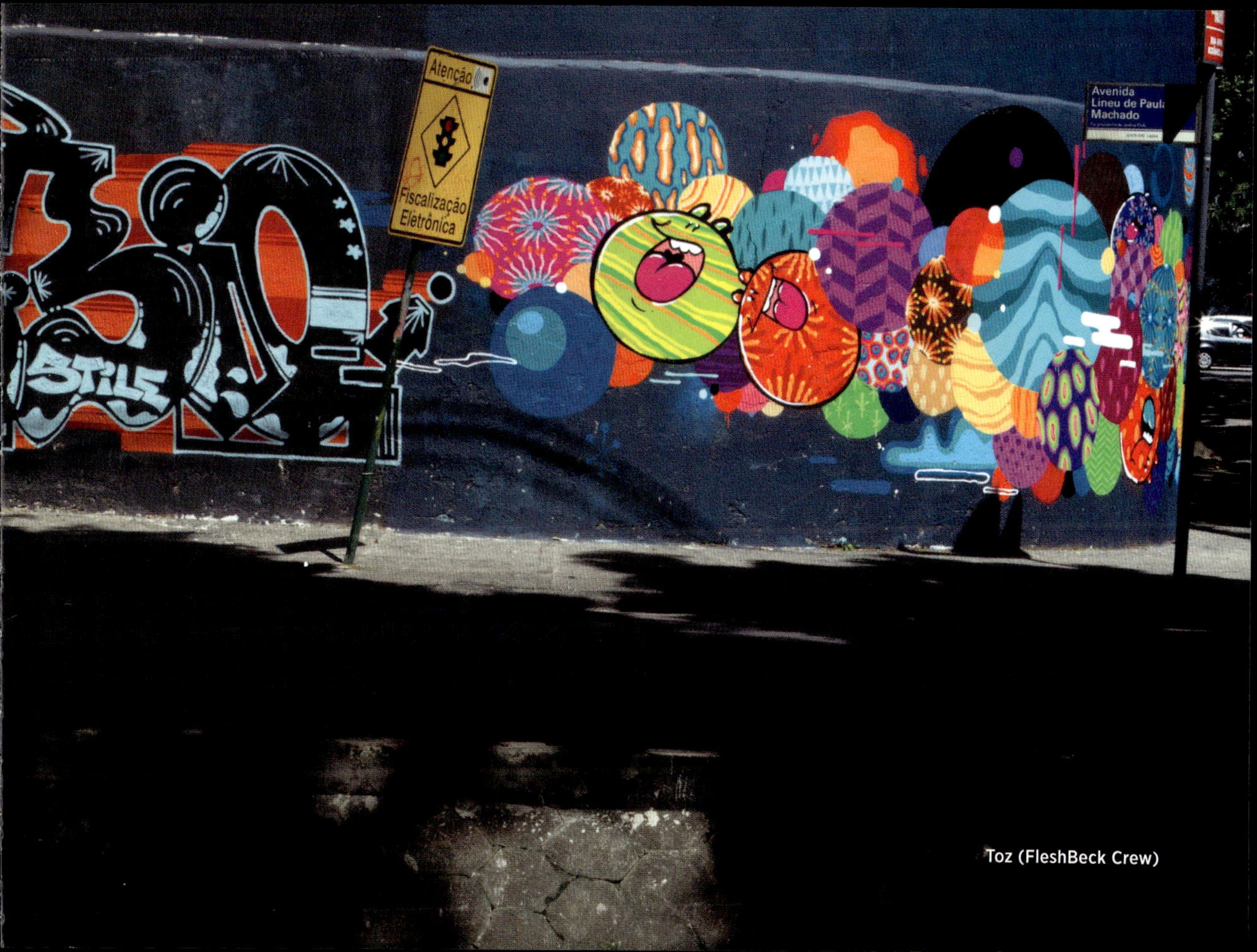

Toz (FleshBeck Crew)

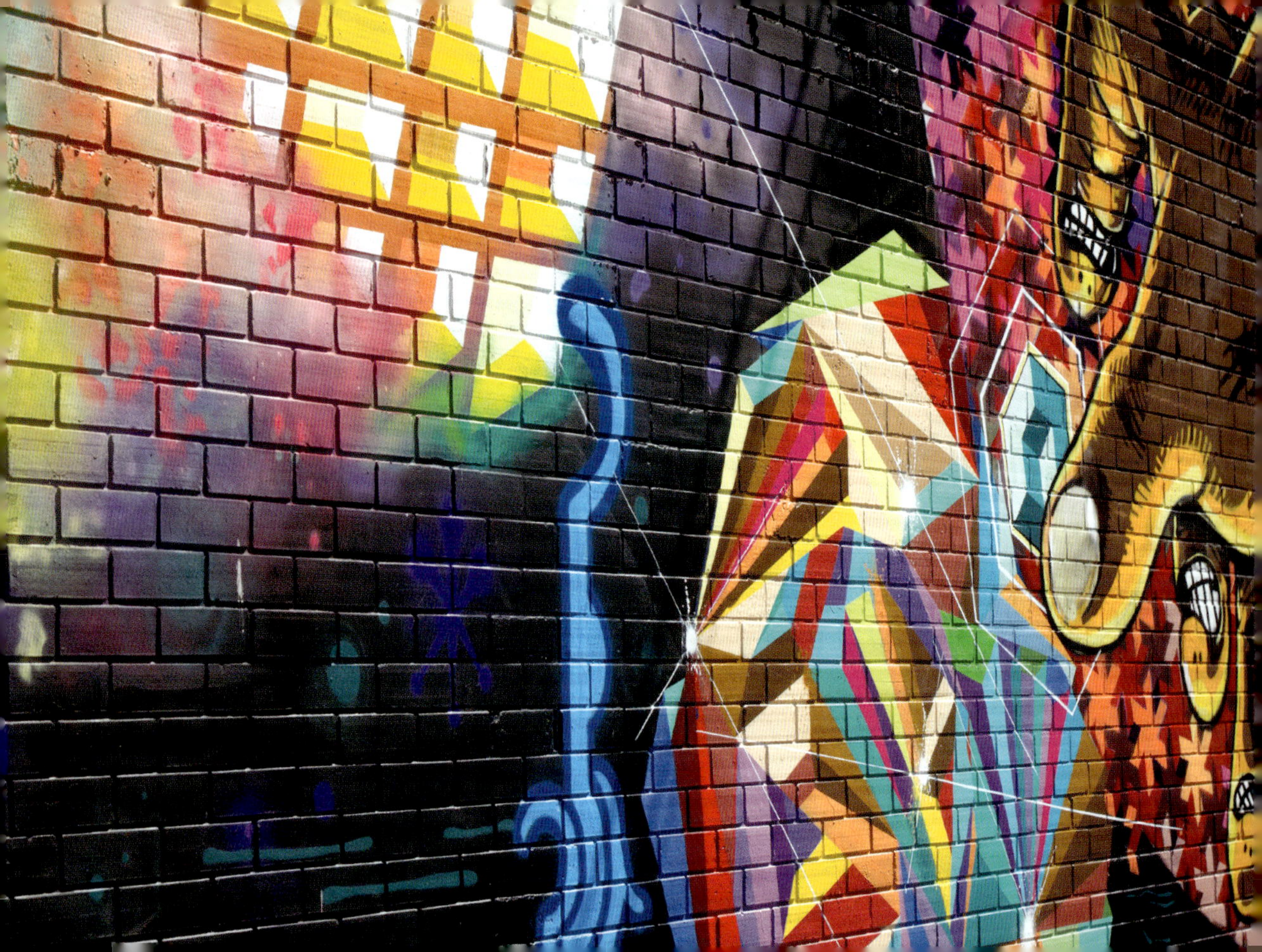

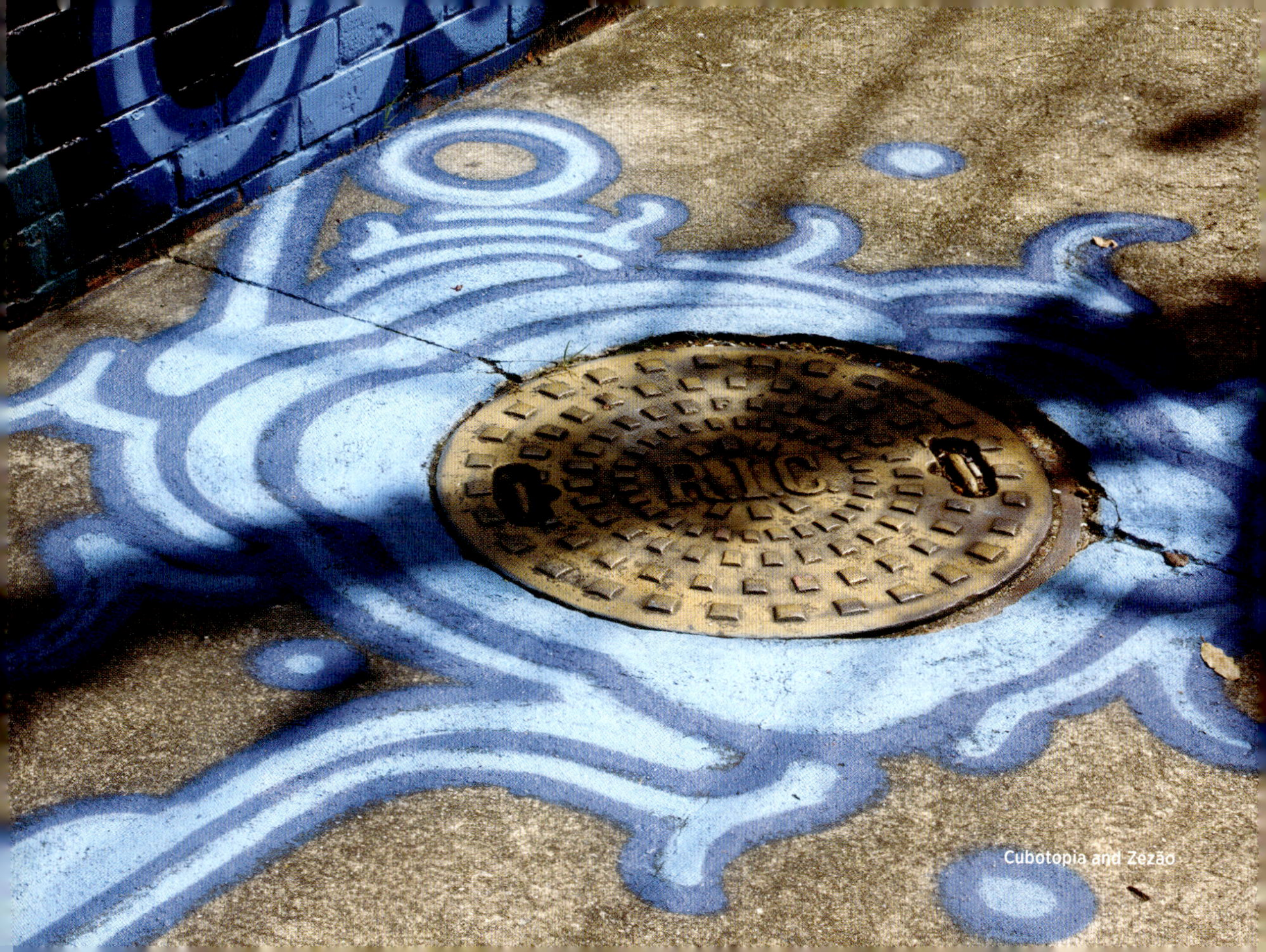

Cubotopia and Zezão

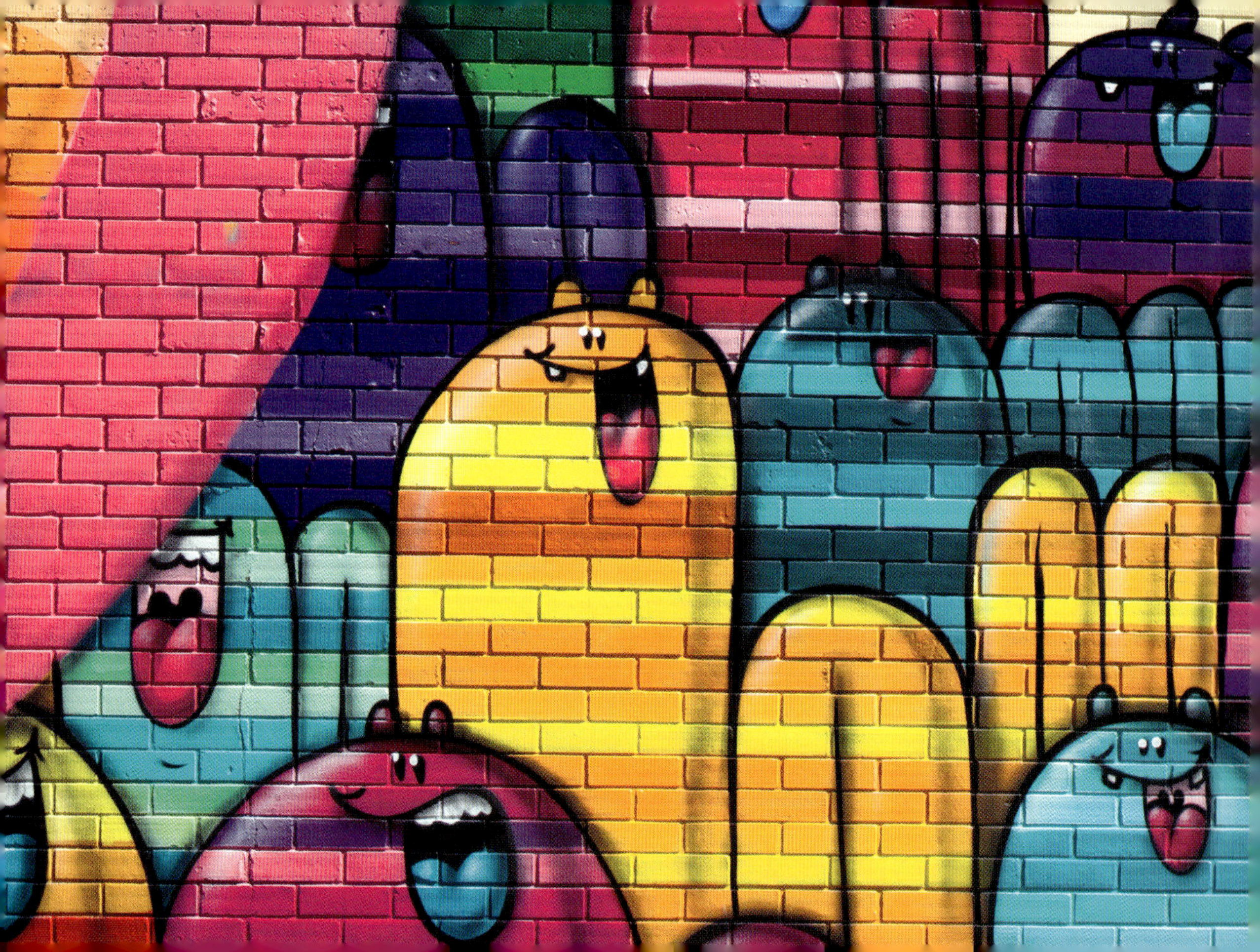

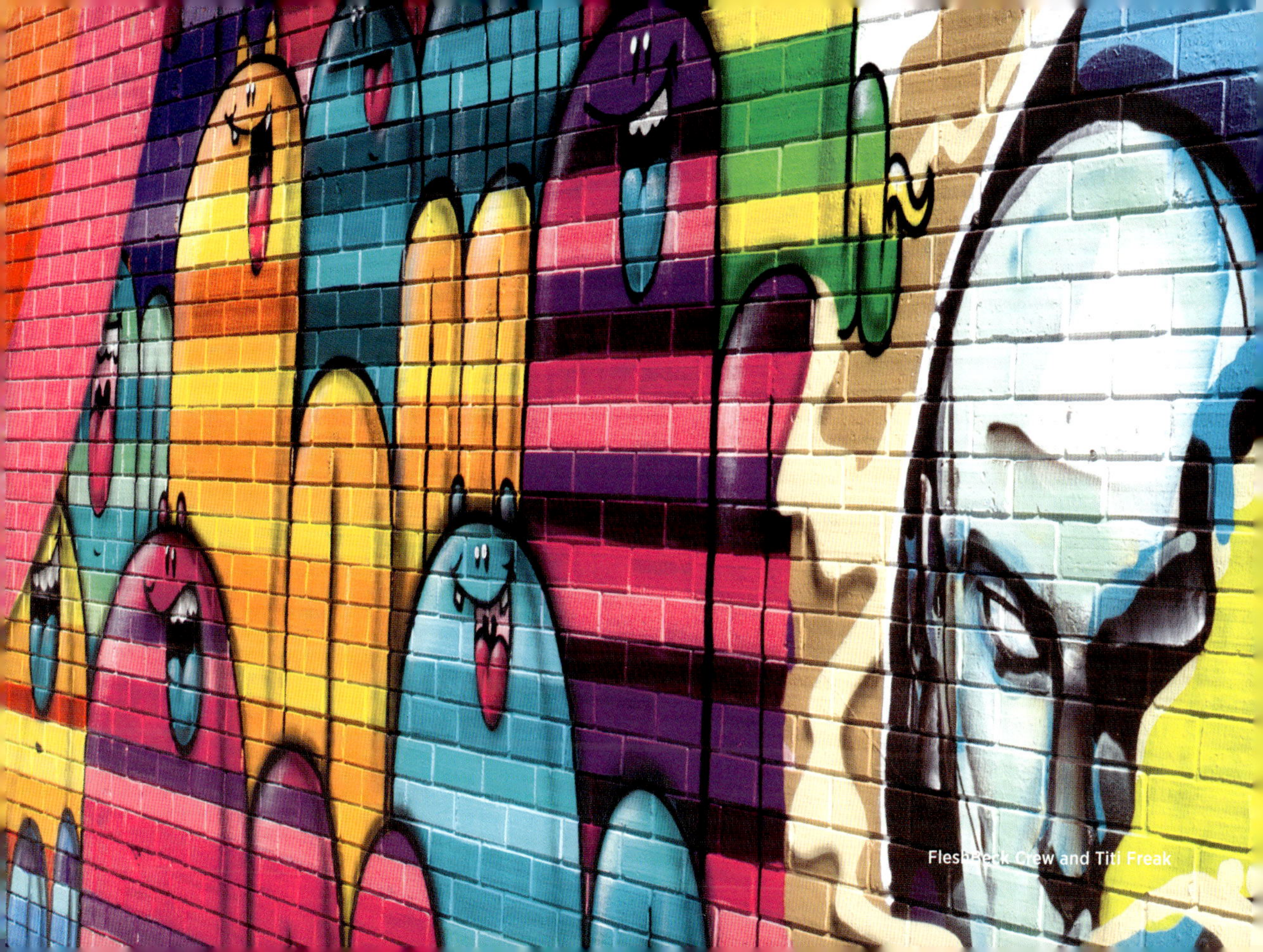

FleshBeck Crew and Titi Freak

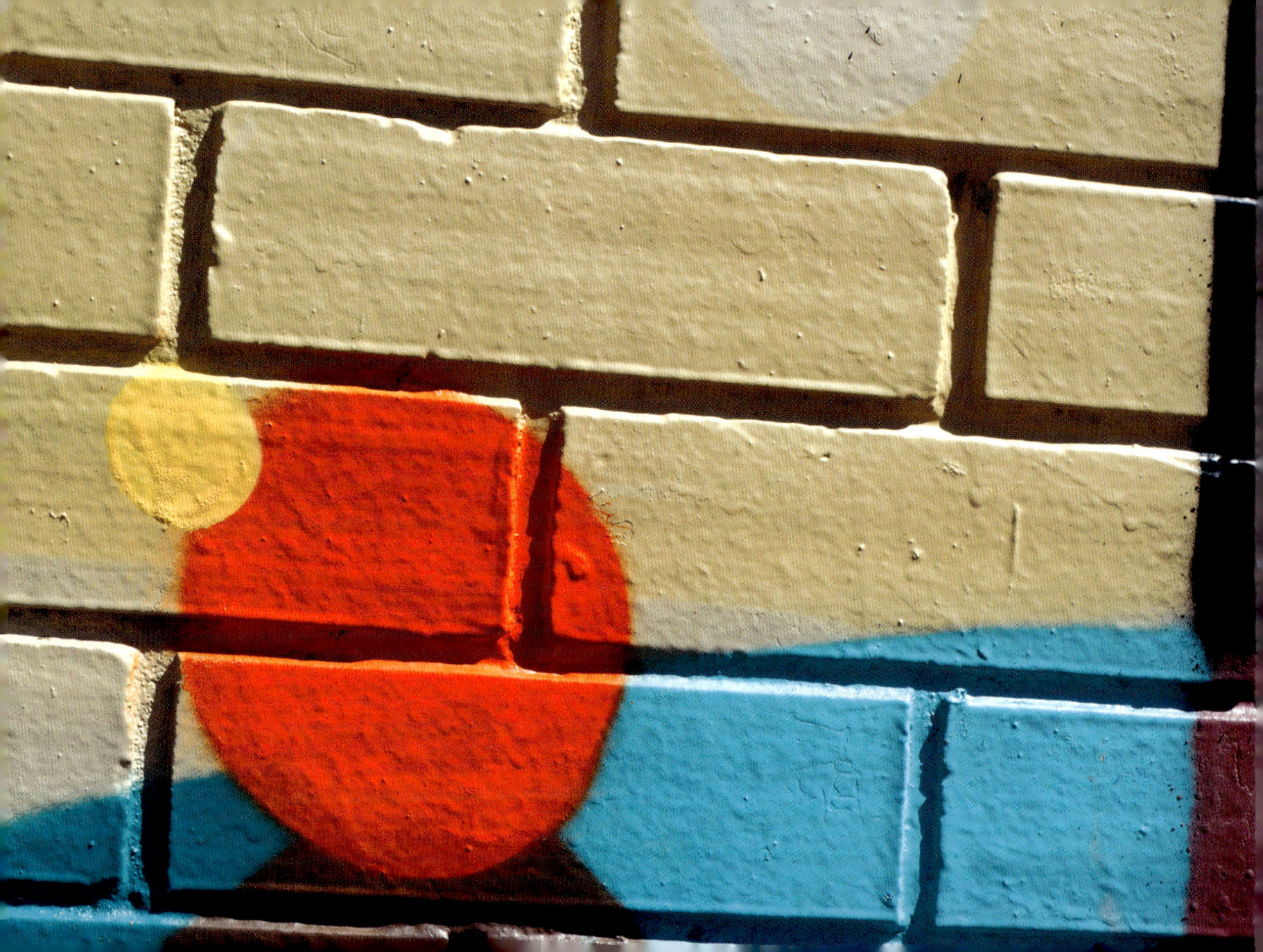

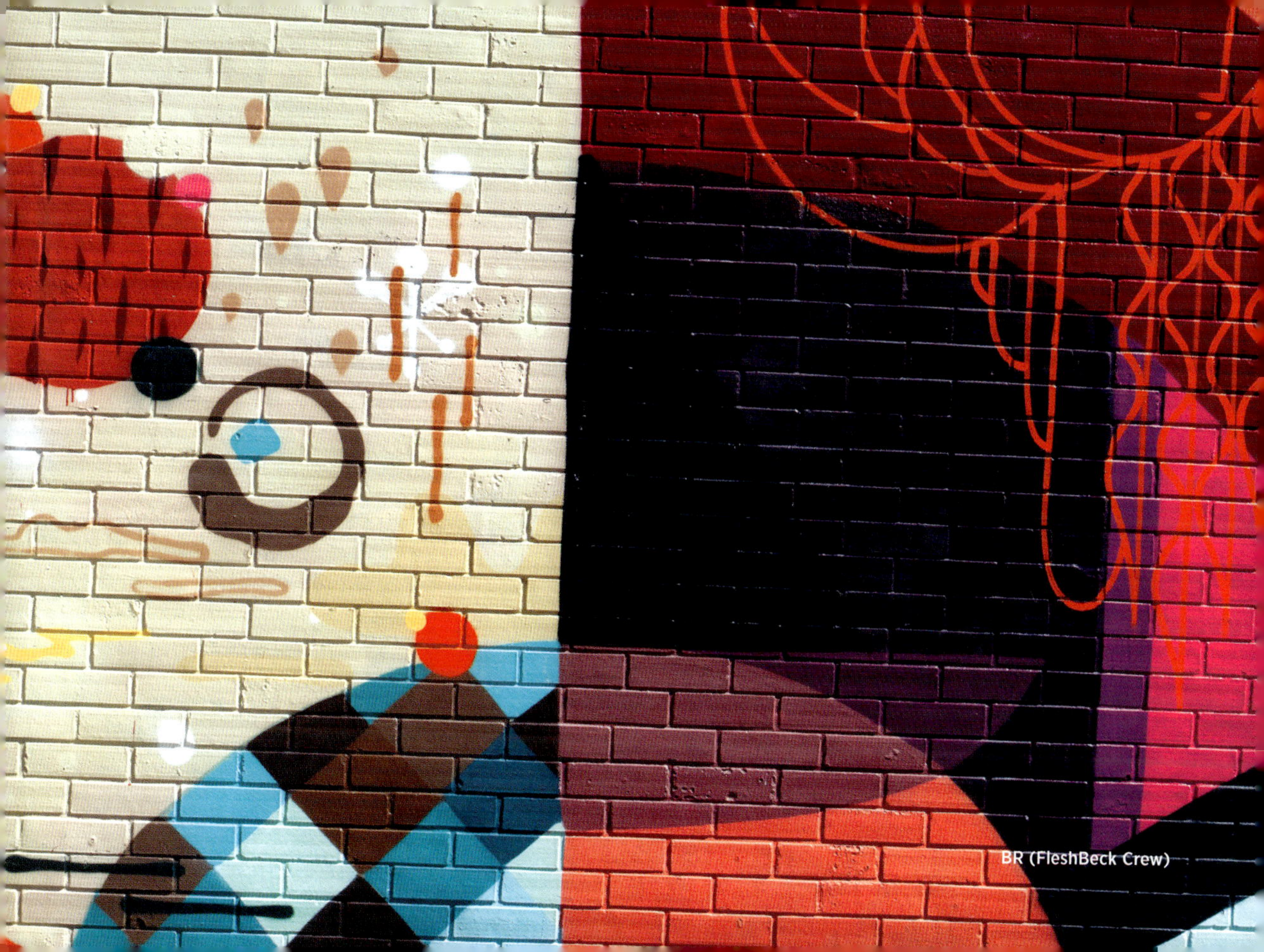

BR (FleshBeck Crew)

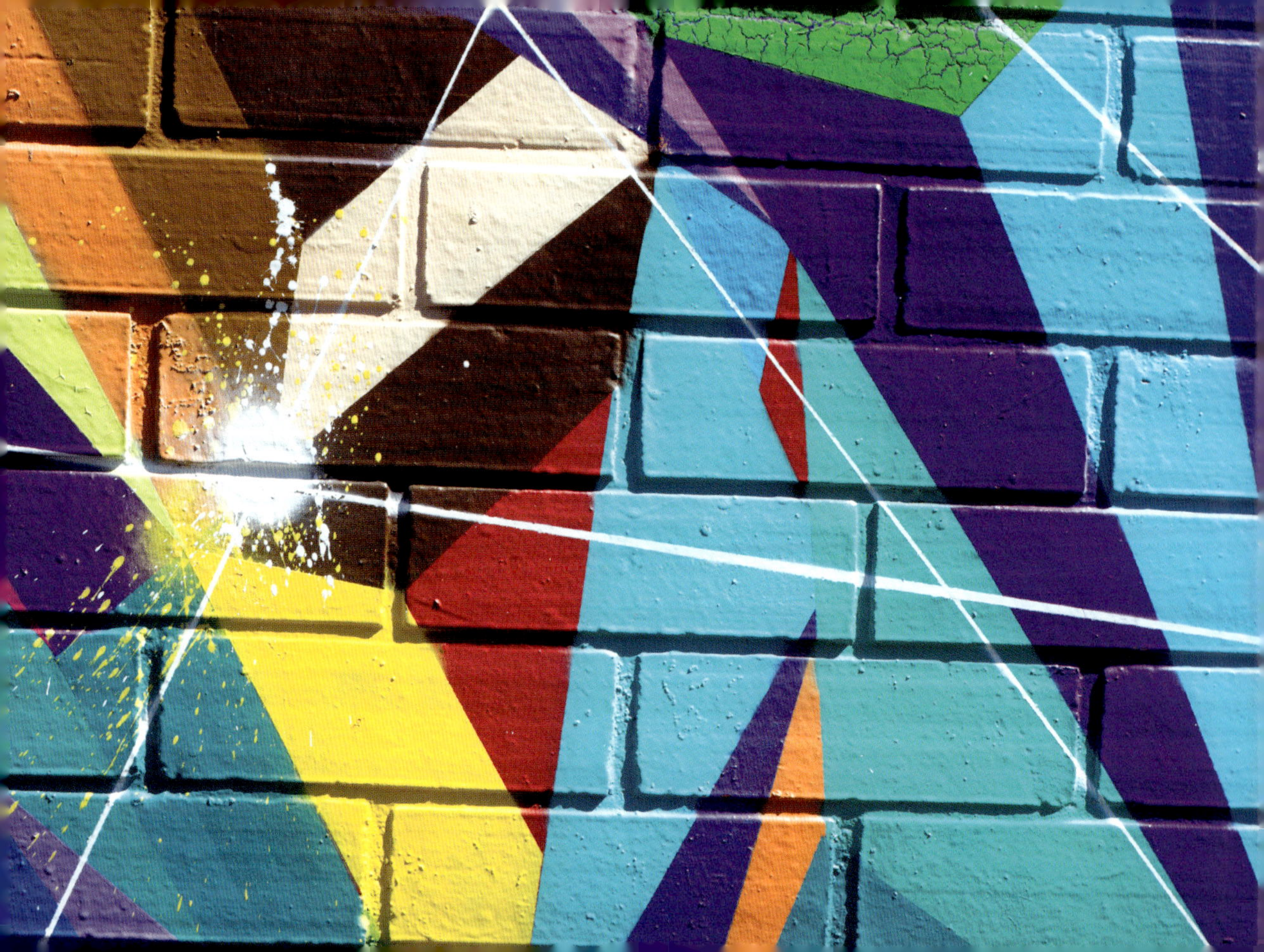

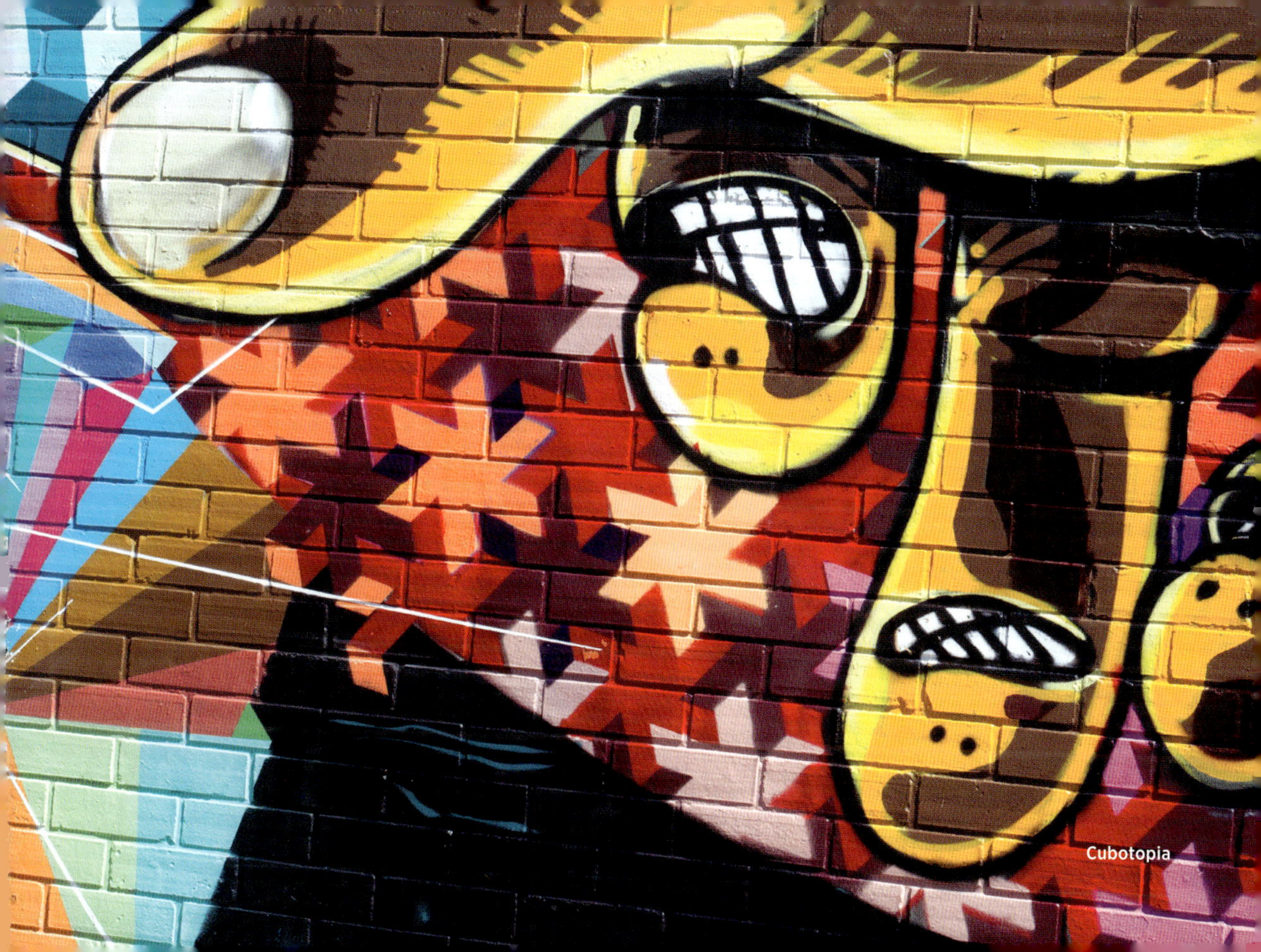

Cubotopia

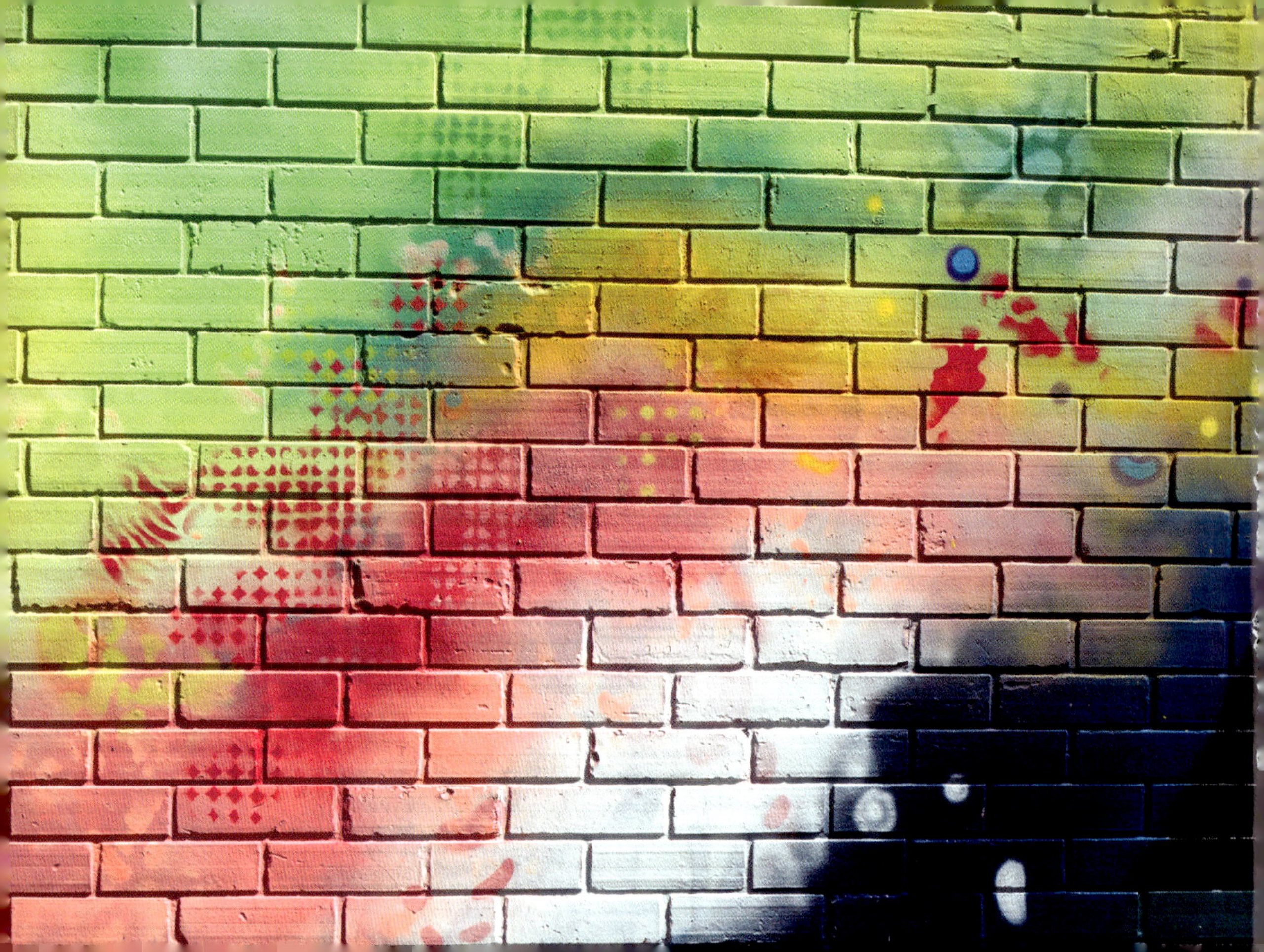

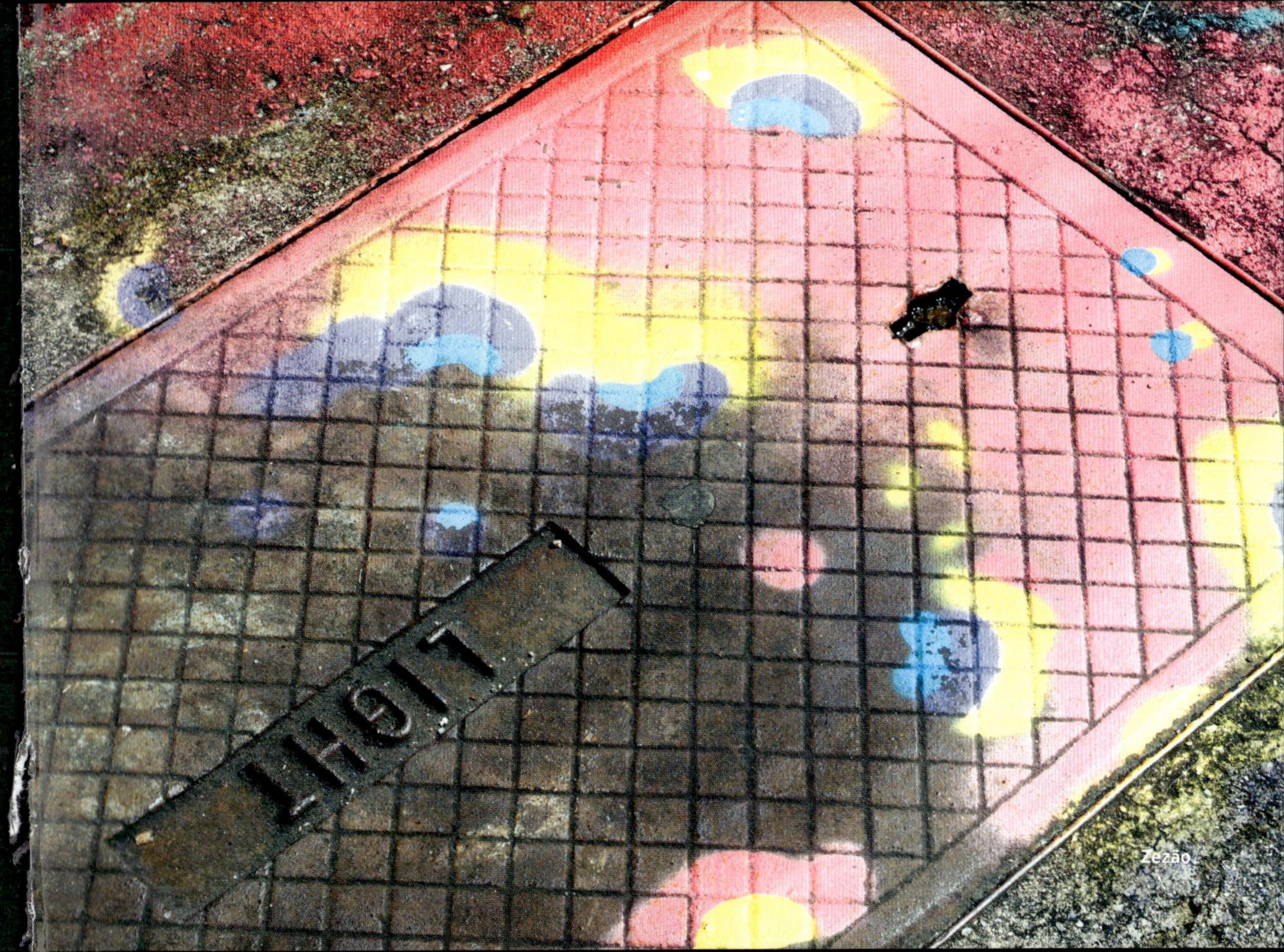

Zezão

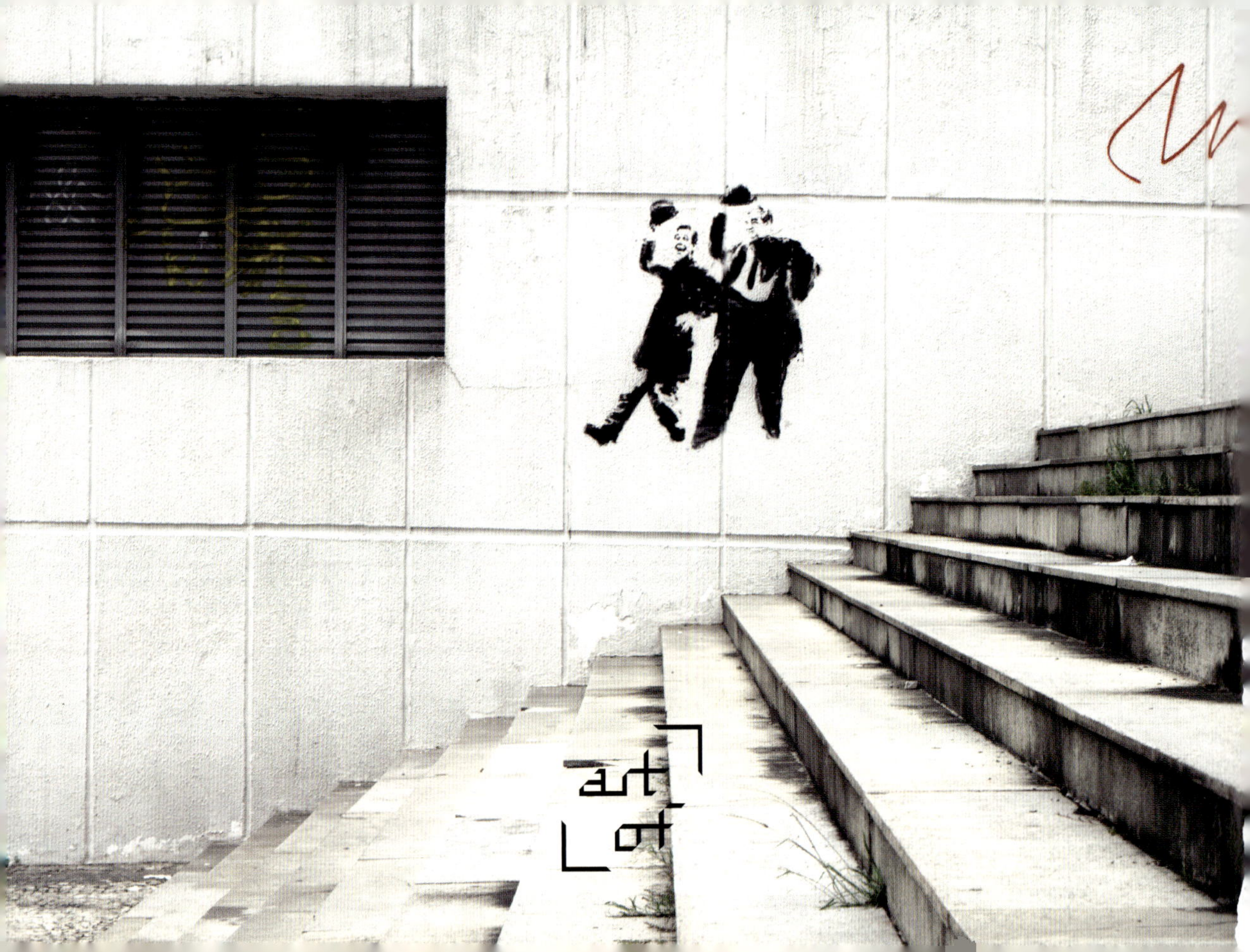
art
of